Have Dog Will Travel
Washington Edition

Barbara Whitaker

Ginger & Spike Publications

© 1999 by Barbara Whitaker

Protected under the Berne Convention. All rights reserved. No part of this book may be reproduced in any form or by any electronic or mechanical means, including information storage and retrieval systems, without written permission from the publisher. Written permission is not needed for brief quotations in reviews.

Printed in the United States of America.

First printing

Publisher's Cataloging-in-Publication
(Provided by Quality Books, Inc)

Whitaker, Barbara.
    Have dog will travel / Barbara Whitaker. —
Washington ed.
    p. cm.
    Includes bibliographical references and index.
    ISBN: 0-9660544-5-8

    1. Hotels—Pet accommodations—Washington—Directories. 2. Dogs—Housing—Washington—Directories. 3. Pets and travel—Washington.
I. Title.

TX907.3.W3W455 1999   647.94797
                                      QBI99-1123

Cover and interior illustrations by Bob Sleeper

The author and publisher of this book have worked very hard to verify the accuracy of all information included in this book. However, they make no warranty of any kind, expressed or implied, regarding the instructions and listings information herein. The author and publisher shall not be liable in the event of incidental or consequential damages in connection with, or arising out of, the furnishing, performance, or use of any information contained in these pages.

Ginger & Spike Publications
PO Box 937
Wilsonville, OR 97070-0937
503/625-3001

Acknowledgments

I want to thank all the wonderful folks who helped bring this second book in the **Have Dog Will Travel** series to completion.

First of all, many thanks to my husband Linn, for his perennial patience and support!

Thanks also to the folks who helped with the original manuscript—Kate Gerity, Susie and Bill Osborn, Dr. Ann Horne, Sharon Anton, Patty Doxtater, Sherry Allmaras, Wendy Bridgewater, Shauna Gonzales and Jo Hibbits. Your suggestions and careful reading of the manuscript were much appreciated.

Kudos to Bob Sleeper for the wonderful illustrations, and to Kohel Haver and Dick Mort for their excellent legal and technical advice, respectively.

And of course, Ginger and Spike kept me motivated to finish the Washington Edition. Thanks again, guys!

In loving memory of
Brujo, Jack, Kala, Jeremiah,
Kaka, Irish and Almond—
faithful companions, all.

Contents

Part I
Help your dog become a well-behaved traveler

1: Touring With Your Well-behaved Traveler   3
   How to have fun–and get invited back   4
   When to bring your dog–and when NOT to   6
   And now a word from Spike   7

2: Puppy Pack Your Bags   9
   Collar and leash   9
   All the proper ID tags   11
   Microchip ID system   13
   Health certificate   14
   First aid kit   15
   Travel crate   16
   Restraints and safety barriers   17
   Food   18
   Water   19

Bedding & towels	20
Grooming aids	21
Cleaning up	21
Last but not least–a flashlight	23
Tote bag checklist	23

3: Good Behavior is a TEAM Effort — 25

What commands are necessary?	25
Before obedience training	26
And after	27
What a difference!	27
Obedience 101	28
Train BEFORE you travel	29
Basic commands	29
Controlling aggression	32
If your dog is a barker	34
Learning to love car rides	35
Reviewing what your dog already knows	37

4: The Well-Behaved Traveler Hits the Road — 39

Tips for traveling in the car	39
Rest stop pointers	41
Room etiquette	42
Mealtime arrangements	43
Walking on the grounds	44
On the trail	45
At the beach	47

Contents

5: When Your Dog Needs First Aid ... 49
Before first aid is needed ... 50
Your dog's first aid kit ... 51
Taking your dog's temperature ... 53
What to do in a life-threatening emergency ... 53
If your dog is choking ... 55
If your dog is drowning ... 56
Cardiac massage ... 57
Artificial respiration ... 57
Restraining an injured dog ... 59
Broken bones ... 59
External bleeding ... 60
If you suspect internal bleeding ... 61
Poisoning ... 62
    Contact poisoning ... 62
    Swallowed poisons ... 63
    A special warning about antifreeze ... 65
Moving an injured dog ... 65
Treating for shock ... 66
Treating burns ... 67
Minor cuts and scrapes ... 68
Removing foreign objects ... 69
Treating an upset stomach ... 71
Treating diarrhea ... 72
Dealing with heat problems ... 72
    Recognizing the danger signs ... 73
    First aid for heatstroke ... 73
Keeping your pet safe in cold weather ... 74
    Watch out for hypothermia ... 74
    Treating for frostbite ... 75

6: If Your Dog Gets Lost — 77
Preparing a Lost Dog poster — 78
Searching for your lost dog — 82
When to call for reinforcements — 83
Putting up Lost Dog posters — 83
May your dog never get lost — 86

Part II
Reference Section

A: Where to Stay in Washington With Your Dog — 89

B: Emergency Clinics — 263

C: Some Useful Books — 269

D: Listings Index — 273

E: Topics Index — 303

Order Form — 312

Part I
Help your dog become a well-behaved traveler

1: Touring With Your Well-behaved Traveler

So you plan to travel around Washington by car, and you want to take your dog along? Well, you're in good company—lots of dogs travel with their owners. My German Shepherd Ginger certainly does. After all, she's part of the family, and a vacation just wouldn't be the same without her.

Traveling with a well-behaved dog can be great fun and a minimum of fuss. But it does involve some advance planning and effort on your part. It also requires extra consideration for your fellow travelers and for the friendly people who provide your accommodations.

Part I of this book shows how you can help your dog become a well-behaved traveler—making your trips more fun for both of you.

Have Dog Will Travel—Washington Edition

In Part II you'll find the reference sections:

- More than 800 Washington hotels, motels, and bed & breakfast inns that welcome you and your dog, listed alphabetically by city name

- Emergency veterinary clinics across the state, just in case your pet needs emergency care during your trip

- Recommended training and dog care books

- 2-part index for locating specific information—listed alphabetically by business name or topic

How to have fun— and get invited back

The numbers of hotels, motels, and bed & breakfast inns that accept pets have been dwindling in recent years. This unfortunate trend is largely due to a small minority of dog owners who have allowed their dogs to run amok. These are the dogs who damage furnishings and landscaping, or behave aggressively toward other guests and their pets.

As responsible dog owners, we can all help to reverse this trend. Preparing in advance and taking appropriate equipment along not only ensures more enjoyable trips

1: Touring With Your Well-Behaved Traveler

for ourselves and our dogs, but also provides positive examples for encouraging more establishments to accept pets.

To prepare for a great trip with your dog, you should:

- Attend obedience training classes with your dog *before* you travel. Once you are both familiar with the basic commands for good behavior, you'll be ready when the unexpected happens. (And believe me, it *does* eventually happen!)

- Pack the appropriate pet travel supplies

- Make advance room reservations, stating clearly that you will be bringing your dog

- Prepare a doggy first aid kit—and learn what to do in an emergency *before* taking your dog to the veterinary clinic

- Always be aware of your dog's impact on other guests and on the facilities, both indoor and outdoor, where you're staying

These topics and more are discussed in the chapters that follow.

When to bring your dog—and when NOT to

Obviously you want your dog to travel with you, or you wouldn't be reading this book. But also ask yourself whether or not he *wants* to come along.

Your dog will probably enjoy the trip if:

- You're traveling by car

- Driving time will be fairly short, so he won't be spending long hours in the car

- You've planned lots of activities that your dog can share, like hiking or walking on the beach

But consider traveling *without* your dog when:

- Adverse weather conditions would make him miserably hot or cold

- You're traveling by plane or train—these are more of an ordeal for your pet than a vacation

- Most of your time will be spent in activities that your dog cannot share—after all, would *you* want to spend your entire vacation locked in an empty car or motel room?

1: Touring With Your Well-Behaved Traveler

And now a word from Spike

The feline member of our family ("He Who Must Be Obeyed") wants to point out that he definitely prefers to stay home while Ginger goes traveling. Call him a homebody if you like, but Spike insists that cats as a rule would much rather stay behind in their own familiar places. On Spike's advice, then, this book addresses the issues related to traveling with dogs, but not cats.

Obviously you'll be making arrangements for your cats to be properly cared for in your absence. So, you can rest assured that they will be just fine while you're gone. Though it may hurt to admit it, they probably won't even miss you.

As Spike puts it, "I'm staying here. And as long as I'm properly fed and admired, my servants [that's us mere humans] can go wherever they like!"

2: Puppy Pack Your Bags

It has been said that every successful vacation begins with careful packing. This is just as true for your dog as for yourself—you need to bring along the proper supplies. Use the handy checklist on p. 23 to be sure nothing important gets left behind.

Many of these supplies are as close as your local pet store. You can also check in dog magazines at your library or newsstand for the names of mail order pet supply houses and write or call for their catalogs. You'll be amazed at the variety of new gadgets available to make traveling with your pet easy and fun.

Collar and leash

Every dog should wear a sturdy leather or woven collar at all times, with the appropriate license, identification and rabies tags attached.

Don't use a choke collar as a permanent collar! Properly used, it can be helpful during training sessions, but if left on your dog all the time, the choke collar could snag on a low branch or other obstruction. Don't let your beloved pet become one of the many sad stories of dogs who choked to death when their owners were not there to rescue them.

If your dog is really hard to control, check with a reputable trainer about using a *prong collar* during your training sessions. This type of collar has blunt metal prongs that momentarily pinch the dog's neck, when he pulls against the leash or when you administer a *correction*. Again, this is for use during training sessions only; don't leave it on your dog all the time!

You'll need a 1-ft to 6-ft long leash for walking with your dog close to your side. Woven nylon or leather works better than metal chain, which is noisy and harder to hold onto. Also check out the new retractable leashes that extend to 16 feet or more so your pet can investigate his surroundings without dragging you every which way, and retract fully for close walking. Ginger does just fine with her bright red nylon collar and 6-ft leather leash.

- Attending a basic obedience class with your dog is one of the very best ways to help him master the fine art of walking on leash.

2: Puppy Pack Your Bags

All the proper ID tags

As important as your dog's license and ID tags are at home, they're even more vital when you travel. Should you and your pet lose track of each other, those ID tags will enable his finders to contact you. In addition to the permanent ID tag with your home address and phone number, I also recommend that you add a travel tag to your dog's collar showing where you can be reached *during* your trip if at all possible.

Dog license tag—Among the many other good reasons for licensing your dog, the license number and phone number of your county dog control department that appear on this tag represent another way to trace a lost dog's owner.

Permanent identification tag—This should list your name, home address and phone number, and perhaps your dog's name. (Ginger's tag even has her regular veterinarian's phone number.) Ideally, this information should be permanently engraved or stamped onto a metal tag. The rectangular style of tag that fastens flat to the collar stays cleaner and doesn't add to the jingling of the other tags.

Any number of companies can create permanent ID tags for you. Veterinary offices often have ordering information from several of them. Dog magazines are full of ads for this service—check your library or newsstand. Some mail order catalogs also offer them.

Rabies tag—Provided by your veterinarian. This tag bears a serial number that can be traced back to the veterinarian and then to the dog's owner. There could be dire consequences if your dog were to get picked up as a stray, or (heaven forbid) bite someone, and not have proof of current rabies vaccination.

Travel tag—Very important! This tag shows where you can be reached *during your vacation*. Check your pet store for a two-part tag consisting of a paper liner you can write on, that fits inside a clear plastic case. You can also get a barrel-type tag that unscrews to hold a rolled-up slip of paper—just be sure to tighten the two halves together *very securely* to keep them from separating accidentally.

Write or type the name, address, city and phone number where you're staying. If your trip includes several destinations, either list them all or prepare a separate slip for each destination—then be sure to update the tag at your next destination. As an alternative, list the name and phone number of someone who can receive messages for you.

Also write "Reward Offered" (no specific dollar amount) and "Call collect, or we will reimburse your phone expenses" on the tag.

2: Puppy Pack Your Bags

Microchip ID system

Microchipping is one of the newest and most promising ways to identify a lost pet. While tags or collars can fall off or be removed, a microchip stays with your pet forever. Each chip is programmed with a unique code that can be detected by a hand-held scanner, similar to the ones used in retail stores.

Microchip scanners are now used at thousands of animal control agencies, shelters and veterinary clinics across the country. Once the chip's code has been retrieved, the staff simply calls it in to the national database agency, which is accessible 24 hours a day, 365 days a year through a toll-free number. The database agency immediately notifies you that your dog has been found.

Your veterinarian can implant the microchip, no bigger than a grain of rice, beneath your pet's skin in a safe, quick office procedure. Then all you have to do is register your pet's unique code and your contact information with the national database agency to receive coverage anywhere you travel in the U.S.

The cost of implanting the microchip and the onetime fee to register your pet in the database add up to about $50—pretty inexpensive insurance for your dog's safe return if he should ever get lost.

Health certificate

Get this certificate from your veterinarian not more than 10 days before beginning your trip. Effective for 30 days, it states that your pet is in good health and lists his current vaccinations. While not strictly required within Oregon when traveling by car, you'll *definitely* need this if you plan to travel by air (even just in-state) or to enter Canada. Before traveling to any other countries, check with their embassies for specific vaccinations and other requirements.

If your pet takes medication or has other problems, get a copy of his medical records along with the health certificate. Make sure the paperwork includes your veterinarian's name, address and phone number, in case follow-up information is needed.

The most well known canine vaccination is for rabies, which is required every three years in Oregon. In fact, you can't get a dog license without proof of a current rabies vaccination. And as a caring, responsible pet owner, *of course* you license your dog, right?

In addition, your pet should be immunized against distemper, hepatitis, parainfluenza, leptospirosis and possibly parvo. Depending on where you'll be traveling, your veterinarian may also recommend a preventive for heartworm or Lyme disease.

Also ask about annual booster shots for corona and bordetella. These safeguard your pet against catching something nasty from other dogs, such as kennel cough, and are often required before your dog can attend obedience classes. And you'll be prepared in case you ever have to temporarily place him in a boarding kennel, since many kennels won't accept dogs without proof of these vaccinations.

Bottom line on vaccinations: Your traveling dog is exposed to many new health hazards at rest stops, parks and other public areas. Along with the stress of drinking unfamiliar water and meeting new dogs, these factors add up to very real dangers for the non-vaccinated dog. So be safe—vaccinate!

🐕 Some vaccines can take up to 30 days to develop their full protective strength, so check with your veterinarian and *plan ahead*!

First aid kit

A basic first aid kit is easy to put together and enables you to deal with emergencies until you can get to a local veterinarian. You'll find a list of the items that belong in your first aid kit on pp. 51–52.

Of course you'll also bring along any special medication your veterinarian may have prescribed. If fleas are a problem in the area you're visiting, you may want to include flea-and-tick spray or powder—just be sure to apply it to your dog only when outdoors, never in your motel room.

Travel crate

Many trainers, breeders and veterinarians recommend using a dog carrier, or *crate*, when your dog travels in the car. Obviously, this is more practical with small dogs than with larger ones—it is much easier to fit a Beagle-sized crate into the back seat than one large enough for a Rottweiler.

Several types of crate are available, from collapsible wire mesh panels to heavy molded plastic. A wire crate works especially well in the flat back of a van or station wagon, while the plastic carriers fit better into the back seat of a sedan. Of course, when traveling by plane, your dog *must* be in an airline-approved travel crate.

The crate should be large enough for your dog to turn around, lie down, and stand or sit up without hitting his head. Even if yours is still a puppy, get a crate that will be large enough for his full adult size. However, this is your dog's den, so think *cozy* and *secure*—don't get anything larger than necessary.

To cushion and provide traction underfoot, place a folded blanket on the bottom of the crate. Better yet, cut a thick piece of carpet to fit snugly without slipping—ask your local carpet dealer for a remnant or sample square.

Restraints and safety barriers

If a travel crate isn't the answer for your situation, not to worry—there are a number of other safety options you can use instead for a car-traveling dog.

Seat belts—Available for dogs of all sizes, these consist of a chest harness and a strap that fastens to the car seat or to the regular seat belt. These allow your dog to either sit up or lie down in the passenger seat, yet prevent him from being thrown forward in the event of a sudden stop. Various size ranges and types are available.

Metal barriers—These allow you to close off the back seat, or the back of a station wagon. These may be either temporarily or permanently installed. Your dog can see and hear you through the barrier, but is securely restrained from jumping or being thrown into the front seat.

Elastic mesh nets—These nets create a barrier between front and back seats and can be ordered for specific makes of cars. They prevent your dog from jumping into the front seat.

Stretch nets are also available in generic sizes and shapes to fit most car models. These have elastic bands that fasten to special hardware installed on the interior of the car.

Collapsible window screens—Made of strong plastic struts that expand like a child's safety gate, these fit securely into a partially opened car window. With screens in place on both sides of the car, there is plenty of air circulation but no danger of your dog jumping out—or of someone reaching into the parked car. When removed, the screens take up almost no space and fit easily under a car seat.

Food

First and foremost, you'll need to bring along dog food and a bowl to serve it in. Unless you are absolutely certain that your dog's preferred brand of food is available wherever you plan to travel, pack enough dog food for the entire trip.

If your dog typically nibbles at his food without finishing it all right away, bring a bowl with a snap-on lid that can go back into your dog's tote bag without spilling kibble all over. The shallow containers used for whipped toppings or margarine work very well.

You may also want to bring along a vinyl placemat for catching spills under the food and water bowls. This is

2: Puppy Pack Your Bags

an item you can pick up for pennies at garage or rummage sales. Or you can get really fancy mats and bowls in pet stores or mail order catalogs.

Remember to pack a can opener for canned food, along with a serving spoon and a snap-on lid for covering any portion to be saved for the next meal. If your dog is accustomed to frequent dog treats or snacks, pack those too. And a small cooler may be helpful in hot weather for keeping drinking water or leftover canned food cool.

Water

Pack a plastic gallon jug of water and an unbreakable bowl where they'll be accessible during your travels, since your dog will need a drink of water every few hours. Don't let him drink from streams or puddles—drinking unfamiliar or polluted water can lead to stomach upsets and diarrhea. Also, *never* allow your dog to drink from the toilet in your motel room—some establishments put cleaning products into the toilet tank, which could make him very sick.

Many veterinarians recommend bringing enough water from home to last at least halfway through your trip. By gradually mixing your own water with the local tap water, you can prevent an unpleasant reaction. You can also buy distilled water for less than a dollar a gallon at most grocery stores.

Bedding & towels

You should always travel with your dog's own bed and cleanup towels. Your dog will thank you—and so will the hotel and motel managers, for sparing their furnishings. If your dog is accustomed to sleeping on the bed with you, or on other furniture, bring a sheet from home to protect the bedspread or upholstery. And do consider training your dog to stay off the furniture, at home *and* when traveling.

A travel crate, so useful in the car, also makes the perfect bed. It is reassuringly cozy and safe. If you're not using a crate, then bring along a *familiar* washable blanket or other bedding. Ginger travels with the same trusty sleeping bag that she sleeps on at home. Zipped up and folded in half, it makes a thick, soft bed. Opened out full length, it protects the back seat of the car from dirt, mud and beach sand.

An absolute must is a pair of towels especially for your dog. Use these to rub down a wet coat or wipe muddy or sandy paws. Spread one out under the water bowl if your dog is an enthusiastic drinker.

The sheet, dog towels, and bedding can all be found very inexpensively at garage sales, rummage sales, or second hand stores. Ginger's sleeping bag cost a dollar, and her towels were a quarter apiece. The tote bag which holds her travel supplies was another garage sale find—all for less than three dollars.

2: Puppy Pack Your Bags

Grooming aids

Pack your dog's brush or comb, since you'll probably be going to places that are fun but will result in a dirty or sandy dog. A quick brushing *before* going back indoors will go a long way toward keeping your motel room fresh and endearing you to the housekeeping staff. Not to mention how much your pet probably enjoys being groomed. Ginger jumps up and down with delight at the mere sight of her brush.

Take care of major grooming chores *before* your trip—trim those too-long toenails and brush the loose hair out of his coat. And pack that bottle of pet shampoo if he has a tendency to roll in smelly things. I'll never forget the time one of my husband's dogs found a dead seal on the beach—'nuff said!

Cleaning up

Many hotels and motels lay out free amenities such as shampoo and hand lotion. Wouldn't it be great if they offered guests with dogs the choice of a few disposable pooper scoopers instead! In the meantime, however, it is up to us as dog owners to take full responsibility for cleaning up after our dogs.

Please, please be considerate of others by cleaning up after your dog's rest stops—whether in a park, on the motel grounds, or at a highway rest stop. You can use either disposable pooper scoopers, or a reusable scooper with disposable bags—plus another bag for storing the scooper between uses. For a low cost, "low tech" method, use a plastic produce bag saved from a trip to the grocery store. Zip-top plastic bags also work well.

Place your hand inside the bag and use this "glove" to pick up the doggy doo. With your other hand, turn the bag inside out, then twist the top shut and secure it with a knot. Properly dispose of the bag in a trash can.

Keep several clean, folded bags in your car, ready for the next rest stop. And *always* tuck one in your pocket when taking your dog out for a walk.

🐾 The true Cadillac of disposable pooper scoopers is called the Dispoz-A-Scoop, made by PetPro Products, Inc., 504 North Oak Street, Inglewood CA 90302 (1-800-873-5957). It consists of a small plastic bag with a wire rim and a cardboard handle that neatly slides down the wire to become a lid, for completely hands-free pickup.

Even seasoned canine travelers occasionally have car sickness accidents, so it's a good idea to pack supplies in the car for quick cleanups. Paper towels, pre-moistened towelettes, or a wet washcloth in a plastic bag are all good. Stash them in an easy-to-reach spot in the car, such as under the front seat.

2: Puppy Pack Your Bags

Last but not least—a flashlight

Keep one in the car and another in your dog's tote bag so it will be handy when you leave the motel room for those just-before-bedtime walks.

Tote bag checklist

- First aid kit, health certificate/medical records
- Dog bed (sleeping bag or blanket) and towels
- Dog food, bowl, serving spoon, can opener and snap-on lid, vinyl placemat
- Jug of water, drinking bowl
- Dog brush or comb, shampoo
- Pooper scoopers (reusable or disposable) or a supply of plastic bags
- Paper towels, pre-moistened towelettes, or wet washcloth in a plastic bag
- Flashlight
- One or two favorite chew toys!

3: Good Behavior is a TEAM Effort

Which sort of pet would you rather vacation with: a barky, uncontrollable bundle of energy, or a well-behaved traveler? The answer is obvious, and basic obedience training is the key.

"Obedience" simply means that your dog is reliably under your control, both on and off the leash. Mastering just a few useful commands—and reviewing them often with your pet— can make all the difference in his behavior.

What commands are necessary?

According to noted dog trainer Bruce Sessions, only two commands are truly required for the traveling dog: *come* and *no*. Check your local library for his excellent article "Training the RV Dog" in the September 1985 issue of *Trailer Life* magazine. He explains how to teach these vital commands in just 15 minutes a day for one week. The practice sessions can be fun for both you and your dog, and they help to strengthen the bond between the two of you.

Ginger and I have also learned a few more commands in obedience class that come in very handy: *sit, down, stay* and *heel.* Does your dog absolutely have to know all these commands before he can travel with you? No, but they will definitely make your trips less harried and more relaxed. Compare the following two scenarios…

Before obedience training
It was early morning at the motel, and I had just let Ginger off her leash (my first mistake) in a far corner of the motel grounds for a relief stop. Another guest and her dog suddenly appeared and Ginger ran to investigate the newcomer, ignoring my call to *"Come back here right now!"* I had to chase Ginger and grab her by the collar. The other guest glared indignantly as our two dogs bristled and snarled at each other in the traditional "I'm a tougher dog than you are" dance. On the leash again, Ginger lunged along the path at full speed, dragging me behind her.

In the motel room, Ginger ran back and forth between the window and the closed door, barking at the sounds of people and cars outside—in spite of my repeated

3: Good Behavior is a TEAM Effort

scolding to *"Stop that barking and lie down."* Loaded down with luggage, I opened the door and she ran out ahead of me, nearly tripping another guest in her excitement.

And after
Let's try this again now that Ginger and I have completed our obedience classes: I take her outside *on the leash* for her morning rest stop. If she moves toward an approaching dog, I tell her *"Heel"* and we walk in the opposite direction. If she makes any aggressive move or sound, I say *"No!"* sharply and we keep walking—without her pulling on the leash.

Back in the motel room, if Ginger barks at a sound outside, I say *"No!"* followed by *"Down."* She lies down quietly on her own bed. When checking out of the room, I put her on the leash *before* opening the door, tell her *"Heel"* and she walks politely beside me to the car. Once she's safely inside, I retrieve the luggage and finish loading the car.

What a difference!
Feel the difference in stress levels between these two scenarios? And that's just the beginning of the day—imagine an entire weekend trip with an uncontrollable dog versus a well-behaved traveler.

Obedience 101

You *can* learn about obedience training from books, and there are some excellent ones available. See pp. 269–271 for a list of my favorites.

However, I definitely recommend that you and your dog attend at least a beginners' obedience class. A trained instructor can get you off to a great start and help to avoid behavior problems before they begin.

Professional dog trainers usually offer both group and one-on-one sessions—check the Yellow Pages under "Dog Training." Beginning, intermediate and advanced levels of obedience classes may also be available through your local school district or community college. Call the school office and ask about their Continuing Education or Community Education programs. Class schedules may also be available at the Post Office or your local bank.

🐾 Ginger's favorite class is conducted by trainer and pet innkeeper Susie Osborn at *Susie's Country Inn for Dogs & Cats* in Vancouver, WA. Located not far from the Portland International Airport, this is also where Ginger stays when we must travel without her. Call *Susie's* at 360/576-K9K9 for information about obedience classes or boarding your pet.

3: Good Behavior is a TEAM Effort

Train BEFORE you travel

The time to begin obedience training is *before* your trip—so that your dog can learn the basic commands in a controlled area without distractions. Once he understands the commands, start practicing with him in a public area like a park, surrounded by people and other dogs. He'll soon learn that you expect the same good behavior wherever he goes with you.

Relax and have fun with this training time. Your dog will love the extra attention you lavish on him, and he'll try to please you. Be patient and upbeat even if he gets confused at first. If you reach a stumbling block, go back to an earlier command that he knows well to get his confidence level back up. Then try the more difficult command again.

Keep your training sessions short so that they don't turn into torture for either one of you. And always end with a few minutes of plain old playing—toss a ball for your dog to fetch, or lead him on a run around the yard to release any leftover tension. After all, good behavior is supposed to make your time together more fun, right?

Basic commands

The following discussion is based on the collective expertise of a number of well-known trainers and authors. For more detailed information on training, check your local bookstore or library for their books (listed in the back of this guide).

Come—This is an easy command that most dogs pick up very quickly. You want to get your dog's attention in such an inviting way that there's nothing else he'd rather do than come running to you. While your dog is on a leash or long cord, call his name followed by the command *"Come."* As soon as he starts toward you, praise him lavishly. Giving a small food treat at first for every positive response helps to reinforce the idea that coming when called is a wonderful idea.

No—There is no specific routine for teaching this command. Just belt it out in a very firm tone of voice, whenever your dog is doing something you *really* don't want him to do. Don't overuse it though—save it for when he does something you absolutely will not tolerate; otherwise you risk losing its impact. The sudden loud command should startle him out of whatever he's doing. Then as soon as he begins to pay attention to you, praise him. You may even want to call him over to you for a pat on the head or a good ear-scratching.

Sit—With your dog on the leash, say his name and then *"Sit."* At the same time, pull up gently on the leash and push down on his hindquarters to guide him into the sit position. Praise him (*"Good sit"*) and then release him from this position with *"Okay"* or *"Release."* Only after you give the release command is he is allowed to stand up again. Then give him lots of praise, both verbal and

3: Good Behavior is a TEAM Effort

hands-on. Most dogs will be so delighted with themselves by now that they'll happily repeat this exercise over and over as long as you keep telling them how wonderful they are.

Down—With your dog on the leash, say his name and the command *"Down"* while you pull downward on his leash. At first, you may also need to push down on his hindquarters or shoulders until he is lying down. Again, give lots of praise to reassure him that he's doing well, even if he immediately wants to stand up again. Use patience and lots of repetition here.

Stay—With your dog in the Sit or Down position, hold your hand in front of his face, palm toward him, while saying *"Stay."* Praise lavishly for even the shortest compliance, then release. Gradually increase the time your dog is expected to hold this position, then practice staying while you step further and further away. Always remember to release him from this position before going on to another command or ending the practice session, so he doesn't get the idea that *he* can decide when this command is over!

Heel (walking on leash)—Start with your dog sitting at your left side, leash in your left hand. Say his name, then give the command *"Heel"* just before you step out with your left foot. Take just a few steps the first time, then say *"Sit"* as you stop walking. You want him to learn to stay right beside you, and to immediately sit down when you stop.

Say *"Heel"* and start walking again, and so on. He'll soon learn to follow your steps. In fact, he'll probably anticipate your takeoff and start too soon at first, so be patient. Once he catches on to the routine, stop giving the Sit command every time, so that he learns to do it automatically.

Try carrying a small food treat right in front of his nose to keep him at your side rather than rushing ahead. Give him the treat after you walk a few steps and then stop. And of course, give lots of praise. (If you think this is starting to sound like the secret to obedience training—you're absolutely right!)

Controlling aggression

If you intend to take your well-behaved traveler out in public, he must be reliably *not* aggressive toward people or dogs. Some dogs don't start out being comfortable with other dogs. Their reactions range from defensive postures like raised fur along the back of the neck and fierce stares to outright barking or growling.

The best way to overcome defensive or aggressive tendencies is to get your dog accustomed to the presence of other dogs at an early age. Simply attending obedience classes will go a long way toward helping him relax around dogs and people. Your instructor can also offer specialized help for problem dogs.

3: Good Behavior is a TEAM Effort

The most important step in preventing aggression is to *always* have your dog under your control—this means on the leash—whenever you venture outside your car or motel room. Dog behaviorists say that once you establish yourself as "pack leader,"your dog will follow your lead on whether to charge ahead or hold back.

Ginger has always been uncomfortable around other dogs. She was apparently kept indoors for the first year of her life and didn't develop the normal doggy socializing skills. When I adopted her as a stray at the local Humane Society shelter, she was very defensive toward the other dogs there.

A few months later, she was viciously attacked by two neighbor dogs, one of whom she had previously played with most amiably—which made her even more suspicious of other dogs.

Several obedience classes later, Ginger is still standoffish when meeting new dogs, but she has become pals with a few familiar dogs belonging to friends and neighbors. On the other hand, she is a total people-lover, going happily from person to person to be petted. It doesn't matter to her whether they are longtime friends or first-time acquaintances—she adores all kinds of people.

Have Dog Will Travel—Washington Edition

If your dog is a barker

Simply put, barking is *not* to be tolerated. A barking dog makes everyone around you miserable. If you are in your motel room and someone knocks on the door, a single "alarm bark" is acceptable, but no more than that. You should train your dog to stop barking as soon as you give the all-purpose command *"No!"*

A really insistent barker may need more than a spoken command to break through his mental barriers. I've had good luck with plain water in a plastic squirt bottle. One good squirt in the face doesn't hurt your dog, but it certainly interrupts his train of thought, especially when accompanied by a loud *"No!"* and followed with praise as soon as he stops barking.

Of course, a dog left behind in a motel room, barking incessantly, is absolutely out. Barking like that is a sign of stress, as in "They left me here all alone and I'm scared/bored/frustrated." It isn't fair to your dog any more than it is to the unfortunate neighbors who have to endure the noise.

Never leave your dog alone in the motel room. He should be going with you—isn't that why you brought him on the trip in the first place? If you must leave him for a short time, while you're in a restaurant for example, let him wait in your car, not in the room.

3: Good Behavior is a TEAM Effort

If you already use a travel crate, your dog should be accustomed to sitting or lying down quietly when he's inside it. Put him in the crate for a few minutes to calm down when he becomes upset and barky. Be sure to practice this "time-out in the crate" exercise at home before you travel, so that your dog knows exactly what is expected of him when he is put into his little den.

Learning to love car rides

Many dogs just naturally love going anywhere in the car with you, but others have difficulty getting used to the sound and motion. A few advance preparations will help to ensure a comfortable trip for all concerned.

Getting used to the car—Jumping around in the car, drooling, panting excessively or throwing up are all signs that your dog is nervous about being in the car. A few practice rides can help to reassure him that riding in the car can be fun rather than intimidating. In extreme cases, you may need to start by sitting quietly with him in the car, not even starting the engine. Ignore him for a few minutes—read a magazine article or two—then let him out of the car with a simple word of praise and a pat on the head.

Repeat this exercise until he can enter the car, sit quietly, and exit without any upset. Then try starting the car but not going anywhere. Next, try driving around the block and back home again, and so on. By the time you've progressed to taking him with you on short errands, such as to the grocery store and back, he'll probably just fall asleep.

Arrange some of your practice trips to include a fun destination or activity, like a brisk walk in the park. Ginger loves going to the drive-up bank window with me, because, believe it or not, the teller always has a bowl of doggy treats handy!

Avoiding a "nervous stomach"—Stress can trigger car sickness, so don't give food or water for at least an hour before a practice ride. Allow time for a few minutes of exercise and a chance to relieve himself just before you leave. If he still gets carsick, see pp. 71–72 for some simple remedies.

Riding politely—Train your dog to sit or lie down quietly—no jumping around, and no barking in your ear or out the window. You may want to use one of the safety restraints described on pp. 17–18.

Loading and unloading—For his own safety, your dog *must* learn to wait for your command before getting into or out of the car. Never open the door without checking that the leash is attached to his collar, and that you have a firm grasp on the other end of the leash. Losing control of an excited dog in unfamiliar territory can be disastrous—so use the Stay command to keep him safely in the car until you are ready for him to get out.

3: Good Behavior is a TEAM Effort

Reviewing what your dog already knows

A brief practice session makes a great exercise break during your trip. It also helps to reinforce the idea that obedience is expected even with lots of unfamiliar distractions.

When you stop at a rest area, a park or other open area, start by walking your dog on the leash. Pause a few times to have him sit or lie down, then release him and continue your walk. Or tell him to sit and stay while you walk ahead a few steps—still holding the leash, of course. Then call him to you once more, and so on.

A few minutes of this activity at each rest stop will leave you with a happy dog who settles down politely—and will probably even fall asleep—as soon as you start driving again.

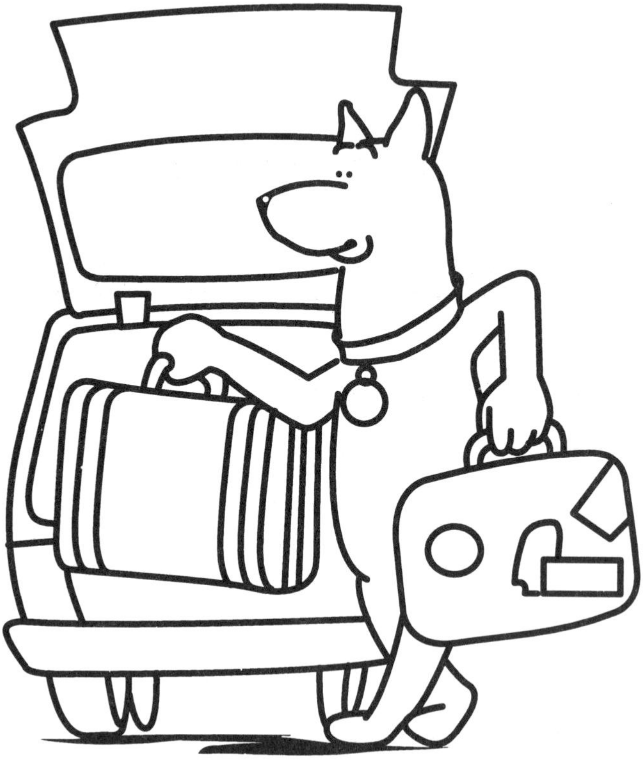

4: The Well-Behaved Traveler Hits the Road

Okay, you've faithfully completed your dog's obedience training, assembled his first aid kit and packed his food, water, and other traveling supplies. You've made your advance room reservations, you're ready to go, and your ecstatic pet is running in circles around the car. This is the payoff for all your preparations—it's time to hit the road!

Tips for traveling in the car

The safest way for a smaller dog to ride in the car is in a travel crate. This protects him in case of a sudden stop and keeps him from jumping around in the car or getting underfoot while you're trying to drive. If your pet is too large for a travel crate, consider using a doggy seat belt that offers similar protection but still allows him to sit or stand up. Whatever form of restraint you decide on, make sure your pet knows that he must stay in his assigned location in the car until you release him. Ginger's travel spot is on her sleeping bag, which has been spread out across the back seat to protect the upholstery.

If your pet is a nervous traveler, reassure him by remaining calm yourself. Praise him for sitting politely in his assigned spot, then ignore him as long as he behaves himself. Don't keep asking anxiously if he's all right, or giving constant reassurance—that will just make him more nervous.

Don't leave your dog's leash attached to his collar while the car is in motion. If you should make a sudden stop, the leash could snag on a door handle or seat back and strangle him. So take the leash off once he's safely inside the car. Just be sure to put it on again *before* opening the car door to let him out.

Open the car window just wide enough for your dog to put his nose into the fresh air, not his whole face. Never let him hang his head out the window of a moving car—not only could he squeeze his whole body out if he decided to chase something, but airborne objects such as insects or flying gravel could injure his ears and eyes. Or the force of the wind could actually give him an earache.

4: The Well-Behaved Traveler Hits the Road

It goes without saying that your pet belongs *inside* the vehicle. A dog riding in the back of an open pickup truck is an accident just waiting to happen. He is exposed to wind-borne hazards and harsh weather, and could be thrown out of the vehicle if you swerve or brake suddenly.

If you need to leave your dog in the parked car—while you stop for lunch, for example—be sure that he won't suffer from heat buildup on a warm day, which can lead to heatstroke or even death. Park under cover if you can, or at least in the shade. For cross ventilation, open one or more windows on each side of the car and insert the collapsible screens described on p. 18. Check frequently to be sure the temperature in the car is still comfortable.

Rest stop pointers

When traveling a long distance, stop every few hours to give both you and your pet a chance to stretch and relax. Keep him on the leash the whole time you're at the rest stop, and stay in the designated pet areas.

If you've been traveling for quite awhile or the weather is warm, he'll appreciate a drink of water. Then give him a few minutes to relieve himself and walk around a bit. Be considerate of others by *always* cleaning up after your dog—use plastic bags or pooper scoopers, and properly dispose of the waste in a garbage can.

This is a great time for a short exercise break, especially if you combine it with a review of obedience commands. Try walking a short distance and have him sit or lie down, then walk for another minute and practice a different command, and so on. A few minutes of activity will have you both feeling refreshed and ready to continue your trip.

Room etiquette

When you arrive at your overnight destination, be sure to remind the staff that your dog is traveling with you. Of course, you should already have stated this when making your advance reservation, but tell them again now that you have arrived. That way, they can be sure not to put you in a "no-pets" room by mistake—many establishments reserve certain rooms for guests who suffer from allergies. Sneaking a dog into a no-pets room hurts all dog owners by jeopardizing the management's willingness to accept dogs in the future.

Ask where on the grounds you can exercise your dog, whether or not they have disposable pooper scoopers available, and if there are designated trash cans you should use for disposal.

Place your pet's bed in an out-of-the-way spot in the room and show him where it is, then make sure that he uses his own bed and not the furniture.

4: The Well-Behaved Traveler Hits the Road

If you allow your pet to sleep on your bed or other furniture at home, bring along one of your own sheets or blankets to cover the motel furnishings—and resolve to begin breaking that habit as soon as your trip is over. Every dog should have his own (washable) bed. Place it on the floor beside you so he's still close, but don't let him sleep on your bed.

If your dog gets bored or rambunctious in the room, offer him a favorite chew toy to play with. Watch that he doesn't damage the furnishings—remember, you are legally and financially responsible for any damage your dog does, both indoors and out.

While it's natural for dogs to bark at unfamiliar sounds, don't tolerate *any* barking in the room, no matter what's going on outside. Incessant barking is the single most common reason given by managers for not allowing dogs to stay.

N*ever* leave your pet alone in the room when you go out, for example, to dinner. Take him along and let him wait for you in the car rather than in the room. He'll feel safer in that familiar place and should settle right down for a nap while you're gone.

Mealtime arrangements

Put your dog's food and water bowls on a dog towel or vinyl placemat in the bathroom—its smooth floor is much easier to clean than the carpet in the main room. If your pet is an especially enthusiastic eater or slobbery drinker, it's easy to rinse the mat off and let it drip-dry in the bathtub. And don't let him drink out of the toilet—cleaning chemicals that may have been added to the water could make him sick.

On checkout day, it's a good idea to withhold food and water at least an hour before starting a long drive. If your pet tends to suffer from car sickness, you may need to do this as much as six hours before departure, meaning the night before if you plan to leave early in the morning.

Walking on the grounds

Shortly after eating or drinking, your dog will need a walk outside, in the designated pet relief area. This is also true after he has been waiting in the car while you were out having your own dinner. And of course, just before bedtime is another important walking time. Be sure to always take along the pooper scooper or plastic bag for cleaning up after him.

Before you and your dog leave the room, make him sit down by the door while you put his leash on. He should remain sitting while you open the door and step outside, then he can follow you out. Don't let him charge through the door ahead of you.

4: The Well-Behaved Traveler Hits the Road

You should always keep your dog leashed while on the premises, of course. And be courteous when taking him for a "relief walk"—use the designated pet area or at least go to the far end of the grounds, away from buildings, major footpaths and children's play areas. (And remember that pooper scooper or disposable bag!) Don't let him romp in landscaped areas like flower beds, decorative ponds or streams. Basically, just be aware of your pet's energy level and potential for destruction, and seek out areas where he can play harmlessly.

When you and your pet return to the room, check him over before stepping inside. Use the dog towel you brought from home to wipe off any mud or sand on his feet. This small courtesy only takes a second, helps to keep the carpet clean, and has a definite effect on the manager's willingness to continue accepting pets as guests.

On the trail

When you go out for the day's activities, remember to bring along the doggy water jug and drinking bowl, just as you would pack your own water bottle for a hike. And of course, the first aid kit should be in your car, not left behind in the room.

Be aware of your pet's effect on other people and animals when you're out in public. You are responsible for making sure that he doesn't cause anyone else discomfort. If you're walking along a trail, for example, rein him in to walk closely beside you when you encounter other hikers. Don't let him monopolize the whole walkway or run up to greet them—or worse yet, to challenge their own pet.

Remember that although your dog is the apple of your eye, not everyone shares your enchantment. In fact, some people are very fearful of even the smallest, meekest dog. So keep your pet on the leash unless you're absolutely sure that no one else is around and that there is no local leash law prohibiting dogs running free. Even then, put the leash back on as soon as you encounter another person or animal. Many towns have enacted ordinances that require dogs to be on leash *at all times*, as do most city, state and national parks.

Watch out for potential hazards underfoot: broken glass, nails or other sharp objects, burning hot pavement, melted road tar, chemical sprays or wet paint could all injure his feet or poison him when he tries to lick them off his fur.

Also remember to clean his feet after walking on snow or ice that may have been treated with salt or other de-icing chemicals.

4: The Well-Behaved Traveler Hits the Road

At the beach

Many dogs love playing in the ocean, and few scenes are more enjoyable to watch than a happy dog chasing waves up and down the beach. However, a naturalist friend has asked me to remind dog owners not to let their pets chase the shore birds, which can cause them to suffer severe or even fatal stress.

Keep a close eye on your pet while he's in the water—don't let him go out too far, as dangerous currents can arise suddenly and carry him away from shore.

Also watch that he doesn't drink too much salt water or he'll be throwing up in the car later. A little bit won't hurt him, and he'll soon learn that he doesn't like the taste after all. Just be sure to offer him a drink of fresh water when he gets back to the car. He may still need to throw up the salt water already in his stomach, so wait a few minutes before bundling him into the car.

After walking your dog on the beach, brush off any sand clinging to his feet or coat. Salt water that dries on his skin can cause lasting irritation, so rinse the salt away as soon as possible—definitely *before* returning to your room. This is where those dog towels you packed in his tote bag come in handy. And of course, the towels provided in your motel room should *never* be used on your dog!

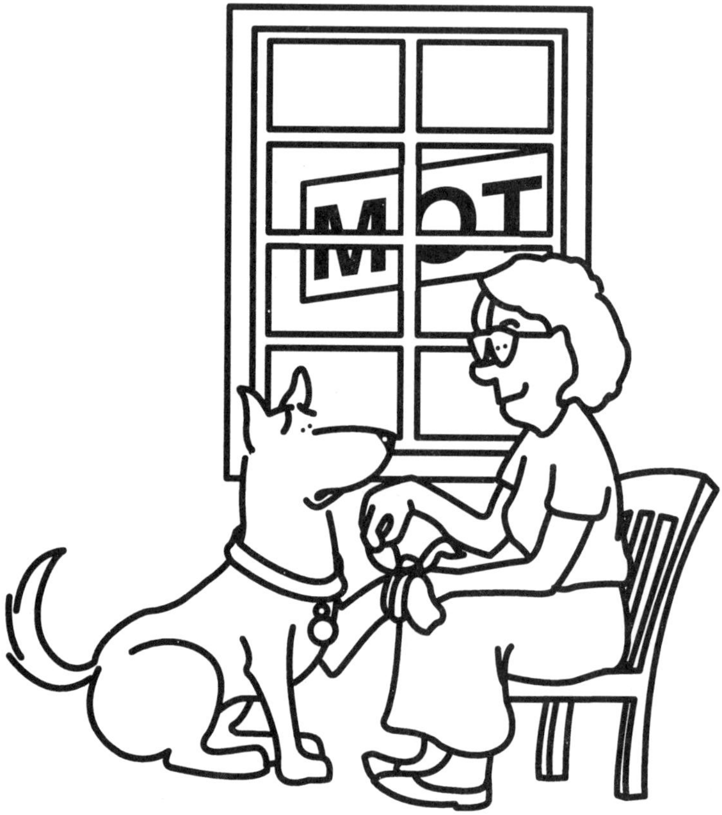
MOT

5: When Your Dog Needs First Aid

Whether your pet sustains a minor scratch or a life-threatening injury, you need to know what first aid measures to take. Then, for all but the most minor problems, your immediate next step is to get him to the nearest veterinary clinic.

If you're not sure just how serious the problem is, call them—most clinics are happy to answer questions over the phone, and can give you exact directions for getting there if it becomes necessary.

Put together your dog's own first aid kit in advance and *always* bring it (and this book) along when he travels with you. Carry it in your car when you're out and about, not back in the motel room with the luggage.

Before first aid is needed

Read through this chapter *now* to get a basic idea of what you would need to do in an emergency, and how to use the supplies in the first aid kit.

Knowing your dog's healthy state will help you to recognize when something is wrong. Sit down on the floor with your dog—he'll love the attention!—and listen to his breathing. Place your palm on his chest just behind the elbow and feel his heartbeat. Check the size and color of his pupils, the color of his gums and tongue, and how warm his body feels normally.

In an emergency, refer to specific sections in this chapter for the proper first aid steps to take. Or better yet, have another person read the steps aloud to you while you perform them on your pet. As soon as you complete the emergency procedures, take him to a veterinary clinic, or at least give call them for further instructions.

🐕 It's a good idea to identify nearby veterinary clinics at your vacation destination *before* the need arises. See the list of 24 hour emergency clinics on pp. 263–267, or check your local Yellow Pages.

5: When Your Dog Needs First Aid

Your dog's first aid kit

This list includes the emergency supplies you'll need until you can get to the clinic. All items are available from your veterinarian or local pharmacy. The dosage of some medicines varies according to body weight, so write your pet's exact dose on a piece of masking tape attached to the medicine container.

Pack it all into a sturdy container, such as a fishing tackle box or one of the colorful new cosmetics travel cases.

Travel papers—copies of your dog's license, health certificate, veterinary records if he has special medical problems, and a master lost-and-found poster with extra photos of your dog as described on p. 78. Store all this paperwork in a zip-top plastic bag

Any medication your dog is currently taking—and a copy of the written prescription

Small packets of **honey**—available in restaurants, or **hard candies** (*but no chocolate*)

Antibacterial ointment—such as *Panalog* from your veterinarian, or *Neosporin* from any pharmacy

Tranquilizers—but *only* if prescribed by your veterinarian *and* you try out the recommended dose on your pet before the trip. The ASPCA recommends against using tranquilizers because their effects can be unpredictable.

Plastic dosage spoon—to measure liquid medicines (available at any pharmacy, often for free).

Paper or **flexible plastic cup**—that you can squeeze into the shape of a pouring spout to administer liquid medicines.

Slip-on muzzle—the quick-release kind that fastens with hook-and-loop tape is especially easy to use.

Kaopectate
Hydrogen peroxide, 3% solution
Activated charcoal
Olive oil
Petroleum jelly
Sterile eye drops
Zip-top plastic bags
Sterile gauze pads
Adhesive tape and **elastic bandages**
Cotton-tipped swabs
Rectal thermometer
Ice pack
Tweezers
Pliers
Blunt-tipped scissors

Emergency stretcher—flat piece of wood or cardboard stored in your car's trunk (see p. 65).

5: When Your Dog Needs First Aid

Taking your dog's temperature

Have another person restrain your dog while you take his temperature, unless he's too weak to put up a fuss. Coat the rectal thermometer with a bit of petroleum jelly or hand lotion to make insertion easier.

Firmly grasp your dog's tail and very gently insert the thermometer about one inch while rotating it back and forth slightly. After one minute, remove it and read the temperature. Wash the thermometer with soap and *cool* water before returning it to its protective case. Normal body temperature is 100° to 101°—anything over 102.5° deserves a phone call to the veterinary clinic.

What to do in a life-threatening emergency

You have to give your pet the first aid he needs to survive until you reach a veterinarian. Remain calm and focused on what you need to do. Speak to him reassuringly while you work.

Each step listed here is described in greater detail in the sections that follow—exact page numbers are indicated for each step.

1. *Do not move him* until you have checked his injuries. The only exception is when it's unsafe to leave him where he is, such as in the middle of a busy street.

2. Check for a heartbeat—if there is none, start cardiac massage *immediately* (p. 57).

3. Check for breathing—if there is none, give him artificial respiration *immediately* (p. 57).

4. Muzzle and restrain him if he's in obvious pain, seems dazed or starts to struggle (p. 59).

5. Check for obvious injuries and take steps to control severe bleeding (p. 60).

6. Check for symptoms of internal bleeding (p. 61).

7. Check for signs of poisoning—depending on the type of poison, induce vomiting or make him swallow an antidote (p. 62).

8. Move him to your vehicle using a board, stiff cardboard or a blanket as a stretcher (p. 65).

9. Treat for shock by keeping him warm (p. 66).

10. Rush him to the nearest veterinary clinic. If possible, have another person call ahead so they can prepare for your pet's arrival.

5: When Your Dog Needs First Aid

If your dog is choking

The traveling dog may encounter chicken bones at picnic areas, fishing line at the river's edge—even more dangerous if a fishhook is still attached—or any number of other choking hazards that can be potentially fatal unless you act quickly.

Signs of choking include violent pawing at his mouth or throat and loud gasping or gagging sounds. In his panic, he may even bite your hand when you try to help.

If possible, have another person hold your pet while you open his mouth wide and pull his tongue out straight with your fingers or a cloth.

If you can see the entire object, pull it out. But *never* pull on a fishline that extends out of sight down his throat—there could be a hook at the other end. Instead, take him to a veterinary clinic for an x-ray.

If you can't see what he's choking on, place your hands on each side of his chest and squeeze in a sudden, forceful movement. The air expelled from his lungs may dislodge the object in his throat.

If he is still choking, head straight for the emergency clinic. Keep him as immobile as possible during the trip, and speak reassuringly to calm him.

If your dog is drowning

If your pet is in the water and can't make it back to shore, *do not* swim out to him. First, try to help him from shore by extending out a board, rope or any floating thing that he can hold or climb onto.

If you still can't reach him, wade part of the way out and try again. If you absolutely must swim out to him, bring something he can cling to—otherwise you could be seriously clawed or even pulled under in his panic to get out of the water.

Once you get him onto the shore, clear any debris out of his mouth and lift his hind legs as high as possible to help drain his airway.

If his heart has stopped, start cardiac massage *immediately* (p. 57).

If he has a heartbeat but is not breathing, give artificial respiration *immediately* (p. 57).

Once he begins breathing on his own, dry him off and keep him warm. If he's willing to drink, give him warm liquids. If his body temperature doesn't quickly return to normal, check with a veterinarian for follow-up treatment.

5: When Your Dog Needs First Aid

Cardiac massage

Place your palm on your dog's chest just behind the elbow. (Practice this at home until you can easily detect his normal heartbeat.) If his heart has stopped beating, you have to restart it *right now*!

Gently lay your dog on his side with head extended—don't move him suddenly, as that can further deepen his shock. Pull his tongue out of his mouth to clear the airway.

Place your hands on each side of his chest just behind the elbow. Squeeze firmly and quickly to compress the chest and then release. Repeat once every second for 1 minute, then check for heartbeat again. If there still is none, repeat the steps above. As soon as his heart starts beating, give artificial respiration to restore his breathing.

Artificial respiration

Check your pet's heartbeat before beginning this procedure. If his heart has stopped, you must perform cardiac massage (see above) before giving artificial respiration.

If your dog has swallowed water while drowning or inhaled vomit or other liquids, lift his back legs as high above his head as possible for 15 seconds and give 3 or

4 downward shakes to drain his airway. Gently pull his tongue out and clear any debris out of his mouth with your hand or a cloth.

Place your hands on both sides of his chest just behind the elbow. Squeeze hard and then immediately release. Repeat once every 5 seconds for 1 minute.

If the movement of air into and out of the lungs seems blocked, open his mouth wide to see if an object is lodged in his throat, and remove it.

If he doesn't start breathing within 1 minute, grasp his muzzle firmly to hold his mouth shut. Take a deep breath, place your mouth over his nose forming an airtight seal, and blow gently. His chest should rise as the lungs expand.

Remove your mouth and listen for air leaving the lungs. Repeat every 5 seconds for 1 minute (10 to 15 breaths). Check to see if he's breathing on his own, then repeat for another 10 to 15 breaths and so on.

Have someone drive you and your dog to the veterinary clinic while you continue helping him to breathe. Don't give up even if there is no immediate response—dogs have been successfully revived after extended periods of artificial resuscitation, as long as the heart keeps beating.

5: When Your Dog Needs First Aid

Restraining an injured dog

An injured dog is also frightened, dazed, and in pain. He may not even recognize you, and may bite when you try to help him. Unless he's unconscious, you'll need to muzzle him before you can check his injuries.

Use the slip-on muzzle in your first aid kit or improvise one from a handkerchief, scarf, or his own leash—whatever is handy. Since a muzzle doesn't work well on a short-nosed dog, loosely place a coat or blanket over his head instead. Whatever you use, be sure not to restrict your dog's breathing. And be ready to remove the muzzle *immediately* if your dog starts to vomit or has trouble breathing.

Broken bones

If your dog is unable to move his leg or holds it at an odd angle, the bone may be fractured. Muzzle and restrain him before checking for broken bones, and handle the injured leg as little as possible. If the bone is protruding from the wound, cover with a clean cloth and control the bleeding with direct pressure.

If you can find a rigid stretcher (see p. 65) for moving your dog, don't waste time applying a splint. But if you have to jostle him in a blanket stretcher or carry him in your arms, you've got to immobilize the broken ends of the bone before moving him.

To apply a temporary splint, wrap a clean cloth around the leg for padding. Fold a newspaper, magazine or piece of cardboard in a U-shape around the leg or lay a strip of wood alongside it. Hold it all in place with adhesive tape or strips of cloth. The splint should extend beyond the joints above and below the fracture in order to hold the broken bones still.

External bleeding

Your first concern is to stop any major bleeding. Minor wounds that are losing only a small amount of blood can wait for the veterinarian. But if blood is spurting out or flowing steadily, you must act *now*.

Cover the wound with a sterile gauze pad or clean cloth if possible, or just place your hand directly over the source of the blood flow. Apply firm, steady pressure until the bleeding stops.

If the wound is on the leg or tail and you cannot slow down the blood loss after a few minutes of direct pressure, you must apply a tourniquet. This may result in having to amputate the appendage, so use this method only as a last resort—*always* try direct pressure first. And *never* place the tourniquet over a joint or a fractured bone.

Wrap a handkerchief or other strip of cloth in a loose loop around the leg about one inch above the wound.

5: When Your Dog Needs First Aid

Tie it with a double knot, then place a strong, short stick in the loop. Twist the stick to tighten the loop until the blood flow stops.

Now take him to the emergency clinic, *fast*. On the way to the clinic, you *must* loosen the tourniquet every 10 minutes to allow some blood to flow through the appendage. Apply direct pressure to the wound to prevent further bleeding, and tighten the tourniquet again only if absolutely necessary.

If you suspect internal bleeding

Hidden bleeding inside your dog's body can result from a traumatic blow, or from certain kinds of poison. Even if he has no visible wounds, his internal organs may be seriously damaged. He may go into fatal shock without immediate veterinary care.

Signs of internal bleeding include: pale skin, gums and tongue; bleeding from ears, mouth or anus; bloody vomit or stool; difficulty breathing; extreme sleepiness. Symptoms may appear right after the accident or hours later, even if he seemed fine initially.

Use a rigid stretcher (see p. 65) if at all possible to move your dog to and from your car on the way to the emergency clinic. Keep him warm and don't jostle him any more than you absolutely have to.

Poisoning

Your dog can be poisoned by eating or drinking a toxic substance, by inhaling it, by licking it off his coat or paws or by absorbing it through his skin.

Poisons your pet might encounter when traveling include spilled antifreeze, toxic bait put out for insects or rodents (or their dead bodies), garbage that contains poisonous substances or chemical sprays on plants that your dog chews or rolls in. Even your own prescription medicine can poison your pet if he discovers it in the motel room and accidentally swallows some while playing with this new "toy."

Symptoms of poisoning include: drooling or difficulty swallowing; trembling; cringing; abdominal pain or vomiting; rapid, shallow breathing; twitching; coma.

Contact poisoning

Rinse his coat *immediately* with lots of water—fresh water, sea water, mud puddle by the side of the road—whatever it takes to dilute the chemical and wash it away. Wear rubber gloves if you can, to avoid getting the toxic chemicals on your hands.

Then wash him with mild hand soap or dog shampoo and rinse thoroughly again with clean water. Repeat until all traces of the chemicals are removed.

5: When Your Dog Needs First Aid

Watch your pet closely over the next few hours. If his skin appears irritated or he shows any symptoms of internal poisoning, see or call a veterinarian.

Swallowed poisons

Your first step is to determine what kind of poison your pet has swallowed. If the product container is available, it may identify the ingredients, the antidote and whether or not to induce vomiting.

Depending on the type of poison, you must choose between two very different first aid treatments—see **Method A** and **Method B** on the following page.

If you can't identify the type of poison, examine your dog's mouth and throat. If the tissues look burned or raw, treat for acid/alkali poisoning—Method A.

Try to collect a sample of the poison in one of the zip-top plastic bags from your first aid kit, or bring the poison container itself if at all possible. Also collect some of the material your dog vomits up. These samples will help the veterinarian identify the exact antidote your dog needs.

Then take him to the nearest veterinary clinic immediately!

Method A. When the poison IS an acid, alkali, or petroleum product:
   DO NOT INDUCE VOMITING!
These extremely corrosive poisons will injure your dog's throat and mouth even more if he throws up.

Rinse his mouth with water to wash away any remaining chemicals. Make him swallow 2 to 3 tablespoons of olive oil or up to a cup of milk.

Keep him warm with a blanket or coat while you rush him to the nearest veterinary clinic.

Method B. When the poison is NOT an acid, alkali, or petroleum product:
   INDUCE VOMITING IMMEDIATELY!
Mix equal parts of hydrogen peroxide and water. Make him swallow $1\frac{1}{2}$ tablespoonfuls of this mixture for every 10 pounds of body weight.

> Example: the dose for a 60-lb dog would be 6 x $1\frac{1}{2}$ = 9 tablespoons.

If he doesn't vomit within 10 minutes, repeat this dosage, but not more than three doses altogether.

After he vomits, make him swallow a mixture of 3 to 4 tablespoonfuls of activated charcoal in a cup of warm water.

Keep him warm with a blanket or coat while you rush him to the nearest veterinary clinic.

5: When Your Dog Needs First Aid

A special warning about antifreeze—sweet but deadly

Every year, dogs die from drinking antifreeze that dripped onto the ground from leaking car radiators, or was spilled by careless humans. This coolant has a sweet smell and taste that attracts many pets to try it—but even a tiny spoonful can be deadly.

If your dog has swallowed even the tiniest amount of antifreeze, induce vomiting *immediately* and rush him to a veterinarian for an antidote injection—but you must work *fast*. Minutes can make the difference between losing him or saving his life.

🐕 Pet-safe antifreeze is now available at auto supply stores and some service centers; ask for it the next time you have the radiator fluid in your car changed!

Moving an injured dog

The safest way to move your pet is on a *stretcher*, a flat rigid surface that won't flex under his weight. A piece of wood, heavy cardboard will do, or even an air mattress blown up as firm as you can make it. If that's unavailable, use a blanket, tarp or piece of clothing that you can carry by its corners to make as flat a surface as possible.

Slide your dog onto the stretcher without twisting or shaking him. If possible, have a helper lift his hindquarters and abdomen at exactly the same moment that you lift his head and shoulders.

If you are alone and can't find a rigid stretcher, you'll have to carry him in your arms. Place one arm around his hindquarters and the other around his front legs at the shoulder, supporting his head on your arm. Keep his spine as straight as possible.

Treating for shock

Shock is a sudden collapse of your dog's circulatory system brought on by sudden injury or other trauma. Be very careful not to jostle or quickly move him—any rapid movement can bring on the *fatal* stages of shock.

Symptoms of shock include: extreme muscle weakness; loss of bladder and bowel control; shallow, rapid breathing and pulse; pale or whitish gums and mouth; body feels cold; appears asleep or semiconscious.

Pull his tongue straight forward to clear the airway—be very cautious, as even the most gentle dog may bite when dazed from great pain or fear.

Try to get his head lower than his body to encourage circulation. However, if he has a head injury, keep his head level with his body.

5: When Your Dog Needs First Aid

Cover him with a warm blanket or coat—unless the shock is caused by heatstroke and his temperature is already too high. Now take him to a veterinarian for follow-up care, and have someone call ahead so they can prepare for the emergency procedures he will need as soon as he gets there.

Treating burns

Watch for hazards that can lead to your dog being accidentally burned: sparks from a beach bonfire, boiling hot liquids spilled from a tiny kitchen unit, licking meat juices from a hot barbecue grill or brushing against a space heater. Chewing on an electrical cord can lead to burns in the mouth as well as unconsciousness, shock, and even death—be sure to *unplug the cord* before touching your dog.

If the burned skin is red but not broken, run cold water over it, or cover with an ice pack or a cold wet towel. If the burned area is heavily blistered, raw, weeping or bleeding, blackened or whitish, *do not apply ice or water*—just cover with a sterile gauze pad or clean cloth.

Treat for shock (see p. 66) and get your dog to the nearest veterinarian *immediately*.

Minor cuts and scrapes

When Ginger is on the trail of a squirrel (though she never catches them) she'll gleefully charge into the thickest blackberry patch. She returns covered with thorns and scratches—grinning like a fool and enormously pleased with herself. So I've gotten plenty of practice at removing stickers and cleaning up her scrapes and scratches.

I have a running joke with Ginger's regular veterinarian that the next time she needs stitches for a torn-up ear—which means shaving a bald strip around the ear to keep fur out of the wound as it heals—we're going to give her a gold earring to go with her Mohawk haircut.

Rinse away any dirt in your pet's wound with clean water, then swab with hydrogen peroxide. If it's still bleeding, cover with a gauze pad and apply pressure until the bleeding stops. Then lightly apply an antibiotic ointment such as *Panalog* or *Neosporin*.

If the wound is large or your dog just won't leave it alone, cover with a gauze pad held in place with adhesive tape or an elastic bandage. And of course, for anything more than a minor scratch or scrape, you should have a veterinarian take a look at it.

5: When Your Dog Needs First Aid

Removing foreign objects

Use common sense in deciding whether or not to try removing an embedded object such as a burr or porcupine quill. In some cases, incorrect removal can do more harm than if you just keep your dog as motionless as possible while taking him straight to the nearest clinic to let the veterinarian do the job.

From the ears—Use tweezers to gently remove seeds or burrs from the *outer* ear canal. If your dog still shakes his head or scratches repeatedly at his ear, seeds may also be deeper inside the ear canal and must be removed by a veterinarian.

From the eyes—If your pet paws at his eye or rubs his face along the ground, gently hold the eyelid open and check for seeds or debris. To wash away a loose object, apply sterile eye drops. Don't try to remove an object that is embedded into the eye's surface. Instead, take him to the nearest veterinary clinic *right away*.

From everywhere else—You're already familiar with this routine if your dog loves to crash through the underbrush like Ginger does. Run your hands gently over his face, body and feet to check for thorns. If he's limping or holding up his paw, he's already zeroed in on the problem for you.

Use tweezers to pull out embedded stickers. If there's any bleeding or tearing of the skin, swab with hydrogen peroxide. When a foreign object is buried too deeply to find, either soak the affected body part in salt water (1 teaspoon salt per cup of lukewarm water) several times a day until the object works its way up to the surface where you can remove it, or else have a veterinarian remove it to begin with.

Remove sharp objects—such as porcupine quills or a fishhook—with pliers. Begin by using the wire cutter notches at the center of the pliers to clip off each porcupine quill tip, or the barbed point of the fishhook *if it is exposed.* When finished, rinse all the wounds with hydrogen peroxide. But if the fishhook point is hidden below the skin surface, or your dog won't submit to having the quills pulled out, take him straight to a veterinarian.

And watch out for ticks—Examine your dog closely after outdoor activities, especially his head, shoulders and feet. Forget the old wives' tales about using a match to burn the tick off, applying gasoline or petroleum jelly to make it let go, and so on. However, dousing the tick with alcohol or nail polish remover *may* make it easier to remove.

Use tweezers to grab the tick by its head, very close to the dog's skin, and firmly pull it out. Don't squeeze its fat abdomen—doing so might force disease-carrying blood back into the bite wound.

5: When Your Dog Needs First Aid

Above all, *don't use your fingers*. Ticks can carry Lyme disease and Rocky Mountain spotted fever, both of which are dangerous to humans. Swab the bite area with hydrogen peroxide. If the skin becomes red or irritated, see a veterinarian for follow-up treatment.

Treating an upset stomach

Car sickness is one of the most common complaints for the traveling dog—whether it's because he's fearful of the car, or just overly excited about coming along. Try reducing his stress level with practice rides as described on p. 35. Don't give food or water for at least an hour before traveling. And always allow him a few minutes of exercise and a last-minute chance to relieve himself.

If your dog still gets carsick, give him a small spoonful of honey, a piece of hard candy or a spoonful of plain vanilla ice cream to calm his stomach. *However, you should never give your dog any food containing chocolate, as it can be toxic!*

If these simple remedies don't help, ask your regular veterinarian about stronger medicines for motion sickness.

An upset stomach can also be caused by eating unfamiliar or spoiled food, or drinking unfamiliar water—contaminants in the water or a different mineral content can throw your pet's system for a loop.

Give him 2 teaspoons of Kaopectate for each ten pounds of body weight, once every four hours. If the problem doesn't clear up within a day, this may be a symptom of a more serious illness, so take him to a veterinarian.

Treating diarrhea

This may be a temporary upset caused by the stress of unfamiliar surroundings, food or water, or a symptom of a more serious illness. Give 2 teaspoons of Kaopectate per ten pounds of body weight, once every four hours.

See a veterinarian if the diarrhea doesn't clear up within a day or if other symptoms appear, such as labored breathing, bloody stool, either a rise or drop in body temperature, listlessness or loss of appetite.

Dealing with heat problems

Summer can mean added hazards for your pet. Short haired dogs can be sunburned just as easily as people can. Older or overweight pets are more prone to heat problems, as are short-nosed breeds and dogs who are taking certain medications. Heat problems are even more likely if the humidity is also high.

When walking your dog, pay special attention to the surface underfoot—if it's too hot for your bare feet, then it's too hot for your dog's paws as well.

5: When Your Dog Needs First Aid

Heatstroke can be caused by too much exercise in the hot sun, not drinking enough water, or simply from sitting in a hot car. On a sunny 80° day, the temperature inside your parked car (even with the windows partly rolled down) will climb well above 100° in just minutes, putting your pet in danger of permanent damage to the brain and internal organs, and even death.

Recognizing the danger signs

Symptoms of heatstroke may include some or all of the following: frenzied barking; a vacant expression or wild-eyed stare; rapid or heavy panting; rapid pulse; dizziness or weakness; vomiting or diarrhea; deep red or purple tongue and gums (the normal color is light pink, except in breeds where the gums and tongue are naturally black); twitching, convulsions or coma.

Use a rectal thermometer to check your dog's body temperature. Normal body temperature is 100° to 101°—but it can rise to 106° or more with heatstroke.

First aid for heatstroke

First, get your dog out of the sun. Then cover him with towels soaked in cool water, or pour cool water over him every few minutes. *Do not* immerse him in ice water or apply ice directly to his skin, but an ice pack is okay if wrapped in a towel.

Give him a small amount of cool water to drink, or let him lick ice cubes or a bit of plain vanilla ice cream. (Remember—no chocolate!) As soon as his body temperature begins to come down, take him to the nearest veterinarian for follow-up care.

Keeping your pet safe in cold weather

Many dogs, Ginger included, love outdoor activities in snowy weather. But don't assume that your dog is as safe and comfortable as you are in your insulated boots and down-filled clothing. Wintertime hazards include hypothermia, frostbite, and irritation from road salt and other de-icing chemicals.

After playing outside, wash off any remaining ice or road salt, and towel him dry. Then give him a well-deserved rest in a warm place—but not too close to a fireplace or space heater. If he's really chilled, he could burn himself before even realizing it.

Watch out for hypothermia

Smaller or older dogs are most likely to suffer from hypothermia. However, exposure to the cold *when wet* can be extremely hazardous for any dog, especially if immersed in icy water for even a few minutes.

5: When Your Dog Needs First Aid

When your pet starts to lag behind you instead of bounding ahead, that's the signal to get him back indoors and warmed up. If he becomes listless, ignores your calls and just wants to lie down in the snow, you've stayed out too long—get him indoors!

Dry him off and help to restore his circulation by rubbing vigorously with a towel. Wrap him in a warm blanket, and offer warm (not hot) water if he's willing to drink. If his body temperature drops below 98.5° take him to a veterinarian *immediately*.

Treating for frostbite

When the weather turns windy, check frequently to see if your dog's feet, ears, and tail are getting pale or numb. If so, bring him indoors right away. Massage the affected areas *very gently* with your hands or a soft dry towel to encourage circulation—rough handling can bruise damaged tissues. Soak frostbitten paws or tail in lukewarm (90°) water to gradually restore circulation. Keep him warm and see, or at least *call*, a veterinarian for follow-up care.

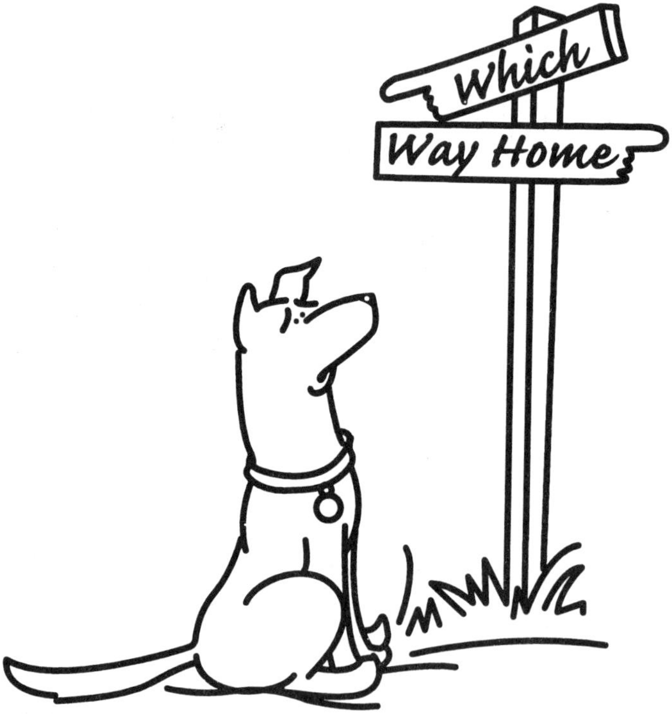
Which
Way Home

6: If Your Dog Gets Lost

You've heard the saying "if you carry an umbrella, it won't rain." Hopefully, being prepared in case your dog gets lost will work the same way for you. And it will remind you of how important—and easy—it is to *prevent* losing him.

The basic prevention measures (you've seen all these before) include:

- Make sure your dog is *always* wearing his collar with ID tags attached. (See p. 11 for information on proper travel tags.)

- Put his leash on *before* letting him out of your car or motel room—and hold onto the other end!

- *Never* leave him alone and unrestrained—he should be in his travel crate or at least inside your car, with adequate ventilation and shade.

That said, if by some fluke you and your dog do get separated, don't panic. Your cool-headed actions now, plus a few advance preparations, will maximize your chances of finding him as quickly as possible.

Preparing a Lost Dog poster

Your first advance effort should be in creating a master lost-and-found poster, complete with your dog's photo and detailed description. Feel free to copy the fill-in-the-blanks poster on the following pages and use it to create your own poster.

First, write a brief description of your pet. Include his name, age, breed, sex (and if neutered or spayed), coat and eye color, height (at top of head or ears when standing), weight, and any special characteristics, such as a crooked tail or a limp.

Second, dig out a close-up photo of your pet, or take a new one right now. It should clearly show his color, any distinctive markings and his relative size. Photograph your dog standing beside a person or a car, for example. Have copies made of this photo that you can attach to multiple copies of your completed lost-and-found poster when needed.

List your home phone number—for leaving a message—and if possible, also list another number that will be answered by a live person who can receive and relay

LOST DOG

Name: **Ginger** Breed: **German Shepherd** Age: **5 yrs**
Sex: **Spayed female** Ht: **30"** Wt: **60 lbs**
Collar: **red nylon** Eye color: **golden brown**
Coat color & length: **tan w/black markings, short straight hair**
ID tags: **Yamhill County license #3617, Rabies tag #03756**
Distinctive markings or behaviors:

Very friendly with people but standoffish with other dogs.

Black ears, muzzle, back and tip of tail

Last seen at:

east end of Memorial Park, near corner of Market & First Sts, approx 3:15 p.m. Monday August 1

Owners: **Linn & Barbara Whitaker**
Staying at: **The Beach Place**
Address: **555 Hwy 101, Lincoln City OR**
Local Phone: **541-555-1212**
Dates at this location: **August 1-3**
Home Phone: **503-625-3001 after August 4**

(Call collect or leave message and we will reimburse you.)

REWARD!

LOST DOG

Breed: Age:

Ht: Wt:

Eye color:

Attach photo of your dog here

Name:

Sex:

Collar:

Coat color & length:

ID tags:

Distinctive markings or behaviors:

Last seen at:

Owner's name:

Staying at:

Address:

Local Phone:

Dates at this location:

Home Phone :

(Call collect or leave message and owner will reimburse you)

REWARD!

messages for you. Of course, if you have a mobile phone that works in the area you're visiting, list that number as well. Leave blank spaces for the name, address and phone number of your motel. You'll add that information when you actually need to use the poster.

Store the master poster and photos with your dog's other travel papers, which I recommend keeping in a plastic bag inside his first aid kit. Also tuck in a broad tipped marking pen.

Searching for your lost dog

As soon as you realize your pet is missing, begin searching the immediate area in an ever-widening spiral pattern. Keep calling your dog's name—if he's within the sound of your voice, *he'll* find *you*.

It's important to search *on foot*, not in your car, for several reasons. First, if you're walking, your dog is more likely to catch your scent and come back to you. Second, when you're cruising along in the car, your pet may hear you call him, but by the time he runs to that location, you could be a block—or a mile—away, missing him altogether.

Try to enlist the aid of other people in your search, and offer them a reward. Children are especially good at finding lost animals.

When to call for reinforcements

If you've already searched for an hour or two without finding your dog, it's time to move on to public announcements. Place calls to the police or county sheriff's office, the dog pound or humane society, and the local veterinary clinics to see if they've already found your pet.

Remember to tell everyone if your dog has been implanted with an identification microchip (see p. 13 for more information).

Leave your local phone number with everyone you speak to, and check back periodically. Also ask if there is a local radio or TV station that broadcasts lost pet announcements as a public service. (Then after you find your dog, be sure to let all these folks know, so they don't continue to put out the alert!)

Putting up Lost Dog posters

If you've already checked with local authorities and still haven't found your dog, you'll need to start posting Lost Dog notices around the area. That way, when someone does find him, they'll know how to contact you.

Get out your master poster and fill in the name, address, and phone number of the place where you're staying. Then take it to the local quick print shop, or any other store with a copy machine available, and run off multiple copies for posting around town. Use white or light-colored paper—neon yellow is especially eye-catching from a distance and still light enough to be readable.

Attach a photo of your pet to each poster copy. If you only have one original photo, you could attach it to your master poster and then make multiple *color copies* at the quick print shop.

Beginning at the location where your dog was last seen and spiraling outward again, start putting up your posters wherever people congregate:

- On bulletin boards in parks, shopping malls, or in front of convenience stores
- In store windows—ask for permission first!
- At bus stops or parking lot entrances
- On street signs or light posts, especially where cars are likely to be stopping or moving slowly
- Near schools or churches

Since the motel's phone number appears on each poster, notify them of your situation right away. If you can, have a family member stay by the phone in your room in case that all-important "found dog" call comes in while you're

6: If Your Dog Gets Lost

out searching. If not, see if the folks at the front desk can take messages for you.

Keep checking back at the place where your dog disappeared, in case he returns there. By the end of the day, he will be increasingly hungry, thirsty, and anxious about being separated from you. Leave a handful of his food there, along with something that has your scent on it, such as a dirty sock. Finding this sign of you during the night may encourage him to stay there until you come back in the morning.

Stay in the local area as long as possible—even if you don't find your pet right away, he may reappear after another day or two. For example, a compassionate resident may take him in overnight, then deliver him to the local dog pound or animal shelter the next day.

When you do have to leave town, be sure to leave your home phone number with everyone—motel management, police, dog pound, local veterinarians—along with instructions to call you *collect*.

And of course, check your home phone often for messages. If your dog is picked up and traced by his license number, rabies tag number or microchip ID, you'll be contacted at your *permanent* address and phone number, so keep those lines of communication open as well.

May your dog never get lost

Your pet is a beloved member of your family, and I sincerely hope you never lose him. Please, spend just a minute or two reviewing the simple steps at the beginning of this chapter to prevent losing him in the first place.

Happy travels to you and your dog from Ginger and myself— and Spike too!

Part II
Reference Section
Hotels—Motels—B & B Listings
Emergency Clinics
Useful Books
Listings Index
Topics Index

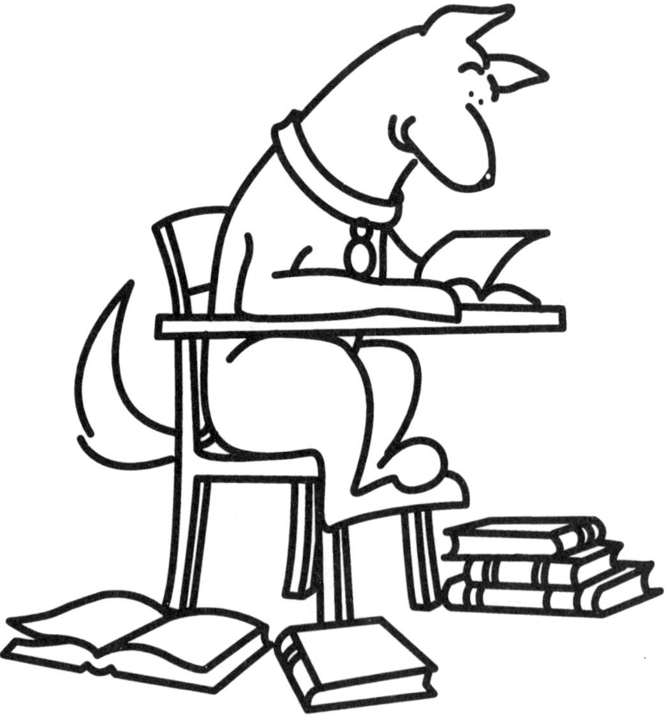

A: Where to Stay in Washington With Your Dog

This directory is alphabetized by city, then business name. If you know the name but not the city, you can look it up in the Listings Index on pp. 273–301. All the hotels, motels and bed & breakfast inns listed here allow dogs in some but not necessarily all rooms. Always call ahead to reserve one of their dog-friendly units. Also be aware that many establishments accept dogs "at the manager's discretion only," meaning they reserve the right to refuse overly dirty, large or out-of-control pets.

The room rates shown are "before tax" in most cases, and are accurate as of the time each location was contacted prior to the publication of this book. However, as in most industries, all rates are subject to change without notice, so ask for the current prices when you call for reservations.

If you don't see one of your favorite establishments listed here, don't despair. Some folks said that although they do accept dogs occasionally, they didn't wish to "go public" with that information and requested not to be included in this directory. Most of them also said that they will continue to accept return customers who've stayed there with their dogs in the past.

Deciphering these listings
I've tried to include as much useful information as possible in each listing, especially dog-related tips. As more and more dog-friendly lodgings were discovered, some abbreviations became necessary!

food/beverage
R = restaurant on the premises
L = lounge in or attached to the restaurant
B&B= bed & breakfast

free
C = complimentary coffee (sometimes also tea or hot chocolate) in the room or in the lobby
CB = continental breakfast
FB = full breakfast

How each listing is laid out:

name	phone #	# of units
address	toll-free #	price range
city-state-zip	email or website address	

A: Where to Stay in Washington with Your Dog

kitchen
K = full kitchen or kitchenette in the room
R = refrigerator, either included or on request
M = microwave oven, same note as refrigerator

pet fee
$ = fee shown is for each dog, either per day or the entire stay, as indicated
ref dep = refundable damage deposit; can be in the form of an open credit card charge slip or a check—either of which is then returned at checkout if no damage has occurred

pool (may be seasonal or year round)
in = indoor or covered
out = outdoor
htd = heated

spa/sauna/hot tub
sp = spa/Jacuzzi
tb = hot tub
sa = sauna or steam room
rm = in-room Jacuzzi

other features
items of further interest to dog owners

food/bev	free	kitchen	pet fee	pool	spa	other features
R & L	C CB FB	K R M	$ per day	in out htd	X	additional information about rules, features or nearby attractions that would be of interest to dog owners

Have Dog Will Travel—Washington Edition

Washington cities with dog-friendly lodgings

City	Number	City	Number
Aberdeen	5	Chehalis	1
Airway Heights	2	Chelan	3
Amanda Park	2	Cheney	2
Anacortes	9	Chewelah	2
Anatone	1	Clallam Bay	2
Anderson Island	1	Clarkston	5
Arlington	2	Cle Elum	7
Ashford	1	Clinton	4
Auburn	5	Colville	4
Bainbridge Island	2	Conconully	4
Belfair	2	Concrete	1
Bellevue	6	Connell	2
Bellingham	13	Conway	1
Bingen	1	Copalis Beach	3
Birch Bay	1	Coulee City	4
Black Diamond	1	Coulee Dam	2
Blaine	5	Coupeville	2
Bothell	1	Curlew	1
Bow	1	Darrington	1
Bremerton	6	Davenport	2
Brewster	1	Dayton	4
Buckley	1	Deer Harbor	1
Camano Island	1	Deer Park	1
Carson	2	Deming	2
Cashmere	1	Des Moines	1
Castle Rock	1	East Wenatchee	2
Centralia	7	Easton	1

A: Where to Stay in Washington with Your Dog

City	Number	City	Number
Eastsound	4	Ione	2
Eatonville	2	Issaquah	1
Edmonds	4	Kelso	5
Elk	1	Kennewick	11
Ellensburg	3	Kent	6
Elma	2	Kettle Falls	3
Entiat	1	Kingston	1
Enumclaw	2	Kirkland	3
Ephrata	1	La Conner	3
Everett	8	La Push	2
Federal Way	5	Lacey	1
Ferndale	4	Lakewood	4
Fife	5	Langley	9
Forks	13	Leavenworth	19
Freeland	4	Lilliwaup	1
Friday Harbor	7	Long Beach	17
Fruitland	1	Longview	6
Gig Harbor	7	Loomis	1
Glacier	2	Loon Lake	2
Goldendale	2	Lynnwood	4
Grand Coulee	2	Mansfield	1
Grandview	1	Maple Falls	1
Granite Falls	1	Marysville	3
Grayland	4	Mazama	1
Hoodsport	1	Metaline Falls	3
Hoquiam	3	Moclips	4
Ilwaco	3	Monroe	2
Inchelium	2	Montesano	2
Index	1	Morton	3

Have Dog Will Travel—Washington Edition

City	Number	City	Number
Moses Lake	16	Pateros	1
Mossyrock	1	Peshastin	2
Mount Vernon	8	Point Roberts	1
Mountlake Terrace	1	Pomeroy	1
Naches	1	Port Angeles	13
Nahcotta	1	Port Hadlock	1
Naselle	1	Port Ludlow	1
Neah Bay	2	Port Orchard	2
Nespelem	1	Port Townsend	9
Newman Lake	1	Poulsbo	1
Newport	3	Prosser	3
North Bend	1	Pullman	7
Oak Harbor	3	Puyallup	3
Oakesdale	1	Quilcene	2
Ocean City	4	Quinault	1
Ocean Park	7	Quincy	2
Ocean Shores	12	Randle	4
Odessa	1	Raymond	2
Okanogan	3	Renton	2
Olalla	2	Republic	6
Olga	1	Richland	6
Olympia	6	Rimrock	1
Omak	5	Ritzville	4
Orcas Island	1	Rockford	1
Oroville	2	Rockport	3
Othello	2	Roslyn	3
Pacific Beach	3	Salkum	1
Packwood	5	SeaTac	2
Pasco	10	Seattle	36

A: Where to Stay in Washington with Your Dog

City	Number	City	Number
Seaview	5	Tumwater	4
Sedro Woolley	2	Twisp	2
Sekiu	5	Union	1
Sequim	10	Union Gap	3
Shelton	6	Usk	1
Shoreline	1	Valley	1
Silver Creek	1	Vancouver	12
Silver Lake	1	Vantage	1
Silverdale	1	Vashon Island	6
Skykomish	1	Walla Walla	11
Snohomish	2	Washougal	1
Snoqualmie	1	Waterville	1
Snoqualmie Pass	1	Wenatchee	13
Soap Lake	5	Westport	15
South Bend	3	White Salmon	1
Spokane	51	Wilbur	2
Sprague	1	Winthrop	7
Stevenson	1	Woodland	4
Sultan	2	Yakima	19
Sumas	1	Yelm	1
Sumner	1	Zillah	1
Sunnyside	3	Total	829
Tacoma	15		
Tahuya	1		
Thorp	1		
Tokeland	1		
Tonasket	2		
Toppenish	3		
Tukwila	2		

Have Dog Will Travel—Washington Edition

Aberdeen — Anacortes

Nordic Inn Motel 1700 S Boone St Aberdeen, WA 98520	360-533-0100 800-442-0101	66 units $40–$80
Olympic Inn Motel 616 W Heron St Aberdeen, WA 98520	360-533-4200 800-562-8618	55 units $52–$95
Red Lion Inn 521 W Wishkah St Aberdeen, WA 98520	360-532-5210	67 units $55–$109
Thunderbird Motel 410 W Wishkah St Aberdeen, WA 98520	360-532-3153 ramatb@techline.com	36 units $52–$58
Trave-Lure Motel 623 W Wishkah St Aberdeen, WA 98520	360-532-3280	24 units $35–$60
Lantern Park Motel West 13820 Sunset Hwy, PO Box 567 Airway Heights, WA 99001	509-244-3653 lanternpark@aol.com	13 units $29–$57
Solar World Estates Motel Alternat. 1832 S Lawson St, PO Box 1420 Airway Heights, WA 99001	509-244-3535 800-650-9484	15 units $50–$60
Amanda Park Motel & Rv Park 8 River Dr, PO Box 624 Amanda Park, WA 98526	360-288-2237 800-410-2237	8 units $45–$70
Lochaerie Resort 638 N Shore Rd Amanda Park, WA 98526	360-288-2215	5 units $60–$70
Anaco Inn 905 20th St Anacortes, WA 98221	360-293-8833 888-293-8833	8 units $44–$90

See pp. 90-91 for a key to the

A: Where to Stay in Washington with Your Dog

food/bev	free	kitchen	pet fee	pool	spa	other features
	C	R M	$5 $10 /day			adjacent to walking trail
	C CB	K R M	$5 per day			laundry facilities, 9 blocks to public park
	C CB					10 blocks to riverfront walk, restaurants within walking distance
	C	R M			sp	laundry facilities, riverfront park approximately 1 mile away
	C	R M	$5 per day			2 blocks to public park
	C	K R M	$3 per day			grassy lawn for walking dogs, less than ½ mi to public park
		K	$100 per stay		rm	$200 deposit ($100 is refundable), laundry facilities, area for walking dogs, 6 blocks to public park
		R	$5-$10 /day			grassy riverfront yard and view, close to public park
		K	$25 per stay			fully equipped lakeside cottages, shorthaired dogs only, advance reservations required, close to park
	C CB FB	K R M	$10 per day		tb rm	laundry facilities

abbreviations used in this section   97

Anacortes — Anderson Island

Anacortes Inn 3006 Commercial Ave Anacortes, WA 98221	360-293-3153 800-327-7976	44 units $50–$100
Guemes Island Resort 4268 Guemes Island Rd Anacortes, WA 98221	360-293-6643 800-965-6643 guemesresort@juno.com	8 units $80–$220
Holiday Motel 2903 Commercial Ave Anacortes, WA 98221	360-293-6511	10 units $30–$55
Islands Inn 3401 Commercial Ave Anacortes, WA 98221	360-293-4644	36 units $60–$120
Lake Campbell Lodging 6676 SR 20 Anacortes, WA 98221	360-293-5314	10 units $39–$80
Old Brook Inn B & B 7270 Old Brook Ln, Anacortes, WA 98221	360-293-4768 800-503-4768 www.oldbrookinn.com	2 units $80–$90
San Juan Motel 1103 6th St Anacortes, WA 98221	360-293-5105 800-533-8009	30 units $36–$60
Ship Harbor Inn 5316 Ferry Terminal Rd Anacortes, WA 98221	360-293-5177 800-852-8568 www.shipharborinn.com	26 units $65–$95
Boggan's Oasis 61376 State Hwy 129 Anatone, WA 99401	509-256-3372	23 units $30–$60
Inn at Burg's Landing B & B 8808 Villa Beach Rd Anderson Island, WA 98303	253-884-9185 800-431-5622	4 units $70–$110

A: Where to Stay in Washington with Your Dog

food/bev	free	kitchen	pet fee	pool	spa	other features
	C	R M	$10 per stay	out htd		adjacent to park and playground
		K		out		fully furnished beachfront cabins, store, well-mannered off-leash pets preferred
		R				public park across street
R & L	C CB	R	$5 per day	out	tb	laundry service
	C CB	K R M	$5 per day			close to public park
B & B	C CB	R				children & pets welcome, 9 acres of forest trails for birdwatching & walking dogs
		K	$5 per stay			laundry facilities, area for walking dogs, 1 block to public park, 4 blocks to waterfront
R	C CB	K R M	$5 per day		tb rm	cabins, in-room hot tubs, laundry facilities, playground, miniature horses & goats, 1 mi to public park
R & L		K R				cabins & RV sites, laundry facilities, riverfront trails, 10 mi to state park
B & B	C FB				tb	dogs allowed in 1 unit only, large beachfront area for walking dogs, close to public parks & walking trail

abbreviations used in this section   99

Arlington — Bainbridge Island

Arlington Motor Inn 2214 SR 530 NE Arlington, WA 98223	360-652-9595	42 units $50–$65
Smokey Point Motor Inn 17329 Smokey Point Dr Arlington, WA 98223	360-659-8561	54 units $44–$65
Stormking Spa at Mt Rainier PO Box 126 Ashford, WA 98304	360-569-2964 www.mashell.com/~strmking/	1 unit $110–$125
Comfort Inn 1 16th St NE Auburn, WA 98002	253-833-1222 800-228-5150	53 units $58–$85
Howard Johnson 1521 D St NE Auburn, WA 98002	253-939-5950 800-446-4656	66 units
Microtell Inn & Suites 9 16th St NW Auburn, WA 98001	253-833-7171 888-771-7171	97 units $50–$70
Nendels Inn-Auburn 102 15th St NE Auburn, WA 98002	253-833-8007	35 units $40–$75
Val U Inn 9 14th St NW Auburn, WA 98001	253-735-9600	96 units $60–$105
Bainbridge House 5257 Lynwood Ctr Rd Bainbridge Island, WA 98110	206-842-1599	4 units $125–$150
Island Country Inn 920 Hildebrand Ln NE Bainbridge Island, WA 98110	206-842-6861 800-842-8429	46 units $69–$169

See pp. 90-91 for a key to the

A: Where to Stay in Washington with Your Dog

food/bev	free	kitchen	pet fee	pool	spa	other features
	C	R M	$25 per stay		sp	area for walking dogs
R	C CB	K R	$8 per day	out htd	tb	seasonal pool, large grassy area, ½ mi to county park on the lake
B & B	C CB	R M	$20 ref dep		tb	dogs allowed at owner's discretion and by advance reservation only, fully equipped cabin
	C CB	R M	$15 per stay	in htd	sp	open field for walking dogs
	C CB	R M	$10 per day	out	sp	large grassy area for walking dogs between the motel and a small airport
	C CB	K	$10 per stay			adjacent to walking trail
	C CB	K R M	$10 per day			large open area behind motel for walking dogs
	C CB	K R M	$5 per day		sp	area for walking dogs, laundry facilities
B & B	C CB	K R M				fully furnished apts, 3 night min stay, laundry, large wooded lot w/stream, near state park
	C CB	K R M	$10 per day	out htd	sp	

abbreviations used in this section 101

Bainbridge Island – Bellevue

Monarch Manor Rentals and B&B 7656 Madrona Dr NE Bainbridge Island, WA 98110	206-780-0112 www.monarchmanor.com	4 units $250
Waterfront Bed & Breakfast 3314 Crystal Springs Dr NE Bainbridge Island, WA 99203	206-842-2431	1 unit $60
Belfair Motel 23322 NE State Highway 3, PO Box 1135 Belfair, WA 98528	360-275-4485	28 units $50–$60
Silver Moon Resort 4071 NE North Shore Rd, PO Box 1167 Belfair, WA 98528	360-277-3611	1 unit $50–$60
Doubletree Hotel Bellevue Ctr 818 112th Ave NE Bellevue, WA 98004	425-455-1515 800-222-8733 www.doubletreehotels.com	208 units $120–$154
Homestead Guest Studios 3700 132nd Ave SE Bellevue, WA 98006	425-865-8680	149 units $64–$89
Homestead Village Guest Studios 15805 NE 28th St Bellevue, WA 98008	425-885-6675	162 units $79–$114
La Residence Suite Hotel 475 100th Ave NE Bellevue, WA 98004	425-455-1475 800-800-1993 laresidencesuite@hotmail.com	24 units $120–$160
Residence Inn by Marriott 14455 NE 29th Pl Bellevue, WA 98007	425-882-1222 800-331-3131	120 units $80–$195
Westcoast Bellevue Hotel 625 116th Ave NE Bellevue, WA 98004	425-455-9444 800-426-0670 www.westcoasthotels.com	176 units $99–$159

See pp. 90-91 for a key to the

A: Where to Stay in Washington with Your Dog

food/bev	free	kitchen	pet fee	pool	spa	other features
B&B	C	K R M	$10 per stay		sp tb rm	continental breakfast by request only, resident dog, laundry, located on Puget Sound waterfront
	C	K				private suite w/separate entrance, kitchen access, waterfront walking area for dogs
	C	K	$10 per stay			close to natural area for walking dogs
	C	K				cabin on Hood Canal, area for walking dogs, ¾ mi to Belfair State Park
R&L	C	K R M	$30 per stay	out htd	sp	refundable damage deposit, exercise room, 3 blocks to Bellevue Park
	C CB	K	$75 per stay			$5 pass to local health club, laundry facilities, area for walking dogs, 10-15 min drive to public parks
	C	K	$75 per stay			fully equipped kitchens, laundry facilities, area for walking dogs, 1½ mi to large public park
			$20 per stay			1 & 2 bdrm suites w/full kitchens, weekly & monthly rates avail, adjacent to 2 public parks
	C CB	K R M	$ per stay	out	tb	laundry facilities, 3 hot tubs, pet fee varies by length of stay ($50 to $150), area for walking dogs
R&L	C	R M		out		dogs under 20 lbs only, exercise room, suites, close to Wilburton Hill Park/Botanical Gardens

abbreviations used in this section   103

Have Dog Will Travel—Washington Edition

Bellingham

Aloha Motel 315 N Samish Way Bellingham, WA 98225	360-733-4900	28 units $30–$65
Best Western Lakeway Inn 714 Lakeway Dr Bellingham, WA 98226	360-671-1011 888-671-1011 www.bestwesternwashington.com	132 units $72–$99
Cascade Inn 208 N Samish Way Bellingham, WA 98225	360-733-2520	44 units $32–$50
Coachman Inn Motel 120 N Samish Way Bellingham, WA 98225	360-671-9000 800-962-6641	60 units $39
Days Inn-Bellingham 125 E Kellogg Rd Bellingham, WA 98226	360-671-6200 800-831-0187 www.daysinn.com	71 units $45–$120
Holiday Inn Express-Bellingham 4160 Meridian St Bellingham, WA 98226	360-671-4800 800-holiday	101 units $68–$98
Mac's Motel 1215 E Maple St Bellingham, WA 98225	360-734-7570	30 units $26–$42
Motel 6-Bellingham 3701 Byron St Bellingham, WA 98225	360-671-4494 800-466-8356	60 units $30–$40
Quality Inn-Baron Suites 100 E Kellogg Rd Bellingham, WA 98226	360-647-8000 800-900-4661 see website at right	86 units $60–$100
Rodeway Inn-Bellingham 3710 Meridian St Bellingham, WA 98225	360-738-6000 800-476-5413	74 units $45–$95

See pp. 90-91 for a key to the

A: Where to Stay in Washington with Your Dog

food/bev	free	kitchen	pet fee	pool	spa	other features
	C	K	$5 per day			or $15 per week, large garden area for walking dogs
R & L	C	R M	$5 per day	in htd	sp sa	dogs under 20 lbs only, exercise room, laundry facilities, area for walking dogs, 8 blks to public park
	C	K R M			sp	laundry facilities, area for walking dogs, 6 blocks to public park
	C CB		$10 per day	out	sp	small dogs only
	C CB	K	$7 per day	out htd	tb	laundry facilities, area for walking dogs, 1 mi to public park
	C CB	R M	$10 per stay	in htd	sp	dog walking area
	C			out htd		laundry facilities, area for walking dogs, 5 mi to Eastsound waterfront
	C CB	R M	$25 per stay	out htd	sp rm	laundry facilities, exercise room www.hotelchoice.com/hotel/WA054/
	C CB		$10 per stay		sp tb	laundry facilities, area for walking dogs, 2 blocks to walking trail & park

abbreviations used in this section

Have Dog Will Travel—Washington Edition

Bellingham — Blaine

Shangri-La Downtown Motel 611 E Holly St Bellingham, WA 98225	360-733-7050	19 units $35–$65
Travel House Inn 3750 Meridian St Bellingham, WA 98225	360-671-4600	124 units $40–$75
Val-U Inn 805 Lakeway Dr Bellingham, WA 98226	360-671-9600 800-443-7777	82 units $54–$80
City Center Motel 208 Steuben St, PO Box 14 Bingen, WA 98605	509-493-2445	9 units $32–$64
Driftwood Inn Resort Motel 7394 Birch Bay Dr Birch Bay, WA 98230	360-371-2620 800-833-2666	12 units
Sunrise Resort-Lake Sawyer 30250 224th Ave SE Black Diamond, WA 98010	360-886-2244	7 units $30–$40
Bayside Motor Inn 340 Alder St, 1529 Blaine, WA 98230	360-332-5288	24 units $30–$44
Birch Bay Vacation Rental Cottages 8068 Birch Bay Dr Blaine, WA 98230	206-325-3500 877-222-1051	2 units $750–$900 (weekly)
Harbor House Bed & Breakfast 5157 Drayton Harbor Rd Blaine, WA 98230	360-371-9060 888-705-9060	1 unit $75
Motel International 758 Peace Portal Dr Blaine, WA 98230	360-332-8222	23 units $40–$48

See pp. 90-91 for a key to the

A: Where to Stay in Washington with Your Dog

food/bev	free	kitchen	pet fee	pool	spa	other features
	C	K R M	$5 per day			small dogs allowed at manager's discretion only, 1 mi to public park
	C CB	R M	$10 per stay	out htd	sp	laundry facilities
	C CB		$5 per day		sp	small dogs only, area for walking dogs, no dogs left alone in rooms
		K R				4 blocks to riverfront walking area for people and dogs
	C	K	$7 per day	out htd		one small dog allowed in cottages Sept thru June only, laundry facilities, beach access across street
		K	$20 per stay		tb	2 bdrm cabins & trailers, RV & tent sites, laundry facilities, walking trails
	C	R M		out htd		open field across street for walking dogs
		K R M				located on Birch Bay waterfront, laundry facilities, area for walking dogs
B & B	C FB				tb	full suite w/private entry sleeps 5, area for walking dogs, waterfront location near public park
R	C	R				laundry facilities, area for walking dogs, 3 blocks to Peace Arch State Park

abbreviations used in this section   **107**

Have Dog Will Travel—Washington Edition

Blaine — Brewster

Westview Motel 1300 Peace Portal Dr Blaine, WA 98230	360-332-5501	13 units $30–$40
Residence Inn by Marriott 11920 NE 195th St Bothell, WA 98011	425-485-3030 800-331-3131	120 units $110–$185
Alice Bay Bed & Breakfast 11794 Scott Rd Bow, WA 98232	360-766-6396 800-652-0223 www.alicebay.com	1 unit $95–$115
Chieftain Motel 600 National Ave Bremerton, WA 98312	360-479-3111	45 units $36–$49
Dunes Motel 3400 11th St Bremerton, WA 98312	360-377-0093 800-828-8238	64 units $50–$60
Illahee Manor 6680 Illahee Rd NE Bremerton, WA 98311	360-698-7555 800-693-6680	2 units $175–$275
Midway Inn 2909 Wheaton Way Bremerton, WA 98310	360-479-2909 800-231-0575	60 units $55–$70
Oyster Bay Inn 4412 Kitsap Way Bremerton, WA 98312	360-377-5510 800-393-3862 www.oysterbaymotel.com	78 units $60–$125
Super 8 Motel 5068 Kitsap Way Bremerton, WA 98312	360-377-8881 800-800-8000 www.super8.com	77 units $45–$50
Brewster Motel 801 S Bridge St, PO Box 1303 Brewster, WA 98812	509-689-2625	10 units $35–$66

See pp. 90-91 for a key to the

A: Where to Stay in Washington with Your Dog

food/bev	free	kitchen	pet fee	pool	spa	other features
		K R M				area for walking dogs, high bank across street offers great view of sunsets over Drayton Harbor
	C CB	K	$10 per day	out	sp	full kitchens in all suites, laundry facilities, 1½ mi walking trail around pond & business park
B&B	C FB	K			tb	3-room beachfront suite, dogs allowed by advance reservations only, laundry, walking trails
	C	K R M	$5 per day	out		$25 refundable deposit, laundry facilities, area for walking dogs, 6 blocks to Oyster Bay State Park
	C CB	K	$20 per stay		sp	laundry facilities
	C	K			tb rm	fully equipped cabins on 6 acres, picnic area, laundry facilities, short path to beach
	C CB	K R M	$10 per stay			small dogs only, laundry facilities, adjacent to open area for walking dogs, 1 mi to public park
R&L	C CB	K R M	$20 per stay			laundry facilities, located on Oyster Bay, enclosed premises for walking dogs
	C CB	M	$25 ref dep			primary local motel for yearly dog shows, cat shows and kennel club events, laundry facilities
		K		out htd		1 block to city park & boat launch on Columbia River

abbreviations used in this section   109

Have Dog Will Travel—Washington Edition

Buckley — Centralia

Mt View Inn 29405 Highway 410 E, PO Box 1681 Buckley, WA 98321	360-829-1100 800-582-4111	41 units $45–$68
Hueter Haus 619 N Sunset Dr Camano Island, WA 98292	360-387-8492	1 unit $85–$125
Carson Mineral Hot Springs Resort 372 St. Martin Rd, PO Box 1169 Carson, WA 98610	509-427-8292 800-607-3678 www.carson-hotsprings.com	24 units $10–$80
Wind River Motel 1261 Wind River Rd, PO Box 777 Carson, WA 98610	509-427-7777 877-816-7908 www.windrivermotel.qpg.com	9 units $45–$65
Grandview Orchard Inn B & B 5105 Moody Rd, PO Box 792 Cashmere, WA 98815	509-782-2340	3 units $60–$70
7 West Motel 864 Walsh Ave NE Castle Rock, WA 98611	360-274-7526	24 units $35–$58
Centralia Travelodge 1325 Lakeshore Dr Centralia, WA 98531	360-736-9344 800-666-8701	40 units $59–$65
Days Inn 702 W Harrison Ave Centralia, WA 98531	360-736-2875 800-329-7466 www.daysinn.com	89 units $59
Ferryman's Inn-Centralia 1003 Eckerson Rd Centralia, WA 98531	360-330-2094	84 units $483–$57
Grand Mound Motel 20333 Old Hwy 99 SW Centralia, WA 98531	360-273-2129	13 units $27–$30

See pp. 90-91 for a key to the

A: Where to Stay in Washington with Your Dog

food/bev	free	kitchen	pet fee	pool	spa	other features
	C CB	M	$10 per stay	out htd	tb	microwave in lobby, laundry facilities, walking trail to town and public park
	C CB	K				cabin w/kitchen, great view of the water, quiet road for walking dogs, 5 mi to state park
R	C	K	$20 per day		sp	dogs allowed in 12 cabins, RV sites, walking trails that lead down to Columbia River
	C	K R M	$5 per day			cottages w/kitchens, oversized motel rooms, RV sites, 1 mi to Columbia River
B&B	C FB				tb	quiet country roads and open orchards for walking dogs
R	C					1 dog allowed per room, area for walking dogs, 4 blocks to riverfront trail
	C CB	R M	$5 per day			laundry facilities, all rooms open onto a grassy area and lake, close to fairgrounds for dog shows
	C CB	R M	$10 per day	out htd		laundry facilities, RV sites avail in park behind hotel, 1 mi to state park w/lake & trails
		K R		out	sp	field across street for walking dogs, also 2 parks located within 2 blocks of motel, laundry facilities
		K	$25 ref dep			fenced yard for walking dogs

abbreviations used in this section

Centralia — Chewelah

Motel 6-Centralia 1310 Belmont Ave Centralia, WA 98531	360-330-2057 800-440-6000	123 units $30–$40
Park Motel 1011 Belmont Ave Centralia, WA 98531	360-736-9333	30 units $33–$41
Peppertree West Motor Inn 1208 Alder St Centralia, WA 98531	360-736-1124	25 units $35–$55
Howard Johnson 122 Interstate Ave Chehalis, WA 98532	360-748-0101 800-446-4656	71 units $50–$100
Beachfront Mobile Homes 1230 W Woodin Ave, PO Box 1090 Chelan, WA 98816	509-682-5419	1 unit $120
Best Western Lakeside Lodge 2312 W Woodin Ave Chelan, WA 98816	509-682-4396 800-468-2781 www.4-westview.com	65 units $55–$220
Kelly's Resort 12801 S Lakeshore Dr Chelan, WA 98816	509-687-3220 800-561-8978 www.kellysresort.com	16 units $90–$200
Rosebrook Inn 304 W 1st St Cheney, WA 99004	509-235-6538 888-848-9853 rosebinn@worldnet.att.net	12 units $36–$60
Willow Springs Motel 5 B St Cheney, WA 99004	509-235-5138	42 units $39–$54
49er Motel & RV Park 311 S Park St Chewelah, WA 99109	509-935-8613 www.theofficenet.com/~49er/	13 units $35–$67

A: Where to Stay in Washington with Your Dog

food/bev	free	kitchen	pet fee	pool	spa	other features
	C			out		laundry facilities
		K	$2 per day			area for walking dogs, 1 block to public park
		K R M	$5 per day			laundry facilities, RV sites, area for walking dogs
	C CB	R M	$25 per stay	out htd	sp	laundry facilities, 1 block to public park
		K M	ref dep			fully equipped vacation home sleeps 6-10, laundry facilities, less than 1 mi to 2 public parks on lake
	C CB	K	$10 per day	in out htd	sp	small dogs allowed at manager's discretion only, laundry facilities, adjacent to public park
	C	K	$10 per stay	out htd		20 acre resort on Lake Chelan, cottages w/full kitchens, laundry facilities, BBQ, walking trails
	C	K				laundry facilities, across street from public park, 2 mi to paved trail for hiking-biking-rollerblading
R	C CB	K	$5-$10/stay			laundry facilities, large open area for walking dogs, ½ mi to "Rails to Trails" walking trail to Fish Lake
	C	K R M	$4 per day	in htd	sp	28 RV sites, area for walking dogs, 2 blocks to public park

abbreviations used in this section   113

Chewelah – Cle Elum

Nordlig Motel 101 W Grant Ave Chewelah, WA 99109	509-935-6704	14 units $39–$55 see website at right
A-View Mobile Home Park 122 8th St, PO Box 383 Clallam Bay, WA 98326	360-963-2394	2 units $25–$75
Andre Court 81 Frontier St, PO Box 432 Clallam Bay, WA 98326	360-963-2481	1 unit $35
Astor Motel 1201 Bridge St Clarkston, WA 99403	509-758-2509	8 units $26–$30
Golden Key Motel 1376 Bridge St Clarkston, WA 99403	509-758-5566	16 units $26–$40
Highland House 707 Highland Ave Clarkston, WA 99403	509-758-3126	5 units $45–$85
Motel 6-Clarkston 222 Bridge St Clarkston, WA 99403	509-758-1631 800-466-8356	85 units $38–$50
Sunset Motel 1200 Bridge St Clarkston, WA 99403	509-758-2517	10 units $26–$50
Aster Inn 521 E 1st St Cle Elum, WA 98922	509-674-2551 888-616-9722	9 units $30–$85 starbird@eburg.com
Cascade Mountain Inn 906 E 1st St Cle Elum, WA 98922	509-674-2380 888-674-3975	43 units $50–$95

A: Where to Stay in Washington with Your Dog

food/bev	free	kitchen	pet fee	pool	spa	other features
		C CB	R M	$3 per stay		sp	lawn areas with picnic tables, www.panoramaland.com/nordlig/index.html
			K M	$5 per stay			1 cabin, 1 house, dogs allowed by advance reservation only, area for walking dog, 3 blocks to waterfront
			M	$5 per day			dogs allowed in 1 motel unit, waterfront location
			K				RV sites, area for walking dogs, 10 blocks to riverfront trails
		C	R M				
B&B		C FB		$5 per day		sp	large fenced yard, 2 blocks to riverside walking trail, 4 blocks to public park
		C	R M		out htd		adjacent to walking trail along riverfront Green Belt, laundry facilities
			K				walking & biking trails nearby
		C	K R M			rm	walking trail, 1 block to river
		C CB	K	$5 per day		rm	large open field for walking dogs

abbreviations used in this section

Cle Elum — Colville

Chalet Motel 800 E 1st St Cle Elum, WA 98922	509-674-2320	11 units $35–$50
Cle Elum Travelodge Inn 1001 E 1st St Cle Elum, WA 98922	509-674-5535	33 units $35–$65
Stewart Lodge 805 W 1st St Cle Elum, WA 98922	509-674-4548	36 units $46–$65
Timber Lodge Motel 301 W 1st St Cle Elum, WA 98922	509-674-5966 800-584-1133	35 units $45–$70
Wind Blew Inn Motel 811 Highway 970 Cle Elum, WA 98922	509-674-2294 888-674-2294	10 units $40–$70
B's Getaway B & B 4750 Orr Rd, PO Box 15 Clinton, WA 98236	360-341-4721	1 unit $85–$95
Home By The Sea Cottages 2388 E Sunlight Beach Rd Clinton, WA 98236	360-321-2964 homebytheseacottages.com	2 units $150–$175
Sunset Beach Cottage 7359 S Maxwelton Beach Rd Clinton, WA 98236	360-579-1590	1 unit $125–$150
Sweetwater Cottage 6111 S Cultus Bay Rd Clinton, WA 98236	360-341-1604	1 unit $120
Beaver Lodge Resort 2430 Highway 20 E Colville, WA 99114	509-684-5657 beaver@triax.com	47 units $8–$60

A: Where to Stay in Washington with Your Dog

food/bev	free	kitchen	pet fee	pool	spa	other features
		R	$5 per day			dog-walking area nearby, walking distance to restaurants
	C CB	R M				
	C CB	R	$5 per stay	out htd	sp tb	laundry facilities, walking trail nearby, 1 block to public park
	C CB	R M	$10 per stay		tb	laundry facilities, exercise room, 2 blocks to walking trail
		K	$5 per day			½ mi to Yakima River, 1 mi to trail for hiking-biking-horseback riding
B & B	C FB					dog allowed by advance reservation only, water view, on 2½ acres for walking dogs, ½ mi to public park
	C CB	K			sp tb rm	small pets welcome, whirlpool tubs, woodstoves, fully stocked kitchens, close to beachfront & state park
	C	K	$10 per day			fully equipped beachfront cabin, dog allowed by advance reservation only, outdoor kennel also available
B & B	C FB	K R	$10 per stay	sa		
R		K R M				laundry facilities, RV sites, adjacent to Lake Gillette, terrific fishing & swimming, trails for hiking/biking

abbreviations used in this section

Colville — Connell

Benny's Colville Inn 915 S Main St Colville, WA 99114	509-684-2517 800-680-2517 www.colvilleinn.com	106 units $40–$105
Comfort Inn 166 NE Canning Dr Colville, WA 99114	509-684-2010 800-228-5150 www.comfortinn.colville.com	53 units $42–$115
Downtown Motel 369 S Main St Colville, WA 99114	509-684-2565	18 units $36
Conconully Motel 402 N Main, PO Box 189 Conconully, WA 98819	509-826-1610	4 units $35
Gibson's North Fork Lodge 100 W Boone, PO Box 205 Conconully, WA 98819	509-826-1475 800-555-1690	2 units $55–$65
Jack's RV Park & Motel 116 Avenue A, PO Box 98 Conconully, WA 98819	509-826-0132 800-893-5668	57 units $16–$62
Kozy Kabins & RV Park 111 E Broadway Ave Conconully, WA 98819	509-826-6780 888-502-2246 kozykabins@northcascades.net	8 units $8–$35
Ovenell's Heritage Inn B & B 46276 Concrete Sauk Valley Rd Concrete, WA 98237	360-853-8494 www.ovenells-inn.com	6 units $75–$115
M & M Motel 730 S Columbia Ave, PO Box 597 Connell, WA 99326	509-234-8811	43 units $27–$46
Tumbleweed Motel 433 S Columbia Ave, PO Box 796 Connell, WA 99326	509-234-2081	20 units $23–$40

A: Where to Stay in Washington with Your Dog

food/bev	free	kitchen	pet fee	pool	spa	other features
R&L	C CB	R M	$5 per day	in htd	sp	guest pass to nearby fitness center, area for walking dogs, near public park
	C CB		$50 ref dep	in	sp	laundry facilities
		K	$10 per stay			6 blocks to public park
	C	K R M				adjacent to creek with grassy area for walking dogs, BBQ available 2 blocks to park and 2 lakes
		K R M				dogs must be kept on leash and never left alone in rooms, creek & miles of walking trails
		K				dog allowed by advance reservation only, laundry facilities, riverfront trails, RV sites
		K R				also 15 RV & tent sites, across street from state park, 2 lakes within 2 blocks, walking trails
B&B	C FB	K R M	$5 per day			guest house w/doghouse & fenced yard, dog allowed on deck but not inside house, 600-acre ranch
	C					area onsite for walking dogs, 2 blks to walking trail, 4 blocks to public park, laundry facilities
	C			out		close to walking trail, 2 blocks to public park

abbreviations used in this section

Have Dog Will Travel—Washington Edition

Conway — Coulee Dam

South Fork Moorage House Boat 2187 Mann Rd, PO Box 633 Conway, WA 98238	360-445-4803 www.virtualcities.com/ons/wa/	2 units $95–$115
Beachwood Resort 3009 SR 109, PO Box 116 Copalis Beach, WA 98535	360-289-2177	18 units $65–$80
Iron Springs Ocean Beach Resort 3707 State Highway 109, PO Box 207 Copalis Beach, WA 98535	360-276-4230	28 units $66–$104
Linda's Low Tide Motel 14 McCullough Rd, PO Box 551 Copalis Beach, WA 98535	360-289-3450	12 units $60–$125
Ala Cozy Motel 9988 Highway 2 E Coulee City, WA 99115	509-632-5703 landerson@odessaoffice.com	10 units $40–$65
Blue Lake Resort 31199 Highway 17 N Coulee City, WA 99115	509-632-5364	10 units $13–$69
Blue Top Motel & RV Park 109 N 6th St, PO Box 687 Coulee City, WA 99115	509-632-5596	13 units $29–$38
Main Stay B & B 110 W Main St, P O Box 367 Coulee City, WA 99115	509-632-5687	2 units $40–$50
Coulee House Motel 110 Roosevelt Way Coulee Dam, WA 99116	509-633-1101 800-715-7767 $54–$120 www.couleehouse.com	61 units
Victoria's Cottage 209 Columbia Coulee Dam, WA	509-633-2908 www.reitpro.com/columbiarivercottage	1 unit $110–$150

A: Where to Stay in Washington with Your Dog

food/bev	free	kitchen	pet fee	pool	spa	other features
	C	K R				whimsical Skagit River houseboat, full galley, lots of dog-walking area, call for reservations and pet rules
		K	$5 per day	out htd	sa tb	dog walking area
	C	K	$10 per day	in htd		oceanfront location, fireplaces, great beach for walking dogs
	C	K	$6 per day			beachfront location, great for walking dogs
	C	R	$10 per day	out		$25 pet deposit, all but $10 is refundable, mini-golf on premises, ½ mi to lakefront park
		K	$2-$5 per day			10 fully equipped rustic cabins & trailers, 80 RV & tent sites, area for walking dogs, close to public park
	C	K R	$5 per stay			RV sites, 4 blocks to lakeside park, 5 mi to state park w/golfing-hiking trails-Interpretive Center
B&B	C CB					walking distance to public park & lake
	C	K	$15 per day	out htd	tb	laundry facilities, overlooking Grand Coulee Dam, near walking trails
B&B	C CB	R M			tb	romantic 3-rm suite w/BBQ & private hot tub, fenced yard, walking trail along Columbia River

wavacdex.htm

abbreviations used in this section   **121**

Coupeville – Dayton

Tyee Motel & Restaurant 405 S Main St Coupeville, WA 98239	360-678-6616	9 units $40–$50
Victorian Bed & Breakfast 602 North Main St, PO Box 761 Coupeville, WA 98239	360-678-5305	3 units $60–$100
Wolfgang's Riverview Inn 2320 Hwy 21 N, 2 Valhalla Ln Curlew, WA 99118	509-779-4252 www.televar.com/wolfgang	4 units $45–$60
Stagecoach Inn 1100 Seemann St Darrington, WA 98241	360-436-1776	20 units $45–$68
Davenport Motel 1205 Morgan St, PO Box 904 Davenport, WA 99122	509-725-7071	9 units $40–$57
Deer Meadows Motel RR 1 Box 201 Davenport, WA 99122	509-725-8425	17 units $50–$120
Blue Mountain Motel 414 W Main St Dayton, WA 99328	509-382-3040	23 units $36–$75
Dayton Motel 110 S Pine St Dayton, WA 99328	509-382-4503	17 units $34–$65
Purple House Bed & Breakfast 415 E Clay St, PO Box 69 Dayton, WA 99328	509-382-3159 800-486-2574	4 units $85–$125
Weinhard Hotel 235 E Main St Dayton, WA 99328	509-382-4032	15 units $70–$125

A: Where to Stay in Washington with Your Dog

food/bev	free	kitchen	pet fee	pool	spa	other features
R & L			$5 per day			pool room, 2 blocks to walking trail, 1 mi to waterfront
B & B	C FB	K R	$50 ref dep			laundry facilities, 2½ blocks to riverfront walking trail that leads to public park, 2½ mi to beach
	C	K R M	$5 per stay			800 ft to Kettle River, RV sites, laundry facilities, fishing-hiking-birdwatching-hunting in area
	C CB	K R M	$5-$8 per stay			laundry facilities, area for walking dogs, close to public park
	C					open field for walking dogs, no dogs left alone in the room or "rest stops" on the motel grounds
R	C	K	$50 ref dep		sa	small dogs only, motel units & 2 bdrm house, loop road around golf course for walking dogs
			$5 per stay			2 mile-long walking trail that begins 3 blocks from motel
	C	K				plenty of area for walking dogs
B & B	C FB	K R M		out	tb	small pets only, kitchen & Japanese soaking tub in 1 suite, dinners & picnic lunches available
R	C CB				rm	Victorian hotel, great walking trails plus 2 parks nearby, friendly local vet always on call

abbreviations used in this section   **123**

Have Dog Will Travel—Washington Edition

Deer Harbor – Eastsound

Deer Harbor Inn	360-376-4110	12 units
Deer Harbor Rd, PO Box 142	887-377-4110	$109–$199
Deer Harbor, WA 98243	www.sanjuan.com/DeerHarborInn	
Love's Victorian B & B	509-276-6636	3 units
31317 N Cedar Rd		$75–$115
Deer Park, WA 99006	www.bbhost.com/lovesvictorian	
The Guest House	360-592-2343	1 unit
5723 Schornbush Rd		$50
Deming, WA 98244	WeissSmith@aol.com	
The Logs Resort	360-599-2711	5 units
9002 Mt Baker Hwy		$75–$135
Deming, WA 98244	www.telcomplus.net/thelogs	
Ramada Inn	206-824-9920	41 units
22300 7th Ave S	800-272-6232	$69–$139
Des Moines, WA 98198		
Cedars Inn-East Wenatchee	509-886-8000	94 units
80 9th St NE	800-358-2074	$61–$122
East Wenatchee, WA 98802		
East Wenatchee Motor Inn	509-884-7300	10 units
10 13th St NE		$22–$35
East Wenatchee, WA 98802		
C B's Motel	509-656-2248	4 units
1781 Railroad St, PO Box D	800-347-2336	$40–$65
Easton, WA 98925		
Bartwood Lodge	360-376-2242	16 units
RR 2 Box 1040		$59–$185
Eastsound, WA 98245	www.orcasisland.com/bartwood	
North Beach Inn	360-376-2660	11 units
Mt Baker Rd, P O Box 80		$95–$175
Eastsound, WA 98245		

See pp. 90-91 for a key to the

A: Where to Stay in Washington with Your Dog

food/bev	free	kitchen	pet fee	pool	spa	other features
B&B	C CB	R M			sp	dogs allowed in 3 cottages, ⅓ mi to beach, quiet country roads for walking dogs
B&B	C FB				tb	resident pets, country setting, lots of area for walking dogs, afternoon tea & cookies, evening cider
	C	K			tb	no dogs left alone in guest house, rural area for walking, less than 1 mi to river
		K R	$5 per day	out		rustic log cabins located 2 mi west of Glacier, on 68 acres of forest along the river for walking dogs
R&L	C CB	K R M			sp sa	small dogs only, 2 blocks to public park
	C CB	R M	$6 per day	in htd	tb	laundry facilities, ski packages Dec thru April, across street from walking trail
		K	$25 ref dep			RV sites, adjacent to Columbia River loop trail
						area for walking dogs, less than 1 mi to Lake Easton State Park
R	C	K R M	$10 per day			private beach, 10 min drive to Moran State Park, 3 min drive to Back Park
		K R	$10 per day			fully equipped 1, 2 and 3 bdrm cottages, ⅓ mile of pebble beach frontage, 90 acres of woods & fields

abbreviations used in this section   **125**

Eastsound — Ellensburg

North Shore Cottages 271 Sunset Ave, PO Box 1273 Eastsound, WA 98245	360-376-5131 www.northshore4kiss.com	3 units $165–$305
West Beach Resort 190 Waterfront Wy Eastsound, WA 98245	360-376-2240 877-937-8224 www.westbeachresort.com	16 units $80–$165
Eagle's Nest Alder Lake Motel 52120 Mountain Hwy E Eatonville, WA 98328	360-569-2533 888-877-2533	10 units $50
Mountain View Cedar Lodge 36203 Pulford Rd E Eatonville, WA 98328	360-832-8080 888-903-5636	3 units $85–$115
Edmonds Harbor Inn 130 W Dayton St Edmonds, WA 98020	425-771-5021 800-441-8033 www.nwcountryinns.com/harbor	60 units $69–$135
Hudgens Haven 9313 190th SW Edmonds, WA 98026	425-776-2202	1 unit $60–$65
K & E Motor Inn 23921 Highway 99 Edmonds, WA 98026	425-778-2181 800-787-2181 www.kemotorinn.com	32 units $52–$67
Seattle North Travelodge 23825 Highway 99 Edmonds, WA 98026	425-771-8008 800-771-8009 www.travelodge.com	58 units $59–$119
Jerry's Landing Resort 41114 N Lake Shore Rd Elk, WA 99009	509-292-2337	36 units $30–$60
Comfort Inn-Ellensburg 1722 Country Canyon Rd Ellensburg, WA 98926	509-925-7037 800-228-5150	52 units $50–$95

A: Where to Stay in Washington with Your Dog

food/bev	free	kitchen	pet fee	pool	spa	other features
	C	K R M			sp sa rm	fully equipped cottages on Orcas Island, great waterfront views, sauna
		K R M	$10 per day		sp tb	fully equipped cottages, RV sites, laundry facilities, grocery store & espresso bar, sandy pebble beach
	C	K	$10 per stay			overlooking Alder Lake, laundry facilities, area for walking dogs, 1½ mi to public parks, 9 RV sites
B & B	C CB FB	R M				dogs allowed indoors in travel carriers only, fenced yard and dog run, walking trails, RV sites
	C CB	K	$10 per day			close to beaches, ferry, public park
B & B	C FB		$2 per day			fenced yard, 1 block to park, wooded paths in natural setting
	C CB	K R	$5 per day			laundry facilities
	C CB	R M	$25 per stay		tb	laundry facilities, 5 min drive to Edmonds waterfront
		K R M				dogs under 20 lbs only, 2 cabins & 34 RV sites, area for walking dogs
	C CB	R M	$10 per stay	in htd	sp	laundry facilities, area for walking dogs, ½ mi to Irene Rinehart Park on Casey Lake

abbreviations used in this section

Have Dog Will Travel—Washington Edition

Ellensburg — Everett

Nites Inn Motel 1200 S Ruby St Ellensburg, WA 98926	509-962-9600 www.televar.com/~nites	32 units $45–$55
Super 8 Motel 1500 Canyon Rd Ellensburg, WA 98926	509-962-6888 800-800-8000 www.super8.com	101 units $48–$68
Grays Harbor Hostel 6 Ginny Ln Elma, WA 98541	360-482-3119 ghhostel@techline.com	3 units $12/person
Parkhurst Motel 208 E Main St, PO Box 793 Elma, WA 98541	360-482-2541	14 units $50–$55
Entiat Valley Motel 2036 Entiat Way # B, PO Box 34 Entiat, WA 98822	509-784-1402	2 units $40
Best Western Park Center Hotel 1000 Griffin Ave Enumclaw, WA 98022	360-825-4490 800-238-7234 www.bestwesternwashington.com	40 units $70–$80
King's Motel 1334 Roosevelt Ave E Enumclaw, WA 98022	360-825-1626	44 units $49–$59
Lariat Motel 1639 Basin St SW Ephrata, WA 98823	509-754-2437	42 units $22–$55
Everett Inn 12619 4th Ave W Everett, WA 98204	425-347-9099 800-434-9204	72 units $50–$105
Everett/Broadway Travelodge 9602 19th Ave SE Everett, WA 98208	425-337-9090 888-454-9090	113 units $49–$74

See pp. 90–91 for a key to the

A: Where to Stay in Washington with Your Dog

food/bev	free	kitchen	pet fee	pool	spa	other features
	C CB	R M	$6 per stay			large area for walking dogs, laundry facilities, RV sites, close to public park, riverfront walking trail
	C		$25 ref dep	in	sp	area for walking dogs, laundry facilities
	C	K			tb	dogs allowed if kept in travel crates and by advance reservation only, adjacent to open field & fairgrounds
		K				laundry facilities, area for walking dogs, ¼ mi to county park
		R M				open area for walking dogs
R	C	R M	$10 per stay		sp	laundry facilities, exercise room, adjacent to 2 public parks
R	C	K R	$5 per day	out htd		laundry facilities, adjacent to hiking trails, woods and streams
	C CB	K	$5 per stay	out		area for walking dogs, 3 blocks to public park
	C CB	R M	$25 per stay	out	rm	microwave in lobby, close to hiking trail
	C CB	K	$25 per stay	out htd	tb	small dogs allowed at manager's discretion only, laundry facilities, area for walking dogs, 8 mi to beach

abbreviations used in this section 129

Everett — Federal Way

Inn At Port Gardner 1700 W Marine View Dr Everett, WA 98201	425-252-6779 888-252-6779	36 units $90–$185
Motel 6-Everett North 10006 Evergreen Way Everett, WA 98204	425-347-2060 800-440-6000	119 units $35–$45
Motel 6-Everett South 224 128th St SW Everett, WA 98204	425-353-8120 800-440-6000	100 units $46–$58
Royal Motor Inn 952 N Broadway Everett, WA 98201	425-259-5177	35 units $42–$56
Travelodge-Everett 3030 Broadway Everett, WA 98201	425-259-6141 800-578-7878	29 units $37–$65
Welcome Motor Inn 1205 N Broadway Everett, WA 98201	425-252-8828 800-252-5512	42 units $43–$62
Best Western Executel-Federal Way 31611 20th Ave S Federal Way, WA 98003 www.bestwesternwashington.com	253-941-6000 800-346-2874	116 units $99–$159
Comfort Inn-Federal Way 31622 Pacific Hwy S Federal Way, WA 98003	253-529-0101	118 units $59–$140
New Horizon Motel 33002 Pacific Hwy S Federal Way, WA 98003	253-927-2337	50 units $35–$60
Roadrunner Truckers Motel 1501 S 350th St Federal Way, WA 98003	253-838-5763 800-828-7202	59 units $30–$38

A: Where to Stay in Washington with Your Dog

food/bev	free	kitchen	pet fee	pool	spa	other features
	C	R M			rm	small dogs only, adjacent to waterfront & boardwalk
	C			out		
R & L	C					laundry facilities, area for walking dogs, 4 blocks to public park
	C	K R M	$5 per day	out		area for walking dogs, 2 blocks to golf course and state park
	C	R M	$5 per stay			area for walking dogs
	C CB	K R M	$20 per stay			small dogs only, adjacent to restaurant & laundry facilities
R & L	C	R	$25 per day	out	sp tb	3 blocks to Steel Lake Park
	C CB	K R M	$20 per stay	in htd	tb	exercise room, area for walking dogs, ¼ mi to Steel Lake Park
		K	$10 per day			laundry facilities, area for walking dogs, 3 blocks to public park
	C		$20 ref dep			laundry facilities, area for walking dogs, 6 blocks to Wetlands Park, 1 mi to public park

abbreviations used in this section

Federal Way — Fife

Super 8 Motel 1688 S 348th St Federal Way, WA 98003	253-838-8808 800-800-8000 www.super8.com	90 units $49–$68
Executive Inn Express 5370 Barrett Rd, PO Box 551 Ferndale, WA 98248	360-380-4600 888-665-4600 www.executiveinnhotels.com	41 units $89–$119
Scottish Lodge Motel 5671 Riverside Dr Ferndale, WA 98248	360-384-4040	94 units $39–$50
Slater Heritage House B & B 1371 W Axton Rd Ferndale, WA 98248	360-384-4273 888-785-0706 www.nas.com/~divindj/slaterbb	4 units $65–$95
Super 8 Motel 5788 Barrett Rd Ferndale, WA 98248	360-384-8881 800-800-8000 www.super8.com	78 units $47–$61
Econo Lodge-Fife 3518 Pacific Hwy E Fife, WA 98424	253-922-0550 800-424-4777	81 units $48–$55
Hometel Inn 3520 Pacific Hwy E Fife, WA 98424	253-922-0555 800-258-3520	110 units $40–$60
Kings Motor Inn 5115 Pacific Hwy E Fife, WA 98424	253-922-3636 800-929-3509	43 units $35–$65
Motel 6-Tacoma/Fife 5201 20th St E Fife, WA 98424	253-922-1270 800-466-8356	120 units $37–$51
Royal Coachman Motor Inn 5805 Pacific Hwy E Fife, WA 98424	253-922-2500 800-422-3051	94 units $65–$130

A: Where to Stay in Washington with Your Dog

food/bev	free	kitchen	pet fee	pool	spa	other features
	C CB		$25 ref dep			laundry facilities, 4 mi to acquatic center w/walking paths
	C CB	K R M	$25 per stay	out	sp	laundry facilities, area for walking dogs, 8 miles to ocean
	C	R	$5 per day	out htd	sa	laundry facilities, 2 mi to Pioneer Park
B&B	C FB					dogs allowed at owner's discretion only, creekside walking area, 1½ mi to public park, 3 mi to waterfront
	C CB		$25 ref dep	in htd	tb	laundry facilities, dog walking area
	C CB	R M	$10 per day			area for walking dogs, laundry facilities
	C CB	R M	$10 per day	out	rm	area for walking dogs
	C	K	$5 per day			laundry facilities, area for walking dogs
R&L	C			out htd		laundry facilities, area for walking dogs
	C CB	R M	$25 ref dep		sp tb	area for walking dogs, laundry facilities

abbreviations used in this section   133

Fife — Forks

Stagecoach Inn 4221 Pacific Hwy E Fife, WA 98424	253-922-5421	26 units $35
Bagby's Town Motel 1080 S Forks Ave Forks, WA 98331	360-374-6231 800-742-2429	20 units $35–$44
Brightwater House B & B 440 Brightwater Dr, PO Box 1222 Forks, WA 98331 www.northolympic.com/brightwater	360-374-5453	2 units $75–$85
Dew Drop Inn 100 Fernhill Rd, PO Box 1996 Forks, WA 98331	360-374-4055 888-4dewdrop	21 units $39–$54
Forks Motel 351 S Forks Ave, PO Box 510 Forks, WA 98331	360-374-6243 800-544-3416	73 units $68–$75
Hoh Humm Ranch 171763 Highway 101 Forks, WA 98331	360-374-5337 www.olypen.com/hohhumm	2 units $35–$45
Kalaloch Lodge 157151 Hwy 101 Forks, WA 98331	360-962-2271 www.visitklaloch.com	64 units $55–$215
Manitou Lodge B & B 813 Kilmer Rd, PO Box 600 Forks, WA 98331	360-374-6295	6 units $85–$105
Mill Creek Inn 1061 Forks Ave South, PO Box 1182 Forks, WA 98331	360-374-5873 grizzly@olypen.com	3 units $35–$60
Miller Tree Inn 654 E Division St, 1565 Forks, WA 98331 www.northolympic.com/millertree	360-374-6806	7 units $90–$125

See pp. 90-91 for a key to the

A: Where to Stay in Washington with Your Dog

food/bev	free	kitchen	pet fee	pool	spa	other features
			$3 per day			area for walking dogs, 10 min drive to Commencement Bay, 15 min drive to Point Defiance
	C	K R M	$5 per day			exercise room, laundry facilities, close to beaches, rivers, trails for walking dogs
B&B	C FB					dog allowed by advance reservation only, ¾ mi river frontage, 60 acres on Sol Duc river for walking dogs
	C CB	R M	$10 per stay			country roads for walking dogs
	C	K R M	$10 per day	out htd		laundry facilities, area for walking dogs, ¾ mi to public park, 20 min drive to beaches
B&B	C FB		$5 per day			large dogwalking area along Hoh River, dogs must be kept on leash because of resident farm animals
R	C FB	K R	$10 per day			cozy cabins w/fireplaces, beach for walking dogs (must be on leash at all times)
B&B	C FB		$10 per day			10 forested acres for walking dogs, close to Rialto Beach (the only pet-friendly beach in the area)
	C					dog allowed by advance reservation only, area for walking dogs, 15 mi to beach
B&B	C FB	K R M	$10 per day		tb	dogs allowed in suite with kitchen & private bath, dog walking area

abbreviations used in this section

135

Forks — Friday Harbor

Olson's Vacation Cabins 2423 Mora Rd Forks, WA 98331	360-374-3142	2 units $50–$60
Olympic Suites 800 Olympic Dr Forks, WA 98331	360-374-5400 800-262-3433	30 units $45–$75
Three Rivers Resort 7765 La Push Rd Forks, WA 98331	360-374-5300 www.northolympic.com/threerivers	29 units $8–$49
Westward Hoh Resort 5692 Upper Hoh Rd Forks, WA 98331	360-374-6657	3 units $40
Enchanted B & B 5804 Pirate Ln, PO Box 1081 Freeland, WA 98249	360-331-5360 800-282-5292	3 units $135–$200
Garden of Angels Guest House 584 E Dolphin Dr Freeland, WA 98249	360-331-7080 800-619-3960	1 unit $99–$150
Harbour Inn Motel 1606 E Main St, PO Box 1350 Freeland, WA 98249	360-331-6900 harbrinn@whidbey.com	20 units $61–$86
Serenity Pines Waterfront Cottages PO Box 999 Freeland, WA 98249	360-321-2575 www.serenitypines.com	4 units $165–$250
Blair House Bed & Breakfast 345 Blair Ave Friday Harbor, WA 98250	360-378-5907 800-899-3030	8 units $85–$155
Discovery Inn 1016 Guard St Friday Harbor, WA 98250	360-378-2000 800-822-4753 www.discovery-inn.com	20 units $75–$110

See pp. 90-91 for a key to the

A: Where to Stay in Washington with Your Dog

food/bev	free	kitchen	pet fee	pool	spa	other features
	C	K	$10 per day			fully equipped cabin, fenced yard, BBQ, also 1 RV in secluded 5-acre meadow, 2 mi to beach & park
	C	K	$75 ref dep			1 & 2 bdrm suites w/full kitchens, 1mi to walking trails & parks, 8 mi to ocean
R	C	K R	$5 per day			cabins, tent & RV sites, groceries, gasoline, laundry facilities, 1 block to river, 4 mi to ocean beaches
	C	K				rustic cabins w/kitchenettes, off-leash area avail, 12 mi to park, 20 mi to ocean
B&B	C CB				sp	dog allowed by advance reservation only, fenced dog area, off-leash beaches nearby
			$50 ref dep		tb	2 bdrm home, fenced yard, dogs allowed by advance reservations only, path to private beach
	C CB	K R M	$6 per day			3 blocks to waterfront park with beach-boat launch-picnic area, 2 mi to off-leash beach
		K	$25 per stay		tb	fully equipped waterfront vacation homes, laundry facilities, private beaches for walking dogs
B&B	C FB	K		out	tb	dogs allowed in the fully equipped guest cottage only, area for walking dogs
	C	K	$50 ref dep		sp sa	fenced mowed pasture for off-leash exercising, close to walking trails, dog-friendly shuttle service

abbreviations used in this section

137

Have Dog Will Travel—Washington Edition

Friday Harbor — Gig Harbor

Harrison House Suites 235 C St Friday Harbor, WA 98250	360-378-3587 800-407-7933 www.san-juan-lodging.com	5 units $65–$240
Inn At Friday Harbor 410 Spring St Friday Harbor, WA 98250	360-378-4000 800-752-5752 www.theinns.com	72 units
Remax San Juan Island Vacation Rentals 285 Blair Ave, PO Box 1459 Friday Harbor, WA 98250	360-378-5060 800-992-1904 www.sanjuanrealestate.com	1 unit $1,100/wk
Snug Harbor Marina Resort 2371 Mitchell Bay Rd Friday Harbor, WA 98250	360-378-4762 www.snugharbormarinaresort.com	10 units $79–$205
Tucker House Bed & Breakfast 260 B St Friday Harbor, WA 98250	360-378-2783 800-965-0123 www.san-juan.net/tucker	6 units $75–$225
White Willow Motel & Camp 6161 Highway 25 S Fruitland, WA 99129	509-722-3640	15 units $50
Best Western Wesley Inn 6575 Kimball Dr Gig Harbor, WA 98332	253-858-9690 888-462-0002 www.wesleyinn.com	53 units $79–$139
Gig Harbor Motor Inn 4709 Point Fosdick Dr NW Gig Harbor, WA 98335	253-858-8161 888-336-8161	21 units $60–$98
Inn At Gig Harbor 3211 56th St NW Gig Harbor, WA 98335	253-858-1111 800-795-9980	64 units $89–$195
No Cabbages' Bed & Breakfast 10319 Sunrise Beach Dr NW Gig Harbor, WA 98332	253-858-7797 www.gigharbor.com/nocabbages	2 units $55–$75

See pp. 90-91 for a key to the

A: Where to Stay in Washington with Your Dog

food/bev	free	kitchen	pet fee	pool	spa	other features
B&B	C CB FB	K			sp rm	suites w/full kitchens, sleep 2 to 12, laundry facilities, 1 block to public park & ferry
R&L	C	R M	$50 ref dep	in htd	sp sa	laundry facilities, exercise room, area for walking dogs, 4 blocks to harbor
		K				Ask for #117-Tranquility Cottage: fully furnished 2 bdrm 2 ba avail Jun-Sept, 1 week min, beach access
	C	K R M	$5 per day			waterfront cabins, BBQ avail
B&B	C FB	K R M	$15 per day		tb	cottages w/kitchenettes, dogs allowed in 3 units, preferably kept in travel carriers for sleeping
	C	M			tb	laundry facilities, RV sites & teepee rentals, 5 mi to Fort Spokane and river
	C CB	R M	$10 per day	out htd	sp rm	exercise room, 1 mile to harbor, area for walking dogs, close to local parks, dog treats served at arrival
	C	K	$5 per day			wooded acreage w/walking trails, pond, off-leash exercise area, 2 mi to harbor & public parks
R&L	C CB	K R M	$50 ref dep		sp	fitness center, massage studio, close to several public parks, 2 mi to waterfront
B&B	C FB					beach access

abbreviations used in this section

139

Have Dog Will Travel—Washington Edition

Gig Harbor — Grandview

Olde Glencove Hotel B & B 9418 Glencove Road KPN Gig Harbor, WA 98329	253-884-2835 www.narrows.com/glencove	4 units $65–$85
Sunny Bay Cottage 50 Raft Island Dr NW Gig Harbor, WA 98335	253-265-6987	1 unit $100–$125
Westwynd Motel 6703 144th St NW Gig Harbor, WA 98332	253-857-4047 800-468-9963 www.westwyndmotel.com	24 units $44–$72
Glacier Creek Lodge 10036 Mt Baker Hwy, PO Box 5008 Glacier, WA 98244	360-599-2991 800-719-1414	21 units $40–$155
Mt Baker Chalet 9857 Mt Baker Hwy, PO Box 5009 Glacier, WA 98244	360-599-2405 www.mtbakerchalet.com	50 units $75–$150
Barchris Motel 128 N Academy Ave, PO Box 1506 Goldendale, WA 98620	509-773-4325	9 units $35–$48
Ponderosa Motel 775 E Broadway St Goldendale, WA 98620	509-773-5842	28 units $38–$75
Center Lodge Motel 508 Spokane Way Grand Coulee, WA 99133	509-633-0770	17 units $54
Trail West Motel 108 Spokane Way, PO Box 23 Grand Coulee, WA 99133	509-633-3155 www.grandcouleedam.org	24 units $39–$60
Grandview Motel 522 E Wine Country Rd Grandview, WA 98930	509-882-1323	20 units $28–$45

See pp. 90-91 for a key to the

A: Where to Stay in Washington with Your Dog

food/bev	free	kitchen	pet fee	pool	spa	other features
B&B	C FB					waterfront location, area for walking dogs, close to public parks
B&B	C CB	K	$10 per stay		tb	dog allowed by advance reservation only, full kitchen, laundry facilities, adjacent to public parks
		K R				¼ mi to public beach
		K	$5 per day		tb	dogs allowed in 12 cabins only, playground, basketball, picnic area, BBQ, creeks, walking trails
				in out tb	sp sa	vacation homes & condos, walking trails, playground, picnic area, tennis-racquetball-basketball
		K	$8 per stay			suites w/full kitchens, 1 block to public park
	C	K R M	$7-$12/ day			adjacent to riverside trail, close to city park
		K	$5 per day			area for walking dogs, 5 mi to Spring Canyon State Park
	C	K	$5 per stay	out htd		dog allowed by advance reservation only, close to 1-mile long walking trail to Grand Coulee dam
		R	$5 per day	out htd		close to walking & biking trails

abbreviations used in this section

Granite Falls — Ilwaco

Mountain View Inn 32005 Mountain Loop Hwy Granite Falls, WA 98252	360-691-6668	6 units $40–$45
Best Western Shores Motel 2193 SR 105, PO Box 689 Grayland, WA 98547	360-267-6115	8 units $40–$85
Grayland Bed & Breakfast 1678 SR 105, PO Box 89 Grayland, WA 98547	360-267-6026	2 units $60–$75
Ocean Spray Motel 1757 Hwy 105, PO Box 86 Grayland, WA 98547	360-267-2205	10 units $45–$65
Surf Motel & Cottages 2029 SR 105 Grayland, WA 98547	360-267-2244	7 units $39–$67
Sunrise Motel & Resort 24520 N US Highway 101 Hoodsport, WA 98548	360-877-5301	15 units $49–$100
Sandstone Motel 2424 Aberdeen Ave Hoquiam, WA 98550	360-533-6383	24 units $39–$69
Timberline Inn 415 Perry Ave Hoquiam, WA 98550	360-533-8048	25 units $35–$60
Y Motel 408 US Highway 101 Hoquiam, WA 98550	360-532-5265	15 units $40–$60
Columbia-Pacific Motel 214 S 1st St, PO Box 34 Ilwaco, WA 98624-0034	360-642-3177	16 units $60

A: Where to Stay in Washington with Your Dog

food/bev	free	kitchen	pet fee	pool	spa	other features
R	C		$5 per day			also general store, weekly rates during winter, across street from riverfront trails
	C	K	$7.50 per day			located on 23 mi of beach, 30 full RV sites, laundry facilities, across street from state park
B&B	C FB					country style breakfast, 2 separate fenced yards, laundry facilities, 2 blocks to ocean, shared bath
		K R	$5 per day			paved road to beach for walking dogs
		K	$5 per day			coffeemakers in each cabin, short path to beach, doggy towels avail
	C	K				waterfront location, grassy area for walking dogs, beach and dock access
	C	K R M	$7 per day			laundry facilities, area for walking dogs
	C	K R M	$5 per day			open areas for walking dogs, 30 min drive to beaches
	C					20 min drive to beach, 35 min to Lake Quinalt
	C	R M	$5 per day			dogs allowed at owner's discretion only, open area for walking dogs, 1½ mi to beaches

abbreviations used in this section

Ilwaco — Kelso

Harbor Lights 147 SE Howerton Way, PO Box 866 Ilwaco, WA 98624	360-642-3196	19 units $38–$69
Heidi's Inn 126 E Spruce St, PO Box 776 Ilwaco, WA 98624	360-642-2387 800-576-1032	26 units $30–$75
Hartman's Log Cabin Resort 5745 S Twin Lakes Access Rd, HCR 1 Box 156 Inchelium, WA 99138	509-722-3543	59 units $36–$50
Rainbow Beach Resort HC 1 Box 146 Inchelium, WA 99138	509-722-5901	26 units $32–$138
Wild Lily Cabins B & B PO Box 313 Index, WA 98256	360-793-2103	3 units $75–$105
Box Canyon Resort & Motel 8612 SR 31 Ione, WA 99139	509-442-3728 800-676-8883	9 units $29–$116
Ione Motel & Trailer Park 301 S 2nd St, PO Box 730 Ione, WA 99139	509-442-3213	11 units $40–$85
Fraternity Snoqualmie Park PO Box 748 Issaquah, WA 98027	425-392-nude www.392nude.org	3 units $12–$25
Best Western Aladdin Motor Inn 310 Long Ave Kelso, WA 98626	360-425-9660 800-528-1234 www.bestwesternwashington.com	78 units $49–$90
Budget Inn-Kelso 505 N Pacific Ave Kelso, WA 98626	360-636-4610	51 units $37–$61

A: Where to Stay in Washington with Your Dog

food/bev	free	kitchen	pet fee	pool	spa	other features
R & L					rm	located on port docks, near beach & local parks, lighthouses & museums nearby
	C	K	$5 per day		tb	laundry facilities, dog walking area, 3 blocks to port of Ilwaco
R		K R	$3 per day			laundry facilities, lots of natural wooded area for walking dogs
		K	$3 per day			laundry facilities, RV sites, lakefront location, walking trails, swimming
B & B	C CB	R	$10 per day			cedar log cabins, BBQ, forested riverfront location, surrounded by wilderness on Skykomish River
	C	K	$3 per day			river frontage, hiking trails, 1 mi to public park
	C	R M				dog allowed by advance reservation only, 500 ft frontage on Pend Orielle river, near public park
		K		out htd	sp sa tb	nudist park! cabin, A-frame, trailer, RV sites, community kitchen avail, close to walking trails
R & L	C	R M	$5 per day	in htd	tb	laundry facilities, area for walking dogs, 2 blocks from Cowlitz River trail
	C	K	$5 per day			

abbreviations used in this section

Kelso — Kennewick

Doubletree Hotel 510 Kelso Dr Kelso, WA 98626	360-636-4400 800-222-8733 fsherer@cport.com	162 units $59–$195
Motel 6-Kelso 106 N Minor Rd Kelso, WA 98626	360-425-3229 800-466-8356 www.motel6.com	63 units $39–$60
Super 8 Motel-Kelso 250 Kelso Dr Kelso, WA 98626	360-423-8880 800-800-8000 www.super8.com	84 units $50–$80
Best Western Kennewick Inn 4001 W 27th Ave Kennewick, WA 99337	509-586-1332	87 units $65–$119
Cavanaugh's At Columbia Ctr 1101 N Columbia Center Blvd Kennewick, WA 99336	509-783-0611 800-325-4000 www.cavanaughs.com	162 units $69–$150
Columbia Motor Inn 1133 W Columbia Dr Kennewick, WA 99336	509-586-4739	11 units $32–$45
Comfort Inn 7801 W Quinault St Kennewick, WA 99336	509-783-8396 800-221-2222	56 units $45–$55
Green Gables Motel 515 W Columbia Dr Kennewick, WA 99336	509-582-5811	23 units $25–$65
Holiday Inn Express-Kennewick 4220 W 27th Ave Kennewick, WA 99338	509-736-3326 800-465-4329	53 units $69–$125
Nendels Inn 2811 W 2nd Ave Kennewick, WA 99336	509-735-9511 800-547-0106	106 units $43–$63

See pp. 90-91 for a key to the

A: Where to Stay in Washington with Your Dog

food/bev	free	kitchen	pet fee	pool	spa	other features
R&L	C		$10 per stay	out	sp	park located directly behind hotel, riverfront trail nearby
	C			out		close to dog walking area
	C	R M	$25 ref dep	in htd	sp	laundry facilities, adjacent to Tam O'Shanter Park for walking dogs
	C CB	R M	$10 per stay	in htd	sp sa	laundry facilities, all pet rooms on ground floor and open onto area for walking dogs
R&L		R M		out htd	sp	area for walking dogs, 1½ mi to Columbia Park
		R				grassy area for walking dogs, ½ mi to public park on Columbia River
	C CB	R M	$10 per day	out	sp rm	absolutely no dogs left alone in room, area for walking dogs, laundry facilities
		K R M	$5 ref dep			laundry facilities, area for walking dogs, 3 minutes to Columbia River & park
	C CB	K R M	ref dep	in	sp sa	dogs allowed in smoking rooms only, laundry facilities, close to park
	C CB		$5 per stay	out htd		area for walking dogs, 1 mi to public park

abbreviations used in this section

Kennewick — Kent

Ramada Inn-Clover Island 435 Clover Island Kennewick, WA 99336	509-586-0541 800-272-6232	151 units $60–$110
Shaniko Suites Motel 321 N Johnson St Kennewick, WA 99336	509-735-6385 888-321-7512	47 units $41–$64
Super 8 Motel-Kennewick 626 N Columbia Center Blvd Kennewick, WA 99336	509-736-6888 800-800-8000 www.super8.com	95 units $40–$65
Tapadera Inn 300-A N Ely St Kennewick, WA 99336	509-783-6191 800-722-8277	61 units $38–$56
Best Western Heritage Inn 25100 74th Ave S Kent, WA 98032	253-520-6670 800-238-7234 www.bestwesternwashington.com	60 units $73–$130
Comfort Inn-Kent 22311 84th Ave S Kent, WA 98032	253-872-2211	101 units $85–$129
Days Inn-South Seattle 1711 W Meeker St Kent, WA 98032	253-854-1950 800-329-7466 www.daysinn.com	82 units $53–$119
Golden Kent Motel 22203 84th Ave S Kent, WA 98032	253-872-8372	21 units $50–$60
Howard Johnson Inn 1233 Central Ave N Kent, WA 98032	253-852-7224 800-446-4656	85 units $65–$150
Val-U Inn 22420 84th Ave S Kent, WA 98032	253-872-5525 800-443-7777 www.members.aol.com/valuinn	94 units $63–$90

See pp. 90-91 for a key to the

A: Where to Stay in Washington with Your Dog

food/bev	free	kitchen	pet fee	pool	spa	other features
R & L	C		$5 per day	out htd	tb	laundry facilities, large riverfront area for walking dogs
	C CB	K R M	$5 per day	out		laundry facilities, close to dog walking area
	C	M	$25 ref dep	in htd	tb	laundry facilities, area for walking dogs, 5 min to Columbia River Park
	C CB	R M	$5 per day	out htd		laundry facilities, open area for walking dogs, 1 mi to Columbia River Park
	C CB			in htd	sp sa rm	laundry facilities, adjacent to bike trails
	C CB	R M	$10 per day	in htd	sp	dog allowed at manager's discretion only, laundry facilities
	C CB		$10 per stay			laundry facilities, small dogs only, close to dog walking area
		K	$25 per stay			full kitchens, laundry facilities, area for walking dogs, ½ mi to Green River walking & biking trails
	C CB	R M		out htd	sp tb	exercise room, coffeemakers, laundry facilities, area for walking dogs, 2 blocks to public park
	C CB		$5 per day		sp	laundry facilities, cookies and doggy biscuits served 5-7 PM, area for walking dogs

abbreviations used in this section   149

Kettle Falls – La Conner

Barney's Cafe & Motel PO Box 1319 Kettle Falls, WA 99141	509-738-6546	8 units $25–$35
Grandview Inn Motel & RV Park 978 Highway 395 N, PO Box 640 Kettle Falls, WA 99141	509-738-6733 888-488-6733	13 units $36–$55
Kettle Falls Inn 205 E 3rd Ave, PO Box 598 Kettle Falls, WA www.angelfire.com/wa/KettleFallsInn/	509-738-6514 800-701-1927	24 units $37–$56
Smiley's Colonial Motel 11067 NE State Hwy 104, PO Box 7 Kingston, WA 98346	360-297-3622	17 units $40–$45
Best Western Kirkland Inn 12223 NE 116th St Kirkland, WA 98034 www.bestwesternwashington.com	425-822-2300 800-332-4200	110 units $77–$94
La Quinta Inn 10530 Northup Way Kirkland, WA 98033	425-828-6585 800-531-5900	118 units $82–$165
Motel 6-Kirkland 12010 120th Pl NE Kirkland, WA 98034	425-821-5618 800-440-6000	123 units $50–$67
Art's Place B & B 511 E Talbott, PO Box 557 La Conner, WA 98257	360-466-3033	1 unit $60
La Conner Country Inn 107 S 2nd St, PO Box 573 La Conner, WA 98257	360-466-3101 www.laconnerlodging.com	28 units $95–$155
Manor Inn & Inside Out 711 E Morris St, PO Box 1367 La Conner, WA	360-466-3144 www.nwculture.com	2 units $65–$85

See pp. 90-91 for a key to the

A: Where to Stay in Washington with Your Dog

food/bev	free	kitchen	pet fee	pool	spa	other features
R	C		$25 ref dep			rustic rooms located across from Lake Roosevelt, great views, area for walking dog
	C	K R M		out htd	sp	laundry facilities, RV sites, ½ mi to public park, 2 mi to Lake Roosevelt park & recreation area
	C	K R M	$5 per day		sp sa tb	near Lake Roosevelt, laundry facilities, area for walking dogs
		R				dogs allowed in 1 unit, 1 block to vet clinic w/boarding kennels, close to dog walking area
R	C CB	R M	$50 ref dep	out	sp	laundry facilities
	C CB	M		out htd		exercise room, many walking trails nearby, laundry facilities, 3 mi to off-leash park
	C			out		laundry facilities, area for walking dogs
B&B	C CB	R M				separate guest house, area for walking dogs
R&L	C CB		$25 per stay			gas fireplaces
	C CB		$10 per day			small dogs only allowed indoors, larger dogs can stay in fenced "doggy hotel," close to parks

abbreviations used in this section

La Push — Langley

La Push Ocean Park Resort 700 Main St, PO Box 67 La Push, WA 98350	360-374-5267 800-487-1267	55 units $63–$175
Shoreline Resort 770 Main St La Push, WA 98350	360-374-6488 800-487-1267 www.lapushwa.com	54 units $62–$175
Super 8 Motel 4615 Martin Way E Lacey, WA 98516-5385	360-459-8888 800-800-8000 www.super8.com	100 units $53–$74
Best Western Lakewood Motor Inn 6125 Motor Ave SW Lakewood, WA 98499	253-584-2212 800-528-1234 www.bestwesternwashington.com	78 units $62–$78
Colonial Motel 12117 Pacific Hwy SW Lakewood, WA 98499	253-589-3261	34 units $35–$75
Fort Clarke Motel 12704 Pacific Hwy SW Lakewood, WA 98499	253-581-5025	20 units $25–$40
Madigan Motel 12039 Pacific Hwy SW Lakewood, WA 98499	253-588-8697	23 units $35–$65
Angel Cottage B & B 616 Edgecliff Dr, PO Box 736 Langley, WA 98260	360-221-3676	1 unit $95
Beach Cabin 325 Wharf St, 791 Furman Ave Langley, WA 98260	360-221-3960	1 unit $60–$80
Drake's Landing 203 Wharf St, PO Box 613 Langley, WA 98260	360-221-3999	1 unit $70

A: Where to Stay in Washington with Your Dog

food/bev	free	kitchen	pet fee	pool	spa	other features
R		K	$10 per stay			1 & 2 bdrm cabins, laundry facilities, RV sites, beachfront resort area
	C	K	$10 per day			dogs allowed in A-frame units and shoreline cabins, beach access for walking dogs
	C CB		$25 ref dep	in htd		laundry facilities
	C CB	R	$6 per day	out htd		1 dog per room only, laundry facilities, area for walking dogs, cleanup scoopers provided
R		R M	$20 ref dep		rm	area for walking dogs, laundry facilities, 5 min drive to public park
		K	$20 ref dep			laundry facilities, small area for walking dogs, 5 min drive to lake & public park
R	C FB	K	$50 ref dep			1 free breakfast per room, laundry facilities, playground, area for walking dogs, close to public park
B&B	C CB	K				cottage overlooking Puget Sound, dog by advance reservation only, 10 min walk to public park & beach
		K				fully equipped kitchen, laundry facilities, small yard, beach access
	C		$10 per stay			across street from beach

abbreviations used in this section   153

Langley – Leavenworth

Gallery Suite B & B 301 1st St Langley, WA 98260	360-221-2978	1 unit $110–$90
Inverness Inn 15630 SR 525 Langley, WA 98260	360-321-5521	6 units $65–$90
Island Tyme Bed & Breakfast 4940 S Bayview Rd Langley, WA 98260	360-221-5078 800-898-8963 www.moriah.com/island-tyme/	5 units $95–$140
Pine Cottage B & B 3827 S McKay Dr Langley, WA 98260	360-730-1376	2 units $85–$100
Primrose Path Cottage 3191 SE Harbor Rd Langley, WA 98260	360-730-3722	1 unit $145–$185
Rabbit On The Green B & B PO Box 620 Langley, WA 98260	360-321-7254 800-366-0645	1 unit $100–$120
Alpen Inn 405 US Highway 2 Leavenworth, WA 98826	509-548-4326	40 units $70–$90
Alpine Chalets 3601 Allen Ln, PO Box 884 Leavenworth, WA 98826	509-548-5674	2 units $80–$95
Alpine Rivers Inn 1505 Alpensee Strasse St, PO Box 288 Leavenworth, WA 98826	509-548-5875 800-873-3960 www.riversinn.com	26 units $69–$99
Bedfinders 305 8th St Leavenworth, WA 98826	509-548-4410 800-323-2920 www.bedfinders.com	5 units $125–$135

See pp. 90-91 for a key to the

A: Where to Stay in Washington with Your Dog

food/bev	free	kitchen	pet fee	pool	spa	other features
B&B	C CB	K				dogs by advance reservation only, 1 bdrm condo w/waterfront view, next to public park
	C	K R M				every suite has kitchen, dining & living areas, bdrm & bath
B&B	C FB				sp	dogs allowed in 1 room, 2 mi to public park, 5 mi to "off-leash" beach
B&B	C CB	K	$10 per stay			1 room cottage w/fully equipped kitchen & fireplace, ocean view, large yard, 15 min walk to beach
	C	K R M	$20 per stay		tb	dog allowed by advance reservation only, separate cottage kitchenette, ½ block to beach
B&B	C CB				tb	on 10 acres w/very large yard area & pond, beaches nearby
	C CB	R M	$10 per day	out htd	sp	refundable damage deposit, across street from public park & walking trails
		K	$5 per stay	out		A-frame cabins, laundry facilities, walking path to Peshastin River, 1 mi to dog-friendly creek trail
	C	R M	$10 per day	out htd	sp	private riverview balconies, 6 blocks to downtown area and city parks, walking trails to river
		K R M	0-$5 per stay			cabins, laundry facilities, pet fee varies, also have cabins in other parts of the state, call for details

abbreviations used in this section   155

Leavenworth

Der Ritterhof Motor Inn 190 Hwy 2 Leavenworth, WA 98826	509-548-5845 800-255-5845	51 units $76–$98
Evergreen Motor Inn 1117 Front St Leavenworth, WA 98826	509-548-5515 800-327-7212 www.evergreeninn.com	40 units $40–$120
Inn Vienna Woods B & B 12842 Prowell St Leavenworth, WA 98826	509-548-7843 888-548-7843	5 units $75–$125
Kinney Suites 217 8th St, PO Box 726 Leavenworth, WA 98826	509-548-5585 800-621-9676	4 units $100–$145
Lake Wenatchee Hide-A-Ways 19944 Hwy 207 Leavenworth, WA 98826	509-763-0108 800-883-2611 www.bluegrouse.com	13 units $100–$175
Leavenworth Village Inn 1016 Commercial St Leavenworth, WA 98826	509-548-6620	18 units $99–$209
Leirvangen Bed & Breakfast 7586 Icicle Rd Leavenworth, WA 98826	509-548-5165 800-401-6693 wwww.leirvangenbnb.com	3 units $85–$120
Natapoc Lodging 12338 Bretz Rd Leavenworth, WA 98226	509-763-3313 888-6282762 www.natapoc.com	7 units $150–$300
Obertal Motor Inn 922 Commercial St Leavenworth, WA 98826	509-548-5204 800-537-9382 www.obertal.com	26 units $69–$109
Phippen's Bed & Breakfast 10285 Ski Hill Dr Leavenworth, WA 98826	509-548-7755 800-666-9806	2 units $70–$80

A: Where to Stay in Washington with Your Dog

food/bev	free	kitchen	pet fee	pool	spa	other features
R	C	K	$10 per day	out htd	sp	barbecue pits, putting green, RV parking
	C CB	K R M	$10 per stay		sp tb	$20 refundable pet deposit, quiet off-road location, 2½ blocks to riverfront trails
B&B	C FB				tb	dog allowed by advance reservation only, country road for walking dogs, walking trail nearby
	C	K	$15 per stay			small dog allowed at owner's discretion only, furnished suites, laundry, near waterfront park
			$5 per stay		tb	riverfront cabins w/fully equipped kitchens
	C CB	K				area for walking dogs, 2 blocks to public park
B&B	C FB		$5 per day		rm	dog allowed by advance reservation only, dog walking area, across street from public park
	C	K	$10 per day		tb	fully furnished lodges, private hot tubs, laundry facilities, group catering avail, area for walking dogs
	C CB	R M	$10 per day		tb	fireplace rooms, laundry facilities, across street from public park
B&B	C FB	R M		out htd	tb	laundry facilities, 2 fenced yards for walking dogs, ¾ mi to public park & swimming pool

abbreviations used in this section 157

Have Dog Will Travel—Washington Edition

Leavenworth — Long Beach

River's Edge Lodge 8401 Hwy 2 Leavenworth, WA 98826	509-548-7612 800-451-5285	23 units $67–$77
Rodeway Inn & Suites 185 Hwy 2 Leavenworth, WA 98826	509-548-7992 800-693-1225 www.leavenworthwa.com	33 units $59–$123
Saimons Hide-A-Ways 16408 River Rd Leavenworth, WA 98826	509-763-3213 800-845-8638 www.saimons.com	6 units $115–$175
Spring Inn 12620 Spring St Leavenworth, WA 98826	509-548-4115	1 unit $80–$130
Tyrolean Ritz Hotel 633 Front St Leavenworth, WA 98826	509-548-5455 800-854-6365 www.tyrolritz.com	16 units $50–$125
Mike's Beach Resort 38470 N US Highway 101 Lilliwaup, WA 98555	360-877-5324 800-231-5324 mikesbch@hctc.com	8 units $40–$95
Anchorage Cottages 2209 Boulevard North, PO Box 504 Long Beach, WA 98631	360-642-2351 800-646-2351	10 units $60–$120
Anthony's Home Court Motel 1310 Pacific Hwy N, PO Box 1532 Long Beach, WA 98631	360-642-2802 888-787-2754 www.aone.com/~djh	32 units $20–$125
Beach It Rentals 11409 Pacific Way Long Beach, WA 98631	360-642-4697 jklein@pacifier.com	1 unit $120
Boulevard Motel 301 N Ocean Blvd, PO Box 1008 Long Beach, WA 98631	360-642-2434	22 units $50–$110

See pp. 90-91 for a key to the

A: Where to Stay in Washington with Your Dog

food/bev	free	kitchen	pet fee	pool	spa	other features
	C	K		out	sp	
	C CB	R M	$12 per day	in htd	tb	laundry facilities, exercise room, close to Riverfront Park & 1½ mile-long trail that loops through town
	C	K R M			sp tb rm	fully equipped cabins on private ½ to 2 acre lots, area for walking dogs, 1 block to river, 9 mi to lake
		K				2 bdrm suite with fully equipped kitchenette, area for walking dogs, 1 mi to public park & waterfront
R	C		$10 per stay		sp	$20 refundable pet deposit, close to dog walking area
	C	K R M	$10 per stay			2,000 ft beachfront, RV sites, laundry facilities, walking trails nearby
		K R M	$6 per day			fireplaces
	C	K R M	$5 per day			7 motel units, 25 RV sites, laundry facilities, beach access directly across street
		K R M				4 bdrm, 1½ bath fully equipped vacation home sleeps 8, laundry facilities, 1 block to dunes beach
		K	$5 per day	in htd		motel rooms & cottages, area for walking dogs, 3 min walk to public park or beach

abbreviations used in this section   159

Have Dog Will Travel—Washington Edition

Long Beach

Breakers Motel	360-642-4414	116 units
26th & Hwy 103, PO Box 428	800-288-8890	$59–$200
Long Beach, WA 98631		www.v-v-a.com
Chautauqua Lodge Resort	360-642-4401	180 units
304 14th St NW, PO Box 757	800-869-8401	$55–$160
Long Beach, WA 98631		
Edgewater Inn	360-642-2311	84 units
409 SW 10th St, PO Box 793	800-561-2456	$49–$104
Long Beach, WA 98631		
Lighthouse Motel	360-642-3622	21 units
12415 Pacific Way	877-220-7555	$55–$149
Long Beach, WA 98631		rgrambo@aone.com
Ocean Lodge	360-642-5400	64 units
208 Bolstad Ave W, PO Box 337		$52–$100
Long Beach, WA 98631		
Our Place At The Beach	360-642-3793	25 units
1309 S Ocean Beach Blvd, PO Box 266	800-538-5107	$39–$63
Long Beach, WA 98631		tompson@aone.com
Pacific View Motel	360-642-2415	11 units
203 Bolstad Ave, PO Box 302	800-238-0859	$40–$100
Long Beach, WA 98631		www.funbeach.com
Sands Motel	360-642-2100	10 units
12211 Pacific Way		$33–$50
Long Beach, WA 98631		wizbang@willapabay.org
Shaman Motel	360-642-3714	42 units
115 3rd St SW, PO Box 235	800-753-3750	$59–$99
Long Beach, WA 98631		www.shamanmotel.com
Thunderbird Motel	360-642-5700	13 units
201 Boulevard Ave N	888-642-5700	$36–$85
Long Beach, WA 98631		

See pp. 90-91 for a key to the

A: Where to Stay in Washington with Your Dog

food/bev	free	kitchen	pet fee	pool	spa	other features
	C	K R M	$15 per day	in htd	sp	suites, fireplaces, laundry facilities, playground, gazebo w/BBQ, beach access, hiking trails
R & L		K	$8 per day	in htd	sp tb	fireplaces, ocean views, therapy pool, recreation room, paved dune trail
R	C	R M	$8 per day			all oceanfront rooms, across street from ¼ mile-long boardwalk & 2 mile-long bike & hiking trail
		K	$5-$10 /day			fireplaces, beach access
	C CB	K	$5 per stay	out htd	sa tb	fireplaces, ocean view, beach access for walking dogs
	C CB	K R M	$5 per day		sp sa tb	cabins & ocean view rooms, fireplaces, exercise room, steam room, area for walking dogs
	C	K	$5 per day			fireplaces, fenced play area, easy beach and downtown access
			$5 per stay			beach access for walking dogs
	C	K R M	$5 per stay	out htd		fireplaces, laundry facilities, ocean vistas, easy walk to downtown & beach, dune path & boardwalk
	C	K R M	$5 per day	in htd		studios and suites, open area for walking dogs, ¼ mi to beach and boardwalk

abbreviations used in this section　　　　　　　　　　161

Have Dog Will Travel—Washington Edition

Long Beach – Loomis

Tryon by the Beach 2209 60th St Long Beach, WA 98631	360-642-4090 pinky@willapabay.org	2 units $100–$125
Whale's Tale 620 S Pacific Hwy, PO Box 418 Long Beach, WA 98631	360-642-3455 800-559-4253 www.thewhalestale.com	9 units $29–$99
Yett Beach House 601 N Ocean Beach Blvd, PO Box 1344 Long Beach, WA	360-642-8069 888-642-8069 www.boreasinn.com/yetthouse.html	1 unit $115
Budget Inn-Longview 1808 Hemlock St Longview, WA 98632	360-423-6980	34 units $27–$45
Holiday Inn Express-Longview 723 7th Ave Longview, WA 98632	360-414-1000 800-465-4329 kimstan@teleport.com	50 units $59–$89
Hudson Hotel 1306 9th Ave Longview, WA 98632	360-425-7791	30 units $18–$110
Hudson Manor Motel 1616 Hudson St Longview, WA 98632	360-425-1100	25 units $35–$46
Town Chalet Motor Hotel 1822 Washington Way Longview, WA 98632	360-423-2020	24 units $30–$53
Town House Motel 744 Washington Way Longview, WA 98632	360-423-7200	28 units $32–$50
Chopaka Lodge 1995 Loomis Oroville Rd Loomis, WA 98827	509-223-3131	3 units $45–$50

See pp. 90-91 for a key to the

A: Where to Stay in Washington with Your Dog

food/bev	free	kitchen	pet fee	pool	spa	other features
	C	K				2 bdrm rental sleeps 6, fireplace, laundry facilities, area for walking dogs, 1 mi to beach & boardwalk
	C	K R M			sp sa	exercise room, ping pong & pool tables, no fee for one dog, additional dogs are $5 ea per night
		K	$25 per stay			3 bdrm 110 yr old beachfront cottage, fenced lawn, dunes path, $25 pet fee plus $25 cleaning fee
	C CB	K R M	$5-$15/stay			close to dog walking area
	C CB	R M	$15 per stay	in htd	sp	laundry facilities, 1 mi to Lake Sacajawea, 3½ mile walking trail around the lake
		R M	$			pet fee varies by length of stay, laundry facilities, easy walking distance to park & waterfront
	C CB	K R M	$3 per day			
		K R M	$3 per day			lawn area for walking dogs, 2 blocks to public park
	C	R M	$5-$10/day	out htd		1 block to fairground, close to restaurants & dog walking area
		K				fully equipped cabins, tent & RV sites, adjacent to park on Palmer Lake

abbreviations used in this section

Loon Lake — Marysville

Lakeside Motel 3849 3rd Ave Loon Lake, WA 99148	509-233-9060 sumharv@aol.com	13 units $40–$80
West Bay Park On Deer Lake 3800 W Bay Rd Loon Lake, WA 99148	509-233-2233	3 units $50–$75
Best Western Lynnwood/N Seattle 4300 200th St SW Lynnwood, WA 98036	425-775-7447 800-238-7234 www.bestwesternwashington.com	103 units $79–$119
Residence Inn by Marriott 18200 Alderwood Mall Pkwy Lynnwood, WA 98037	425-771-1100 800-331-3131	120 units $145–$199
Rodeway Inn 20707 Highway 99 Lynnwood, WA 98036	425-774-7700 800-228-2000	52 units $69–$89
Rose Motel 20222 Hwy 99 Lynnwood, WA 98036	425-744-5616	10 units $32–$35
Jameson Lake Resort North End 580 Jameson Lake Rd, PO Box 8 Mansfield, WA 98830	509-683-1141	9 units $25–$60
Thurston House Bed & Breakfast 9512 Silver Lake Rd, PO Box 13 Maple Falls, WA 98266	360-599-2261 bzylsra@juno.com	2 units $50–$65
Best Western Tulalip Inn 6128 33rd Ave NE Marysville, WA 98271	360-659-4488	69 units $69–$109
City Center Motel 810 State Ave Marysville, WA 98270	360-659-2424	21 units $39–$44

A: Where to Stay in Washington with Your Dog

food/bev	free	kitchen	pet fee	pool	spa	other features
R&L	C	R M	$10 per stay		rm	1 mi to lake beaches w/snack bar, boat rental, fishing, RV sites, area for walking dogs
		K				cabins sleep 8, RV sites, recreation hall w/kitchen, laundry facilities, next to state lands for walking dogs
	C CB		$10 per day	in htd	sp	
	C CB	K	$10 per day	out	sp	fireplaces in most rooms, laundry facilities, grocery shopping service, close to dog walking area
	C CB	K	$20 per stay			area for walking dogs
			$10 per stay			laundry facilities
R&L		K				9 trailers, 46 RV sites, tent sites, lakefront location with areas for walking dogs
B&B	C FB	K			tb	suite & guest house w/kitchenette, 3 RV sites, area for walking dogs along Silver Lake, 2 mi to park
R	C CB	R M	$10 per day	in htd	sp rm	small dogs only, grassy area for walking dogs, 5 mi to waterfront
	C	K	$10 per day			

abbreviations used in this section   165

Marysville — Monroe

Village Motor Inn 235 Beach Ave Marysville, WA 98270	360-659-0005 877-659-0005	45 units $52–$130
Mazama Country Inn 42 Lost River Rd, HCR 74 Box B-9 Mazama, WA 98833	509-996-2681 800-843-7951 www.mazama-inn.com	3 units $115–up
Circle Motel Highway 31, PO Box 616 Metaline Falls, WA 99153	509-446-4343	8 units $30–$45
Pend O'reille Apts/Historic Miners Hotel 101 W 4th St, PO Box 477 Metaline Falls, WA 99153	509-446-4802	33 units $29–$49
Washington Hotel 225 E 5th Ave, PO Box 2 Metaline Falls, WA 99153	509-446-4415	18 units $35
Barnacle Motel 4816 Pacific Ave, PO Box 44 Moclips, WA 98562	360-276-4318 http://users.olynet.com/kjaquet	2 units $45–$68
Hi-Tide Ocean Beach Resort 4890 Railroad Ave, PO Box 308 Moclips, WA 98562	360-276-4142 800-662-5477	25 units $90–$164
Moclips Motel 4852 Pacific Ave, PO Box 8 Moclips, WA 98562	360-276-4228	11 units $38–$70
Ocean Crest Resort 4651 State Highway 109, PO Box 7 Moclips, WA 98562	360-276-4465 800-684-8439	45 units $58–$129
Best Western Baron Inn 19233 Hwy 2 Monroe, WA 98272	360-794-3111 www.bestwesternwashington.com	58 units $50–$150

A: Where to Stay in Washington with Your Dog

food/bev	free	kitchen	pet fee	pool	spa	other features
	C CB	R M	$12 per day			1 block to open field for walking dogs
		K	$50 ref dep			dogs allowed in 2 of the cabins & vacation homes, laundry facilities, near river & walking trails
	C CB	R M	$5 per day		tb	2 mi from town on 20 country acres w/view & trails, RV sites
	C	K				hotel rooms, studios, 2 bdrm suites, laundry facilities, field & walking trails, near public park & riverfront
						historical building, across street from public park
		K	$5 per day			located on quiet dead-end road, 1 block to beach access
	C	K R M	$10 per day			no pit bulls or rottweilers, close to dog walking area
		K	$3-$6/day			full kitchens, 100 ft to beach
R & L	C	K R M	$12 per day	in htd	sp sa tb	laundry facilities, exercise room, 200 ft to ocean & sandy beach
	C CB	M	$25 per stay	out	sp	laundry facilities, exercise room

abbreviations used in this section   167

Monroe — Moses Lake

Fairgrounds Inn 18950 Hwy 2 Monroe, WA 98272	360-794-5401	62 units $45–$50
Monte Square Motel 518-1/2 1st St S Montesano, WA 98563	360-249-4424	10 units $35–$45
Plum Tree Motel & Apt Rentals 822 Pioneer Ave E Montesano, WA 98563	360-249-3931	22 units $39
Evergreen Motel 121 Front St, PO Box 205 Morton, WA 98356	360-496-5407	12 units $30–$50
Seasons Motel 200A Westlake Ave, PO Box 567 Morton, WA 98356	360-496-6835 877-496-6835 www.whitepasstravel.com	50 units $50–$65
Stiltner Motel 250 Morton Rd, PO Box 474 Morton, WA 98356	360-496-5103	7 units $35
Best Western Hallmark Inn 3000 W Marina Dr Moses Lake, WA 98837	509-765-9211 888-448-4449 www.hallmarkinns.com	160 units $64–$140
Heritage Suites 511 S Division St Moses Lake, WA 98837	509-765-7707 800-457-0271	24 units $40–$79
Holiday Inn Express 1745 E Kittleson Rd Moses Lake, WA www.televar.com/~holiday/mlinn.html	509-766-2000 800-576-7500	75 units $55–$100
IMA El Rancho Motel 1214 S Pioneer Way Moses Lake, WA www.imalodging.com/Lodges/W122.htm	509-765-9173 800-341-8000	20 units $33–$55

A: Where to Stay in Washington with Your Dog

food/bev	free	kitchen	pet fee	pool	spa	other features
	C CB	R M	$5 per day		sp	laundry facilities, area for walking dogs, 10 min to public park
	C	K				open area for walking dogs
		R M				small dogs only, area for walking dogs, 1 mi to Lake Sylvia State Park
		K M				public park across street, only motel in town that takes dogs of any size
R	C		$5 per day			small dogs only, 2½ blocks to public park, ½ mi to riverfront park
		K R M				well-behaved dogs only
R&L	C	K R		out htd	sp	walking-biking trail across lake to state park, doggy sheets & disposable scoopers avail
		K	$100 ref dep		rm	2 night min stay, fully equipped kitchens, laundry facilities, grassy dog walking area, 5 blocks to park
R	C CB	R M		in htd	sp rm	laundry facilities, exercise room, area for walking dogs
	C	K		out htd		picnic area w/BBQ

abbreviations used in this section   169

Moses Lake

Imperial Inn 905 W Broadway Ave Moses Lake, WA 98837	509-765-8626	29 units $34–$71
Inn at Moses Lake 1741 E Kittleson Rd Moses Lake, WA www.televar.com/~holiday/mlinn.html	509-766-7000	44 units $59–$80
Interstate Inn 2801 W Broadway Ave Moses Lake, WA 98837	509-765-1777	30 units $36–$54
Lakeshore Resort Motel 3206 W Lakeshore Dr Moses Lake, WA 98837	509-765-9201	33 units $25–$75
Maples Motel 1006 W 3rd Ave Moses Lake, WA 98837	509-765-5665	44 units $20–$60
Moses Lake Travelodge 316 S Pioneer Way Moses Lake, WA 98837	509-765-8631 800-578-7878	40 units $49–$65
Motel 6-Moses Lake 2822 Wapato Dr Moses Lake, WA 98837	509-766-0250 800-466-8356	89 units $34–$40
Oasis Budget Inn 466 Melva Ln Moses Lake, WA 98837	509-765-8636 800-456-0708	36 units $35–$75
Sage 'n' Sand Motel 1011 S Pioneer Way Moses Lake, WA 98837	509-765-1755 800-336-0454	38 units $32–$65
Shilo Inn-Moses Lake 1819 E Kittleson Rd Moses Lake, WA 98837	509-765-9317 800-222-2344 www.shiloinns.com	100 units $65–$95

See pp. 90-91 for a key to the

A: Where to Stay in Washington with Your Dog

food/bev	free	kitchen	pet fee	pool	spa	other features
	C CB	K R M	0-$5 per day	out htd		newly renovated, area for walking dogs, 1 mi to public park
	C CB	R M				laundry facilities, all non-smoking rooms, area for walking dogs
	C	R M		in htd	sp sa	area for walking dogs, walking distance to public park
		K	$5 per day	out htd		lakefront cabins, boat launch & slips, laundry facilities, close to dog walking area
	C	R		out htd		1 block to walking trail
			$5 per day	out	sp	adjacent to city park
	C	R		out htd		laundry facilities, area for walking dogs, 2 blocks to public park
	C	K R M		out htd	sp	large grassy area for walking dogs, 2 blocks to lake, laundry facilities
	C	K R M	$5 per day	out htd		area for walking dogs
	C CB	R M	$7 per day	in htd	sp sa	exercise room, steam room

abbreviations used in this section

Moses Lake — Mount Vernon

Sunland Motor Inn 309 E 3rd Ave Moses Lake, WA 98837	509-765-1170 800-220-4403	22 units $34–$52
Super 8 Motel-Moses Lake 449 Melva Ln Moses Lake, WA 98837	509-765-8886 800-800-8000 www.super8.com	62 units $49–$75
Mossyrock Inn 120 E State St, PO Box 642 Mossyrock, WA 98564	360-983-8641	6 units $45–$55
Best Western College Way Inn 300 W College Way Mount Vernon, WA	360-424-4287 800-793-4024 www.bestwesternwashington.com	66 units $45–$88
Best Western Cottontree Inn 2300 Market St Mount Vernon, WA 98273	360-428-5678 800-662-6886 www.cottontree-ninn.com	121 units $59–$89
Comfort Inn-Mount Vernon 1910 Freeway Dr Mount Vernon, WA 98273	360-428-7020	68 units $59–$110
Days Inn-Mount Vernon 2009 Riverside Dr Mount Vernon, WA 98273	360-424-4141 800-882-4141 www.daysinn.com	67 units $50–$70
Hillside Motel 23002 Bonnieview Rd Mount Vernon, WA 98273	360-445-3252	5 units $43–$55
West Winds Motel 2020 Riverside Dr Mount Vernon, WA 98273	360-424-4224	40 units $35–$95
Whispering Firs B & B 19357 Kanako Ln Mount Vernon, WA 98274	360-428-1990 800-428-1992	4 units $65–$95

A: Where to Stay in Washington with Your Dog

food/bev	free	kitchen	pet fee	pool	spa	other features
		K R M	$5 per stay			1 block to public park, off-site swimming pool privileges available
	C	R M	$25 ref dep	in htd		laundry facilities, across street from walking trail to the lake
						1 mi to Riff Lake, other lakes within easy driving distance
	C CB	K	$10 per day	out htd	sp	
R & L	C CB	R M	$10 per stay	out htd		laundry facilities, 1 block to river-front walking trails
	C CB	K	$5 per day	in htd	sp	laundry facilities, area for walking dogs, 1 mi to public park
R & L	C		$5 per day	out htd		RV sites, area for walking dogs
	C	K	$5 per day			
	C CB	R M	$5 per stay			walking trails, ½ mi to public park
B & B	C FB				sp	dog allowed by advance reservation only, dinners available on request, on 250 acres with lake

abbreviations used in this section   173

Mount Vernon — Newport

White Swan Guest House 15872 Moore Rd Mount Vernon, WA 98273	360-445-6805 www.cn.com/~wswan/	1 unit $135–$150
Homestead Guest Studios 6017 244th St SW Mountlake Ter, WA 98043	425-771-3139 888-782-9473	118 units $273–$378
Natchez Hotel 222 Naches Ave, PO Box 514 Naches, WA 98937	509-653-1317 888-282-1317	6 units $63–$74
Moby Dick Hotel Sandridge Road, PO Box 82 Nahcotta, WA 98637 www.nwplace.com/mobydick.html	360-665-4543	8 units $70–$95
Sleepy Hollow Motel 1032 SR 4 Naselle, WA 98638	360-484-3232	7 units $35–$40
Cape Motel & RV Park 150 Bayview Ave South, PO Box 136 Neah Bay, WA 98357	360-645-2250	10 units $45–$65
Tyee Motel Bayview Ave, PO Box 193 Neah Bay, WA 98357	360-645-2223 360-645-2450	41 units $35–$95
Reynold's Resort Buffalo Lake Rd, PO Box 556 Nespelem, WA 99155	509-633-1092	4 units $15–$20
Sutton Bay Resort 12016 NW Newman Lake Dr, PO Box 8 Newman Lake, WA 99025	509-226-3660 $45/dy–$475/wk	9 units
Golden Spur Motor Inn 924 W Hwy 2 Newport, WA 99156	509-447-3823	24 units $36–$60

A: Where to Stay in Washington with Your Dog

food/bev	free	kitchen	pet fee	pool	spa	other features
B & B	C FB					dog allowed by advance reservation only, on large acreage for walking dogs
	C	K	$75 per stay			weekly rates, laundry facilities, fully equipped kitchens, adjacent to short walking trail
R	C	R M			tb	fenced yard avail for dogs, 1½ blocks to public park
B & B	C FB		$10 per day		sa	on 7 acres for walking dogs, ½ mi to beach and parks
		K M				coffeemakers available, wooded area behind motel for walking dogs, close to river & park
		K	$7 per day			laundry facilities, 54 RV sites, across street from beach
		K				RV sites, across from waterfront, 3 mi to ocean
						rustic fishing cabins at Buffalo Lake, electricity but no running water, RV & tent sites
		K				dog allowed by advance reservation only, rustic cabins w/kitchenettes, 3 day min stay, RV sites
R & L	C	K	$10 per day			dog allowed by advance reservation only, walking trail across street, ¼ mi to public park

abbreviations used in this section

Have Dog Will Travel—Washington Edition

Newport — Ocean City

Marshall Lake Resort 1301 Marshall Lake Rd Newport, WA 99156	509-447-4158	10 units $25–$50
Newport City Inn 220 N Washington Ave Newport, WA 99156	509-447-3463	13 units $40–$65
Mt Si Motel 43200 SE North Bend Way North Bend, WA 98045	425-888-1621	4 units $35–$40
Acorn Motor Inn 31530 SR 20 Oak Harbor, WA 98277	360-675-6646 800-280-6646	32 units $46–$62
Best Western Harbor Plaza 33175 SR 20 Oak Harbor, WA 98277	360-679-4567 800-927-5478 www.bestwesternwashington.com	80 units $69–$129
Victorian Rose 438 E Sea Breeze Way Oak Harbor, WA 98277	360-675-8197	3 units $600–$675
Hanford Castle B & B 399 Roberts St, PO Box 23 Oakesdale, WA 99158	509-285-4120	2 units $50–$75
Blue Pacific Motel & RV Park 2707 SR 109 Ocean City, WA 98569	360-289-2262 800-453-2262	19 units $14–$51
North Beach Motel 2601 SR 109 Ocean City, WA 98569	360-289-4116 800-640-8053	14 units $35–$75
Pacific Sands 2687 SR 109 Ocean City, WA 98569	360-289-3588	9 units $40–$56

See pp. 90-91 for a key to the

A: Where to Stay in Washington with Your Dog

food/bev	free	kitchen	pet fee	pool	spa	other features
	C	K				swimming lake on 65 acres, walking trails, RV sites, next to national forest lands
						small dogs only, open area behind motel for walking dogs, 6 blocks to public park and riverfront
						dogs under 25 lbs only, grassy areas for walking dogs, near Mt Si Trails, 6 mi to Snoqualmie Falls
	C CB		$10 per day			1 block to beach park
R	C CB	R M	$10 per day	out htd	tb	exercise room, area for walking dogs, 3 mi to beach with walking trails & playground
	C	K			sp	fully equipped apartments, 1 week min stay, dogs allowed on approval by advance reservations only
B & B	C FB					on 5 acres for walking dogs, close to Steptoe Butte state park, John Wayne walking/biking trail
	C	K	$10 per day			dogs under 25 lbs only, 19 RV sites, 4 motel units, across street from beach
	C	K R	$5 per stay			laundry facilities, 5 min walk to beach, 2 mi to Ocean City State Park
		K	$5 per day	out htd		fully equipped kitchens, 5 to 7 min walk to beach

abbreviations used in this section   **177**

Ocean City – Ocean Shores

West Winds Resort Motel 2537 SR 109 Ocean City, WA 98569	360-289-3448 800-867-3448	10 units $38–$100
Coastal Cottages of Ocean Park 1511 264th Pl, PO Box 888 Ocean Park, WA 98640	360-665-4658 800-200-0424 coastalcottages@webtv.net	4 units $65–$75
Ocean Park Resort 25904 R St, PO Box 339 Ocean Park, WA www.aone.com/~opresort/home.html	360-665-4585 800-835-4634	94 units $17–$148
Paulson's Play House 27301 I St Ocean Park, WA 98640	503-861-2288 800-535-8767 epaulson@lektro.com	1 unit $125
Sea Nest in Long Beach PO Box 214 Ocean Park, WA http://vacationspot.com/SeaNest.htm	360-665-3633	1 unit $95–$145
Shakti Cove Cottages 25301 Park Ave, PO Box 385 Ocean Park, WA 98640	360-665-4000 www.shakticove.com	10 units $65–$75
Sunset View Resort 25517 Park Ave, PO Box 399 Ocean Park, WA 98640	360-665-4494 800-272-9199	52 units $65–$185
Westgate Motel & Trailer Court 20803 Pacific Hwy Ocean Park, WA 98640	360-665-4211	46 units $45–$65
Beach Front Vacation Rentals 759 Ocean Shores Blvd NW Ocean Shores, WA www.oceanshoresbeachhouses.com	360-289-3568 800-544-8887	46 units $65–$250
Chalet Village 659 Ocean Shores Blvd NW Ocean Shores, WA 98569	360-289-4297 800-303-4297 www.oceanshoreschalets.com	9 units $75–$105

See pp. 90-91 for a key to the

A: Where to Stay in Washington with Your Dog

food/bev	free	kitchen	pet fee	pool	spa	other features
		K	$5 per day			on 3 acres with creek and walking trail to beach
	C	K	$5 per stay			fireplaces, fully equipped kitchens, picnic area, walking distance to beach
	C	K	$7 per day	out htd	sp	motel units, laundry facilities, tent & RV sites, playground, recreation room, 4 blocks to ocean
		K				dogs allowed at owner's discretion, 2 bdrm 1 ba mobile home, laundry facilities, easy beach access
		K	$150 ref dep			2 bdrm oceanfront vacation home, laundry facilities, nature walk to beach, near Loomis State Park
		K	$5 per day			fully equipped kitchens, ocean view, 5 min walk to beach thru the dunes, 8 mi to state park
	C	K	$10 per stay		sa tb	laundry facilities, 6½ landscaped acres for walking dogs
	C	K				6 fully equipped cabins, 40 RV hookups, easy beach access
		K		out	sp	privately owned vacation homes & condominiums, call for details or visit their website
		K	$10 per day		tb	chalets & beachhouses, laundry facilities, beachfront locations

abbreviations used in this section

Ocean Shores

Discovery Inn Condominium 1031 Discovery Ave SE Ocean Shores, WA 98569	360-289-3371 800-882-8821	22 units $60–$88
Grey Gull Motel, PO Box 1417 651 Ocean Shores Blvd SW Ocean Shores, WA 98569	360-289-3381 800-562-9712 www.seanet.com/~greygull	37 units $70–$325
Nautilus Hotel, PO Box 128 835 Ocean Shores Blvd NW Ocean Shores, WA 98569	360-289-2722 800-221-4541 www.oceanviewcondos.com	24 units $70–$135
Ocean Shores Motel, PO Box 1687 681 Ocean Shores Blvd NW Ocean Shores, WA 98569	360-289-3351 800-464-2526	40 units $49–$130
Ocean View Resort Homes 164 Ocean Shores Blvd NW Ocean Shores, WA 98569	360-289-4416 800-927-6394 ovhomes@techline.com	15 units $70–$250
Polynesian Resort, PO Box 998 615 Ocean Shores Blvd NW Ocean Shores, WA 98569	360-289-3361 800-562-4836 www.v-v-a.com	71 units $79–$179
Sands Resort 801 Ocean Shores Blvd NW Ocean Shores, WA 98569	360-289-2444 800-841-4001	196 units $48–$199
Sands Royal Pacific Motel 781 Ocean Shores Blvd NW Ocean Shores, WA 98569	360-289-3306 800-562-9748	47 units $110–$195
Silver King Motel 1070 Discovery Ave SE Ocean Shores, WA 98569	360-289-3386 800-562-6001	50 units $35–$90
Westerly Motel, PO Box 544 870 Ocean Shores Blvd NW Ocean Shores, WA 98569	360-289-3711 800-319-3711	8 units $40–$70

See pp. 90-91 for a key to the

A: Where to Stay in Washington with Your Dog

food/bev	free	kitchen	pet fee	pool	spa	other features
	C	K	$10 per day	out htd	sp	laundry facilities, across street to open area for walking dogs, close to beach
	C	K	$10 per stay	out htd	sa tb	oceanfront location, kitchen & gas fireplace in every unit, laundry facilities, beach for walking dogs
	C	K	$20 per stay		tb	fully equipped condos, 1 or 2 dogs only, doggy towels & blankets avail, pet "rest area," trail to beach & park
	C CB	K R M	$10 per day		rm	breakfast on weekends only, guest pass for pool & sauna, lawn area for walking dogs that leads to beach
		K	$10 per day		tb	rustic cabins to contemporary homes & condos, ocean views, easy beach access
R & L	C CB	K	$15 per day	in	sp sa	oceanfront location, game room, laundry facilities, private park
	C CB	K	$10 per day	in out htd	tb	continental breakfast on weekends, beachfront & dunes area for walking dogs
	C CB	K	$10 per day	in out htd	tb	continental breakfast on weekends, beachfront & dunes area for walking dogs
	C	K	$10 per day			close to walking trails & bayfront
		K				1 block to beach for walking dogs

abbreviations used in this section   181

Have Dog Will Travel—Washington Edition

Odessa — Olympia

Odessa Motel 609 E 1st Ave, PO Box 295 Odessa, WA 99159	509-982-2412	11 units $35–$48
Okanogan Cedars Inn 1 Appleway (Jct Hwy 97 & Hwy 20) Okanogan, WA 98840	509-422-6431	78 units $45–$57
Ponderosa Motor Lodge 1034 2nd Ave S Okanogan, WA 98840	509-422-0400 800-732-6702 www.okanogan.net/ponderosa	25 units $39–$46
U & I Rivers Edge Motel 838 2nd Ave N Okanogan, WA 98840	509-422-2920	9 units $30–$46
Childs' House 8331 SE Willock Rd Olalla, WA 98359	253-857-4252 800-250-4954	3 units $65–$95
Still Waters Bed & Breakfast 13202 Olympic Dr SE Olalla, WA 98359-9415	253-857-5111	3 units $55–$65
Doe Bay Village Resort 107 Doe Bay Rd, PO Box 437 Olga, WA 98279	360-376-2291 www.doebay.com	32 units $15–$100
Bailey Motor Inn 3333 Martin Way E Olympia, WA 98506	360-491-7515	48 units $45–$48
Best Western Aladdin Motor Inn 900 Capitol Way S Olympia, WA 98501	360-352-7200 800-367-7671 www.bestwesternwashington.com	99 units $64–$200
Cavanaugh's at Capital 8 2300 Evergreen Park Dr SW Olympia, WA 98502	360-943-4000 800-325-4000	185 units $105–$185

See pp. 90-91 for a key to the

A: Where to Stay in Washington with Your Dog

food/bev	free	kitchen	pet fee	pool	spa	other features
	C	K R M				walking trail along creek
R & L	C	K		out htd		laundry facilities, RV sites, large area for walking dogs
R	C	K R M		out		1½ blocks to public park & riverfront, dog walking area, RV sites
	C	K R M				small dogs only, riverfront picnic area, BBQ, 1 block to public park
B & B	C FB					dog allowed by advance reservation only, 5 acres for walking dogs
B & B	C FB		$5 per day		tb	dogs allowed at owner's discretion only, walking trails, 5 to 8 mi to several parks
R		K	$10 per day		sa tb	dogs allowed Sept 15 thru June 15 only, cabins, tent cabins, RV sites, "clothing optional" hot tub & sauna
R & L	C	K	$5 per stay			on 7½ acres with off-leash area, near Cascade Trail, short drive to several public parks
R & L	C	K	$5 per day	out htd	sp	small dogs only, laundry facilities, area for walking dogs, 2 blocks to public park, 4 blocks to lake
R & L	C	R	$25 per stay	out htd	sp	laundry facilities, grass area for walking dogs, ½ mi to Capital Lake

abbreviations used in this section

Have Dog Will Travel—Washington Edition

Olympia — Oroville

Harbinger Inn B & B 1136 East Bay Dr NE Olympia, WA 98506	360-754-0389	6 units $60–$125
Holly Motel 2816 Martin Way E Olympia, WA 98506	360-943-3000	37 units $38–$50
Puget View Guesthouse B & B 7924 61st Ave NE Olympia, WA 98516	360-413-9474 bbonline.com/wa/pugetview	1 unit $99–$119
Motel Nicholas 527 E Grape St Omak, WA 98841	509-826-4611 800-404-4611	21 units $30–$45
Omak Inn 912 Koala Dr Omak, WA 98841	509-826-3822 800-204-4800	49 units $57–$112
Omak Rodeway Inn & Suites 122 N Main St, PO Box 393 Omak, WA 98841	509-826-0400 888-700-6625	70 units $32–$45
Royal Motel 514 E Riverside Dr, PO Box 3273 Omak, WA 98841	509-826-5715	10 units $30–$45
Stampede Motel 215 W 4th St, PO Box 956 Omak, WA 98841	509-826-1161 800-639-1161	14 units $30–$45
Windsong Bed & Breakfast 213 Deer Harbor Rd, PO Box 32 Orcas Island, WA 98280	360-376-2500 800-669-3948	4 units $100–$150
Camaray Motel 1320 Main St, PO Box 923 Oroville, WA 98844	509-476-3684	38 units $33–$60

See pp. 90-91 for a key to the

A: Where to Stay in Washington with Your Dog

food/bev	free	kitchen	pet fee	pool	spa	other features
B&B	C FB					dog allowed by advance reservation only, fenced yard, walking trails, rooms & separate house
	C		$5 per stay			area for walking dogs, 5 mi to state park & hiking trails
B&B	C CB	R M	$10 per day			1 bdrm beachfront cottage, next to 100-acre state park
		R M				adjacent to open area for walking dogs
	C CB	R M	$10 per stay	in htd	sp	laundry facilities, small dogs only, country road for walking dogs
	C CB	K	$5 per stay	out htd	rm	walking distance to several public parks
	C CB	K R M	$20 ref dep			picnic area, 2 blocks to walking trail along river, ½ mi to public park
	C	K R				adjacent to small public park
B&B	C FB				tb	dogs allowed Nov 1-April 30 by advance reservation only, 4 acres for walking dogs, 400 yds to ocean
	C	R		out		well-behaved dogs only, area for walking dogs

abbreviations used in this section 185

Oroville – Packwood

Red Apple Inn 1815 Main St, PO Box 598 Oroville, WA 98844	509-476-3694	37 units $38–$60
Best Western Lincoln Inn 1020 E Cedar St Othello, WA 99344	509-488-5671 800-240-7865 www.bestwesternwashington.com	50 units $59–$115
Cabana Motel 665 E Windsor St Othello, WA 99344	509-488-2605 800-442-4581	56 units $30–$80
Sand Dollar Inn 53 Central Ave, PO Box 206 Pacific Beach, WA 98571	360-276-4525	11 units $40–$105
Sandpiper Beach Resort 4159 SR 109, PO Box A Pacific Beach, WA 98571	360-276-4580 800-567-4737	31 units $60–$170
Shore Line Motel 12 1st St S, PO Box 183 Pacific Beach, WA 98571	360-276-4433	12 units $45–$75
Hotel Packwood 104 Main St, PO Box 130 Packwood, WA 98361	360-494-5431	9 units $20–$38
Mountain View Lodge 13163 Hwy 12, PO Box 525 Packwood, WA 98361	360-494-5555	23 units $31–$73
Peters Inn 13051 US Highway 12, PO Box 369 Packwood, WA 98361	360-494-4000	3 units $43–$66
Tatoosh Meadows Resort & Rentals PO Box 487 Packwood, WA 98361	360-494-2311 800-294-2311 www.tmcproperties.com	25 units $125–$350

See pp. 90-91 for a key to the

A: Where to Stay in Washington with Your Dog

food/bev	free	kitchen	pet fee	pool	spa	other features
	C			out htd		¼ mi to state park, RV spaces, riverfront picnic area
	C CB	K	$10 per day	out htd	sa	laundry facilities, exercise room, ½ block to public park, hunters' bird cleaning station
	C	K R M		out htd	tb	dog allowed at manager's discretion only, field for walking dogs, across street from public park
	C	K	$5 per day		sp	laundry facilities, across road to public beach
		K M	$10 per day			oceanfront studio, 1-2-3 bdrm suites & cottages sleep up to 12, laundry facilities, gift shop
		K	$5 per day			adjacent to beach
	C					dogs allowed by owner's approval only, area for walking dogs, 17 mi to several state parks
	C	K	$5 per day	out htd	tb	walking trails nearby
R & L			$10 per stay			open fields for walking dogs, weekly rates avail, walking distance to public park
	C	K R M	$25 per stay	out	tb	vacation homes near Mt Rainier & White Pass, riverfront cabins & suites, fireplaces, private hot tubs

abbreviations used in this section   **187**

Packwood – Pasco

Timberline Village Motel 13807 Hwy 12, PO Box 394 Packwood, WA 98361	360-494-9224	21 units $35–$59
Airport Motel 2532 N 4th Ave Pasco, WA 99301	509-545-1460 888-323-1460	42 units $30–$48
Doubletree Hotel Pasco 2525 N 20th Ave Pasco, WA 99301	509-547-0701 800-222-tree	279 units $79–$115
King City Truck Stop 2100 E Hillsboro St Pasco, WA 99301	509-547-3475	36 units $33–$65
Motel 6-Pasco 1520 N Oregon Ave Pasco, WA 99301	509-546-2010 800-466-8356	106 units $30–$50
Sage 'n Sun Motel 1232 S 10th Ave Pasco, WA 99301	509-547-2451 800-391-9188	32 units $28–$55
Starlite Motel 2634 N 4th Ave Pasco, WA 99301	509-547-7531	18 units $28–$45
Thunderbird Motel 414 W Columbia St Pasco, WA 99301	509-547-9506	44 units $28–$48
Travel Inn Motel 725 W Lewis St Pasco, WA 99301	509-547-7791	38 units $25–$32
Tri-Cities Sleep Inn 9930 Bedford St Pasco, WA 99301	509-545-9554 800-sleepinn	62 units $55–$100

See pp. 90-91 for a key to the

A: Where to Stay in Washington with Your Dog

food/bev	free	kitchen	pet fee	pool	spa	other features
	C CB	R	$5 per day			lots of area for walking dogs, close to wilderness trails
R	C	K	$5 per day	out htd		laundry facilities, area for walking dogs, ½ mi to public park
R & L	C	R		out htd	tb	laundry facilities, across street from open area for walking dogs, shuttle to walking & biking path along river
R & L	C		$20 ref dep			laundry facilities, area for walking dogs, 10 min drive to Columbia Park
	C	R M		out htd		laundry facilities, area for walking dogs, 1 mi to public park
	C	K		out		laundry facilities, adjacent to cable bridge & recreational area
		K				open area for walking dogs
	C	K	$10 ref dep	out		laundry facilities, walking distance to public park
		R M		out		½ mi to public park
	C CB	K R M	$20 ref dep	in htd	sp rm	laundry facilities, open area for walking dogs, 5 min walk to riverfront park

abbreviations used in this section

Have Dog Will Travel—Washington Edition

Pasco — Port Angeles

Vineyard Inn 1800 W Lewis St Pasco, WA 99301	509-547-0791	165 units $45–$75
Lake Pateros Motor Inn 115 Lake Shore Dr, PO Box 25 Pateros, WA 98846	509-923-2203 800-444-1985	30 units $67–$88
Mount Valley Vista B & B 8695 Larson Rd, PO Box 476 Peshastin, WA 98847	509-548-5301	3 units $65–$75
Timberline Motel 8284 Hwy 2, PO Box 638 Peshastin, WA 98847	509-548-7415	6 units $40–$50
Cedar House Inn B & B 1534 Gulf Rd, PO Box 1117 Point Roberts, WA 98281	360-945-0284	6 units $36–$49
Pioneer Motel 1201 Main St, PO Box 321 Pomeroy, WA 99347	509-843-1559 rsliter@pomeroy-wa.com	13 units $38–$55
Chinook Motel 1414 E 1st St Port Angeles, WA 98362	360-452-2336	52 units $30–$70
Elwha Resort 239521 Highway 101 Port Angeles, WA 98363	360-457-7011	5 units $35–$325
Historic Lake Crescent Lodge 416 Lake Crescent Rd Port Angeles, WA 98363	360-928-3211	52 units $75–$224
Indian Valley Motel & RV Park 235471 Highway 101 Port Angeles, WA 98363	360-928-3266	9 units $36–$41

See pp. 90–91 for a key to the

A: Where to Stay in Washington with Your Dog

food/bev	free	kitchen	pet fee	pool	spa	other features
R	C CB		$5 per day	in htd	tb	laundry facilities, smaller dogs only, area for walking dogs, 4 blocks to walking trails
	C CB		$5 per day	out htd		lake views, rental boats, dock, BBQ & picnic tables, laundry facilities, RV & tent sites, next to state park
B&B	C FB					dogs allowed at owner's discretion only, surrounded by orchards for walking dogs
		K				area for walking dogs
B&B	C CB					ocean views, wooded walking area, laundry facilities, ¼ mi to beach, ½ mi to public pool & hot tub
	C	K R M			tb	1 block to public swimming pool, close to trails & public park
		K	$5 per day			laundry facilities, 7 blocks to waterfront area for walking dogs
		K R				rustic riverside cabins available on monthly basis, lakeside nature trail, RV & tent sites, near national park
R&L	C		$10 per day			lakeside lodge & cottages, gift shop, dogs allowed on lodge premises but not on adjacent national park trails
R						RV sites, close to hiking areas & parks, including several hot springs

abbreviations used in this section

Port Angeles — Port Hadlock

Log Cabin Resort 3183 E Beach Rd Port Angeles, WA 98363	360-928-3325	28 units $48–$122
Ocean Crest Bed & Breakfast 402 South M St Port Angeles, WA 98363	360-452-4832	3 units $65–$85
Pond Motel 1425 W Hwy 101 Port Angeles, WA 98363	360-452-8422	10 units $37–$60
Portside Inn 1510 E Front St Port Angeles, WA 98362	360-452-4015	109 units $60–$74
Red Lion Hotel 221 N Lincoln St Port Angeles, WA 98362	360-452-9215 800-222-tree www.doubletreehotels.com	187 units $59–$155
Sportsmen Motel 2909 E Hwy 101 Port Angeles, WA 98362	360-457-6196	20 units $45–$75
Super 8 Motel 2104 E 1st St Port Angeles, WA 98362	360-452-8401 800-800-8000 www.super8.com	62 units $60–$94
Uptown Inn 101 E 2nd St Port Angeles, WA 98362	360-457-9434 800-858-3812	35 units $49–$160
Whiskey Creek Beach 1385 Whiskey Creek Beach Rd Port Angeles, WA 98363	360-928-3489	6 units $60–$65
Old Alcohol Plant Lodge & Marina 310 Alcohol Loop Rd Port Hadlock, WA 98339	360-385-7030 800-785-7030	28 units $44–$250

A: Where to Stay in Washington with Your Dog

food/bev	free	kitchen	pet fee	pool	spa	other features
R & L		K	$6 per day			laundry facilities, RV sites, on 23 acres, including large off-leash area for dogs to run
B & B	C FB					exercise room, fenced yard, across street from public park
		K	$6 per day			wooded area for walking dogs
	C CB	R	$25 ref dep	out htd	sp	laundry facilities, dogs allowed in 4 rooms, area for walking dogs, 1 mi to walking trail
R & L	C			out htd	tb	laundry facilities, 1 block to ferry, waterfront trail
		K				on 10 acres for walking dogs
	C		$25 ref dep			laundry facilities, area for walking dogs
	C CB	K	$5 per day		sp	dogs up to 20 lbs only, area for walking dogs, 3 blocks to public pool, 4 blocks to walking trail
		K	$2 per day			rustic cabins (propane, but no electricity), RV sites, lots of beach for walking dogs
R & L		K	$10 per day			area for walking dogs, 2½ mi to public park & beach

abbreviations used in this section 193

Have Dog Will Travel—Washington Edition

Port Ludlow — Port Townsend

Heron Beach Inn On Ludlow Bay 1 Heron Rd Port Ludlow, WA 98365	360-437-0411	37 units $125–$450
Guesthouse Inn 220 Bravo Terrace Port Orchard, WA 98366	360-895-7818	56 units $69–$109
Vista Motel 1090 Bethel Ave Port Orchard, WA 98366	360-876-8046	28 units $45–$65
Aladdin Motor Inn 2333 Washington St Port Townsend, WA 98368	360-385-3747 800-281-3747	30 units $65–$85
Annapurna Inn & Spa 538 Adams St Port Townsend, WA 98368 www.annapurnaretreat-spa.com	360-385-2909 800-868-2662	6 units $85–$136
Bishop Victorian Guest Suites 714 Washington St Port Townsend, WA 98368	360-385-6122 800-824-4738 www.waypt.com/Bishop	14 units $79–$159
Harborside Inn 330 Benedict St Port Townsend, WA 98368	360-385-7909 800-942-5960	63 units $64–$175
Palace Hotel 1004 Water St Port Townsend, WA 98368	360-385-0773 800-962-0741 www.olympus.net/palace	15 units $59–$159
Point Hudson Resort 103 Hudson St Port Townsend, WA 98368	360-385-2828 800-826-3854	24 units $49–$79
Swan Hotel 222 Monroe at Water St Port Townsend, WA 98368	360-385-1718 800-776-1718 www.waypt.com/Bishop	9 units $79–$400

See pp. 90-91 for a key to the

A: Where to Stay in Washington with Your Dog

food/bev	free	kitchen	pet fee	pool	spa	other features
R & L	C CB	R	$50 ref dep		rm	jacuzzi tubs & fireplaces in all rooms, waterfront location, next to walking trails
	C CB	R M	$10 per day	in htd	sp	dogs under 25 lbs only, exercise room, meeting room, laundry, open area across street for walking dogs
	C	K	$5 per day	out htd	sp	close to dog walking area
	C CB	R M	$7 per day			beachfront location, laundry facilities
B & B	C FB		$25 ref dep		sp sa	Featured in Fodor's Best Places in Pacific Northwest, healing retreat, close to public park & beach
	C CB	K	$15 per day			athletic club privileges, dog walking area on premises, 1 block to waterfront & walking paths
	C CB	K R M	$5 per day	out htd	tb	private patios, laundry facilities, dogs under 25 lbs only, grass area for walking dogs, 2 blocks to beach
	C CB	K	$20 per stay			laundry facilities, ½ block to beach
R	C					beachfront motel, RV sites, marina, groceries, laundry facilities
	C	K	$15 per day			marine view suites & cottages, across street from waterfront & walking paths

abbreviations used in this section   **195**

Have Dog Will Travel—Washington Edition

Port Townsend — Pullman

Valley View Motel 162 Hwy 20 Port Townsend, WA 98368	360-385-1666 800-280-1666	6 units $40–$60
Victorian Suite at the Club 229 Monroe St Port Townsend, WA 98368	360-385-6560	1 unit $80
Poulsbo Inn 18680 Hwy 305 NE Poulsbo, WA 98370	360-779-3921 800-597-5151	73 units $55–$110
Barn Motor Inn 490 Wine Country Rd, PO Box 818 Prosser, WA 99350	509-786-2121	30 units $45–$110
Best Western Prosser Inn 225 Merlot Dr Prosser, WA 99350	509-786-7977 800-688-2192 www.bestwesternwashington.com	49 units $59–$79
Prosser Motel 1206 Wine Country Rd Prosser, WA 99350	509-786-2555	16 units $30–$46
Carstens Bed & Breakfast 251 Flat Rd Pullman, WA 99163	509-332-6162	3 units $55
Country Bed & Breakfast 2701 Staley Rd Pullman, WA 99163	509-334-4453 ntenwick@aol.com	7 units $50–$100
Hawthorn Inn & Suites 928 NW Olson St Pullman, WA 99163	509-332-0928 800-527-1133 www.bestwesternwashington.com	59 units $72–$199
Holiday Inn Express-Pullman 1190 SE Bishop Blvd Pullman, WA 99163	509-334-4437 800-465-4329	130 units $79–$99

See pp. 90-91 for a key to the

A: Where to Stay in Washington with Your Dog

food/bev	free	kitchen	pet fee	pool	spa	other features
		K				fully equipped kitchens, on 40 acres for walking dogs, 1 mi to walking trails along Lake Anderson
		K				guest pass to local athletic club, area for walking dogs, 10 min walk to public park
	C CB	K	$10 per day	out htd	tb	apartments also, laundry facilities, area for walking dogs, 6 blocks to waterfront park & trails
R		K	$10 per stay	out htd	rm	area for walking dogs, laundry facilities
	C CB	R	$9 per day	out htd	sp	laundry facilities, ⅓ block to public walking area
	C					¼ mi to walking trails
B&B	C FB				tb	laundry facilities, dog run in yard, resident dogs, quiet country road for walking dogs
B&B	C CB FB	R M			tb	RV sites, area for walking dogs
	C FB	K		in htd	sp sa	evening snack, 2 blocks to public park, near WSU Veterinary Hospital (patient rates available)
	C CB	R M		in htd	tb	laundry facilities, area for walking dogs, ¼ mi to walking trail, 5 min walk to public park

abbreviations used in this section 197

Pullman – Quincy

Manor Lodge Motel 455 SE Paradise St Pullman, WA 99163	509-334-2511	31 units $39–$64
Nendels Inn-Pullman 915 SE Main St Pullman, WA 99163	509-332-2646 888-619-1202	60 units $29–$80
Quality Inn Paradise Creek 1050 SE Bishop Blvd Pullman, WA 99163	509-332-0500 800-221-2222	66 units $58–$135
Best Western Park Plaza 620 S Hill Park Dr Puyallup, WA 98373	253-848-1500 800-528-1234	100 units $86–$146
Motel Puyallup 1412 S Meridian Puyallup, WA 98371	253-845-8825 800-921-2700	63 units $48–$65
Northwest Motor Inn 1409 S Meridian Puyallup, WA 98371	253-841-2600 800-845-9490	52 units $41–$80
Maple Grove Motel 61 Maple Grove Rd, PO Box 144 Quilcene, WA 98376	360-765-3410	12 units $40–$50
Quilcene Hotel 11 Quilcene Ave, PO Box 129 Quilcene, WA 98376	360-765-3868	9 units $43–$50
Lake Quinault Lodge 345 S Shore Rd, PO Box 7 Quinault, WA 98575	360-288-2900 800-562-6672 www.visitlakequinault.com	92 units $62–$250
Sundowner Motel 414 F St SE Quincy, WA 98848	509-787-3587	24 units $33–$71

A: Where to Stay in Washington with Your Dog

food/bev	free	kitchen	pet fee	pool	spa	other features
		C	K R M	$3-$10/day			2 blocks to public park
R		C CB	K	$7 per day			laundry facilities, adjacent to public park
		C CB	K R M		out htd	sp sa rm	laundry facilities, close to dog walking area
		C CB	R M	$10 per stay	out htd	tb	area for walking dogs
R		C CB	K	$10 per day			laundry facilities, area for walking dogs, 3 blocks to public park
		C CB	K	$5 per day		tb	laundry facilities, area for walking dogs, 4 blocks to public park
			K				bordering national forest land w/walking trails
		C CB					historic hotel w/shared bathrooms, close to national forest & walking trails, 1 mi to beach
R		C		$10 per day	in htd	sa	historic lakeside lodge, game room, gift shop, adjacent to national forest & walking trails
		C	K	$5 per day	out htd		area for walking dogs, 2 blocks to public park

abbreviations used in this section

Quincy — Republic

Traditional Inns 500 F St SW Quincy, WA 98848	509-787-3525	24 units $41–$81
Medici Motel & Campground 471 Cispus Rd Randle, WA 98377	360-497-7700 800-697-7750	5 units $45–$47
Mount Adams Motel & RV Park 9514 Hwy 12 Randle, WA 98377	360-497-7007	16 units $35–$45
Tall Timber Motel 10023 Hwy 12, PO Box 28 Randle, WA 98377	360-497-2991	6 units $35–$45
Woodland Motel 11890 US Highway 12 Randle, WA 98377	360-494-6766	8 units $40–$60
Maunu Mountcastle Motel 524 3rd St Raymond, WA 98577	360-942-5571 800-400-5571	26 units $40–$60
Willis Motel 425 3rd St Raymond, WA 98577	360-942-5313	3 units $35–$40
Travelodge of Renton 3700 E Valley Rd Renton, WA 98055	425-251-9591	129 units $58–$115
West Wind Motel 110 Rainier Ave S Renton, WA 98055	425-226-5060	21 units $45–$55
Black Beach Resort 80 Black Beach Rd Republic, WA 99166	509-775-3989	13 units $45–$73

See pp. 90-91 for a key to the

A: Where to Stay in Washington with Your Dog

food/bev	free	kitchen	pet fee	pool	spa	other features
		C	R M	$5 per stay			laundry facilities, adjacent to open area for walking dogs
		C	K				on 40 acres with trails for walking dogs
			K R M	$10 per stay			recreation room, laundry facilities, RV sites, adjacent to walking trails
R & L			K	$10 per day			area for walking dogs, 5 min drive to lakes & walking trails
		C	K R			tb	fully equipped kitchens, adjacent to national forest w/walking trails
		C	K				area for walking dogs, 3 blocks to walking trail
R			K				2 blocks to river & public parks
		C CB	K	$10 per day		sp	laundry facilities, close to dog walking area
			K				area for walking dogs, 1 mi to public park
			K				lakefront cabins, duplex & motel, laundry facilities, RV sites, area for walking dogs, groceries & gift shop

abbreviations used in this section

Have Dog Will Travel—Washington Edition

Republic — Richland

Frontier Inn Motel 979 S Clark Ave, PO Box 1031 Republic, WA 99166	509-775-3361	33 units $39–$53
K-Diamond-K Guest Ranch 15661 S Hwy 21 Republic, WA 99166	509-775-3536 www.kdiamondk.com	4 units $75–$105
Klondike Motel 150 N Clark St, PO Box 614 Republic, WA 99166	509-775-3555	20 units $36–$44
Northern Inn 852 S Clark St Republic, WA 99166	509-775-3371 888-801-1068	25 units $39–$47
Pine Point Resort 38 Pine Point Resort Rd Republic, WA 99166	509-775-3643 877-775-3643	13 units $55–$117
Bali Hi Motel 1201 George Washington Way Richland, WA 99352	509-943-3101	44 units $43–$58
Best Western Tower Inn 1515 George Washington Way Richland, WA 99352	509-946-4121 800-635-3980 www.bestwesternwashington.com	195 units $79–$99
Motel 6-Richland 1751 Fowler St Richland, WA 99352	509-783-1250 800-466-8356	93 units $38–$44
Red Lion Hotel-Richland 802 George Washington Way Richland, WA 99352	509-946-7611 800-733-5466	149 units $55–$119
Richland Hampton Inn 486 Bradley Blvd Richland, WA 99352	509-943-4400 800-426-7866	130 units $72–$225

See pp. 90-91 for a key to the

A: Where to Stay in Washington with Your Dog

food/bev	free	kitchen	pet fee	pool	spa	other features
	C CB		$20 ref dep		sa tb	laundry facilities, 2 blocks to public park
B&B	C FB		$5 per day			indoor kennels for dogs to stay in overnight, breakfast-lunch-dinner included in guest fee, river frontage
	C	K	$50 ref dep		sp	dog allowed by advance reservation only, 4 blocks to Wilderness Park trail
	C CB	K R M			rm	area for walking dogs, 2 blocks to public park
						cabins w/fully equipped kitchens, RV sites, laundry facilities, 1 mi to state park, walking trails
	C	R M	$5 per day	out	sp	laundry facilities, across street from Columbia River park
R&L	C	R	$10 ref dep	in htd	sp sa	laundry facilities, live entertainment on weekends, 3 blocks to walking trail along Columbia River
R	C	R M		out htd		laundry facilities, area for walking dogs, 1 block to Columbia River Park
R&L	C	R M		out htd	sp	river view, adjacent to river walking trails & park
	C CB	R M		in htd	sp	laundry facilities, exercise room, adjacent to public park & riverfront, river view

abbreviations used in this section

203

Richland – Rockport

Shilo Conference Hotel 50 Comstock St Richland, WA 99352	509-946-4661 800-222-2244 www.shiloinns.com	150 units $69–$115
Game Ridge Motel 27350 US Hwy 12 Rimrock, WA 98937	509-672-2212 800-301-9354	14 units $37–$185
Best Inn & Suites 1513 S Smittys Blvd Ritzville, WA 99169	509-659-1007 www.bestwesternwashington.com	54 units $49–$149
Colwell Motor Inn 501 W 1st Ave Ritzville, WA	509-659-1620 800-341-8000 www.imalodging.com/Lodges/W123.htm	25 units $40–$65
Empire Motel 101 W 1st Ave Ritzville, WA 99169	509-659-1030	19 units $27–$47
Westside Motor Inn 407 W 1st Ave Ritzville, WA 99169	509-659-1164 800-559-1164	11 units $26–$46
Rockcreek Manor B & B 600 N 1st St, PO Box 10 Rockford, WA 99030	509-291-4008 Bjndan@aol.com	3 units $65–$85
A Cab in the Woods 9303 Dandy Pl Rockport, WA 98283	360-873-4106 www.northcascades.com	5 units $55–$65
Clark's Cabins & Resort 58468 Clark Cabin Rd Rockport, WA 98283	360-873-2250 800-273-2606 www.northcascades.com	30 units $49–$109
Totem Trail Motel & Conf Ctr 57627 Hwy 20 Rockport, WA 98283	360-873-4535	8 units $45–$55

A: Where to Stay in Washington with Your Dog

food/bev	free	kitchen	pet fee	pool	spa	other features
R & L	C FB	K R M	$7 per day	out htd	sp sa rm	laundry facilities, exercise room, steam room, adjacent to riverfront, 2 blocks to public park
	C	K	$10 per day	out htd	tb	motel units, cabins w/private hot tubs, RV sites, adjacent to national forest and river, walking trails
	C CB	K		out htd	tb	complimentary evening snack, laundry facilities, RV sites, adjacent to golf course & public park
	C	R M	$4 per day	out htd	sa rm	$25 refundable pet deposit, laundry facilities, BBQ, self-guided walking tour of historic downtown & homes
	C					area for walking dogs, ½ mi to public park, 2 blocks to downtown, laundry facilities
	C CB	M				5 min drive to public park
B & B	C FB			in htd	tb	dog allowed at owner's discretion by advance reservation only, many resident animals, near hiking trails
		K				fully equipped cabins, walking trails along river
R	C	K R	$10 per day			resident rabbits–so dogs must be well-behaved, cabins, RV sites, walking trails along Skagit River
	C	R	$10 per stay			dogs allowed at owner's discretion only, picnic tables & BBQ, basketball court, adjacent to walking trails

abbreviations used in this section

Roslyn — Seattle

Hummingbird Inn 106 E Pennsylvania Ave, PO Box 984 Roslyn, WA 98941	509-649-2758	3 units $60–$75
Last Resort 14254 Salmon La Sac Rd, PO Box 532 Roslyn, WA 98941	509-649-2222	12 units $45
Roslyn Inns 5th St, PO Box 386 Roslyn, WA 98941	509-649-2936	3 units $90–$190–$290
White Spot Motel 2527 US Highway 12, PO Box 144 Salkum, WA 98582	360-985-2737	6 units $30–$32
Howard Johnson 20045 International Blvd SeaTac, WA 98198	206-878-3310 800-446-4656	58 units $54–$109
Mini-Rate Motel 20620 International Blvd SeaTac, WA 98198	206-824-6930 800-426-5060	50 units $40–$50
Airport Plaza Hotel 18601 International Blvd Seattle, WA 98188	206-433-0400 877-433-0400	123 units $50–$85
Alexis Hotel 1007 1st Ave Seattle, WA 98104	206-624-4844 800-945-2240	109 units $180–$380
Aurora Seafair Inn 9100 Aurora Ave N Seattle, WA 98103	206-524-3600 800-445-9297	63 units $60–$95
Blue Willow Bed & Breakfast 213 W Comstock St Seattle, WA 98119	206-284-4240	3 units $85–$105

See pp. 90-91 for a key to the

A: Where to Stay in Washington with Your Dog

food/bev	free	kitchen	pet fee	pool	spa	other features
B&B	C FB					small dogs allowed if kept in travel crate while in room, shared bath, close to wooded dog walking area
R		R	$10 per day			small dogs allowed by advance reservations only, RV sites, walking trails, near lake
		K				3 historic houses w/fully equipped kitchens, picnic area, BBQ, 3 mi to lake, next to national forest, trails
		K				lots of walking trails, laundry facilities, RV sites
	C CB		$10 per stay			rm small dogs only, refundable deposit, 2 blocks to Engel Lake Park
	C	K				2 min drive to public park, 5 min drive to waterfront
R&L	C CB		$15 per day			rm laundry facilities, open area for walking dogs, 6 blocks to public park
R&L	C	R				sp 24-hr fitness room, 2 blocks to Freeway Park
	C	K	$5 per day			rm laundry facilities
B&B	C FB					dog allowed by advance reservation only, 1 block to public park

abbreviations used in this section

Seattle

Bridge Motel 3650 Bridge Way N Seattle, WA 98103	206-632-7835	13 units $40–$65
Cavanaugh's On Fifth Avenue 1415 5th Ave Seattle, WA 98101	206-971-8000 800-325-4000 www.cavanaughs.com	297 units $155–$195
Crowne Plaza Hotel 1113 6th Ave Seattle, WA 98101	206-464-1980 800-521-2762	415 units $149–$239
Dibble House B & B 7301 Dibble Ave NW Seattle, WA 98117	206-783-0320	5 units $55–$65
Doubletree Hotel-Seattle Airport 18740 International Blvd Seattle, WA 98188	206-246-8600 800-222-tree	850 units $79–$159
Four Seasons Olympic Hotel 411 University St Seattle, WA 98101	206-621-1700 800-332-3442	450 units $295–$1750
Hawthorne Inn & Suites 2224 8th Ave Seattle, WA 98121	206-624-6820 800-437-4867	72 units $89–$199
Hilton-Seattle Airport 17620 International Blvd Seattle, WA 98188	206-244-4800	178 units $189–$174
Holiday Inn-SeaTac 17338 International Blvd Seattle, WA 98188	206-248-1000 877-5seatac	260 units $109–$129
Homewood Suites Hotel 206 Western Ave W Seattle, WA 98119	206-281-9393 800-225-5466	161 units $159–$279

A: Where to Stay in Washington with Your Dog

food/bev	free	kitchen	pet fee	pool	spa	other features
			$25-$50 dep			adjacent to open area for walking dogs, refundable pet deposit
R&L	C	R	$75 ref dep			exercise room, 4 blocks to public park
R&L	C CB	R	$25 per stay		sp sa	exercise room, laundry facilities, adjacent to public park for walking dogs
B&B	C FB					fenced back yard, close to zoo & public park with off-leash area
R&L	C	R		out htd	tb	
R&L	C	R		in htd	sp sa	dogs under 15 lbs only
	C CB FB	K	$50 per stay		sp sa	laundry facilities, 2 blocks to Denny Park
R&L	C	R M		out htd	sp	dogs under 20 lbs only, laundry facilities, area for walking dogs
R&L	C		$20 per day	in htd	sp	dogs under 20 lbs only, exercise room, laundry facilities, area for walking dogs, 1 mi to public park
	C CB	K	$65 per stay		.	full kitchens in all suites, exercise room, 1 block to waterfront

abbreviations used in this section   **209**

Seattle

Homewood Suites-Tukwila 6955 Fort Dent Way Seattle, WA 98188	206-433-8000 800-225-5466	106 units $109–$179
Hotel Monaco 1101 4th Ave Seattle, WA 98101	206-621-1770 800-945-2240	189 units $195–$725
King's Arms Motel 23226 30th Ave S Seattle, WA 98198	206-824-0300	45 units $35–$90
La Quinta Inn 2824 S 188th St Seattle, WA 98188	206-241-5211 800-531-5900	143 units $89–$99
Marriott Seattle Sea Tac 3201 S 176th St Seattle, WA 98188	206-241-2000 800-228-9290	459 units $79–$194
Motel 6-SeaTac Airport 16500 International Blvd Seattle, WA 98188	206-246-4101 800-466-8356	111 units $50–$66
Motel 6-SeaTac South 18900 47th Ave S Seattle, WA 98188	206-241-1648 800-466-8356	146 units $42–$61
Motel 6-Seattle South 20651 Military Rd S Seattle, WA 98198	206-824-9902 800-466-8356	124 units $45–$64
Pargardens Bed & Breakfast 14716 26th Ave NE Seattle, WA 98155	206-367-7066	3 units $60–$75
Pensione Nichols 1923 1st Ave Seattle, WA 98101	206-441-7125 800-440-7125	12 units $75–$175

A: Where to Stay in Washington with Your Dog

food/bev	free	kitchen	pet fee	pool	spa	other features
	C CB	K	$20 per day	out htd	tb	adjacent to walking trail, walking distance to Fort Dent Park
R & L	C				rm	guest pass at health club, laundry facilities, 3 blocks to public park, 6 blocks to waterfront
	C	K	$10 per day	out		area for walking dogs, 5 blocks to public park
	C CB	R		out htd	sp	laundry facilities, exercise room, ¼ mi to public park
R & L	C	R		in htd	sp	open area for walking dogs, next to walking trails
	C					
	C			out htd		dogs under 30 lbs only, laundry facilities, area for walking dogs
	C			out htd	sp	laundry facilities, open area for walking dogs
B & B	C FB		$5 per day			fenced backyard, 3 blocks to public park
B & B	C CB	K				rooms & suites w/full kitchen, sitting room, bedroom & bath, 1 block to public park

abbreviations used in this section   211

Seattle

Ramada Inn-Seattle 2140 N Northgate Way Seattle, WA 98133	206-365-0700 800-272-6232	169 units $99–$159
Residence Inn by Marriott 800 Fairview Ave N Seattle, WA 98109	206-624-6000 800-331-3131	234 units $120–$350
Residence Inn by Marriott-South 16201 W Valley Hwy Seattle, WA 98188	425-226-5500 800-331-3131	144 units $115–$205
Rodeway Inn-SeaTac 2930 S 176th St Seattle, WA 98188	206-246-9300 800-347-9301	59 units $40–$80
Royal Arms Apartments & Motel 1050 SW 151st St Seattle, WA 98166	206-244-6110	2 units $45–$60
Shafer-Baillie Mansion 907 14th Ave E Seattle, WA 98112	206-322-4654 800-922-4654	13 units $89–$145
Summerfield Suites 1011 Pike St Seattle, WA 98101	206-682-8282 800-833-4353	193 units $89–$370
Super 8 Motel-SeaTac 3100 S 192nd St Seattle, WA 98188	206-433-8188 800-800-8000 www.super8.com	119 units $74–$98
Travelodge by the Space Needle 200 6th Ave N Seattle, WA 98109	206-441-7878 800-578-7878	88 units $79–$159
Vagabond Inn 325 Aurora Ave N Seattle, WA 98109	206-441-0400 800-522-1555	58 units $79–$109

A: Where to Stay in Washington with Your Dog

food/bev	free	kitchen	pet fee	pool	spa	other features
R	C CB	K		out htd	sp	laundry facilities
	C CB	K	$10 per day	in htd		exercise room, w/full kitchens, laundry facilities, walking area along Lake Union
	C CB		$10 per day	out htd	sp	kitchens in all units, laundry facilities, adjacent to 27-mile walking trail
	C CB		$5-$10 /day			laundry facilities, area for walking dogs, 5 blocks to public park w/lake & beach
		K				small dogs only, laundry facilities, 3 blocks to public park
B & B	C CB	K	$7 per day			small dogs allowed by advance reservations only, area for walking dogs, 2 blocks to Volunteer Park
	C CB	K	$50 per stay	out htd	sp	rooms & suites, laundry facilities, close to waterfront area
	C		$25 ref dep			fitness room, laundry facilities, adjacent to Angle Lake Park
	C CB		$5 per day	out	sp	3 blocks to city center
	C CB	R	$10 per day	out htd	sp	laundry facilities, close to public park

abbreviations used in this section　　　　　　　213

Have Dog Will Travel—Washington Edition

Seattle — Sekiu

Westcoast SeaTac Hotel 18220 International Blvd Seattle, WA 98188	206-246-5535 800-426-0670	146 units $89–$130
Westin Hotel 1900 5th Ave Seattle, WA 98101	206-728-1000 800-westin1	891 units $165–$1500
Bev's Beach Bungalow 1101 34th St, PO Box 316 Seaview, WA 98644	360-642-3544 www.pacifier.com/~bevrolfe	1 unit $45
Historic Sou'wester Lodge, Cabins, Tch! Tch! & RV Park, Beach Access Rd (38th Pl) PO Box 102, Seaview, WA 98644	360-642-2542	20 units $39–$124
Rose Cottage 4714 L St, PO Box 177 Seaview, WA 98644	360-642-3254 patti@pacifier.com	1 unit $65–$85
Seaview CoHo Motel 3701 Pacific Hwy, PO Box 198 Seaview, WA 98644	360-642-2531 800-681-8153	13 units $35–$110
Seaview Motel & RV Park 3728 Pacific Way, PO Box 548 Seaview, WA 98644	360-642-2450 www.beachdog.com/seaviewmotel	11 units $12–$80
Skagit Motel 1977 Hwy 20 Sedro Woolley, WA 98284	360-856-6001 800-582-9121	46 units $32–$55
Three Rivers Inn 210 Ball St Sedro Woolley, WA 98284	360-855-2626 800-221-5122	40 units $61–$88
Bay Motel & Marina 15562 Hwy 112, PO Box 10 Sekiu, WA 98381	360-963-2444	16 units $45–$69

See pp. 90-91 for a key to the

A: Where to Stay in Washington with Your Dog

food/bev	free	kitchen	pet fee	pool	spa	other features
R & L	C			out htd	sa tb	laundry facilities, exercise room, close to lakeside park
R & L	C	R M		in htd	sp	laundry facilities, 8 blocks to waterfront, area for walking dogs, short drive to several parks
		K				fully equipped kitchen, microwave, fenced yard, easy beach access thru dunes
		K				lodge rooms, cabins, tent & RV sites, fireside discussions & musical events, next to dunes & beach
B & B	C FB	K				children welcome, fully equipped cottage, private entrance, bicycles, close to walking trails
	C	K R M				fully equipped kitchens, BBQ & picnic area, grassy area for walking dogs, 2 blocks to beach
	C	K				11 motel units, RV sites, 1st dog free, additional dogs $5/day, close to park & trails & ocean
	C	K	$5 per stay			area for walking dogs, 1 mi to public park
R	C FB	R	$10 per stay	out htd	tb	rooms & suites, walking distance to riverfront park
	C	K				across street from 2½ mi of beach for walking dogs, ½ mi to county park

abbreviations used in this section   215

Have Dog Will Travel—Washington Edition

Sekiu — Sequim

C-View Resort Highway 112, PO Box 245 Sekiu, WA 98381	360-963-2530	2 units $50
Herb's Motel & Charters 411 Front St, PO Box 175 Sekiu, WA 98381	360-963-2346	12 units $40–$85
Van Riper's Resort & Charter 280 Front St, PO Box 246 Sekiu, WA 98381	360-963-2334 888-462-0803	16 units $50–$135 www.sekiu.com
Winters' Summer Inn B & B 8670 Hwy 112 Sekiu, WA 98351	360-963-2264	4 units $70
Best Western Sequim Bay Lodge 268522 Hwy 101 Sequim, WA 98382	360-683-0691 800-622-0691 www.bestwesternwashington.com	54 units $61–$87
Brigadoon Bed & Breakfast 62 Balmoral Ct Sequim, WA 98382	360-683-2255	1 unit $75
Dungeness Bay Motel 140 Marine Dr Sequim, WA 98382	360-683-3013 888-683-3013 www.northolympic.com/dungenessbay	6 units $75–$120
Econo Lodge 801 E Washington St Sequim, WA 98382	360-683-7113 800-488-7113	43 units $44–$125
Greathouse Motel 740 E Washington St Sequim, WA 98382	360-683-7272 877-683-7272	20 units $39–$69
Groveland Cottage B & B 4861 Sequim Dungeness Way Sequim, WA 98382	360-683-3565 800-879-8859	5 units $80–$110

See pp. 90-91 for a key to the

A: Where to Stay in Washington with Your Dog

food/bev	free	kitchen	pet fee	pool	spa	other features
		C	K			fully equipped duplex & mobile home on 3 acres w/playground, laundry, walking trail to beach
			K	$10 per stay		across street from beach for walking dogs
		C	K	$10 per stay		dogs allowed in 3 cabins and at owner's discretion only, RV sites, waterfront area for walking dogs
B&B	C CB	K	$5 per day			dogs allowed at owner's discretion only, fenced kennel, beachfront home also avail at $225/night
R	C	R M	$10 per day	out htd		area for walking dogs, ½ mi to state park, 1 mi to marina
B&B	C	K				dogs allowed in separate 2 bdrm mobile home w/fully equipped kitchen, large yard, 1½ mi to beach
		K	ref dep			1 dog by advance reservation only, fully equipped kitchens, area for walking dogs, private beach access
	C CB	R M	$6 per day			miniature golf, laundry facilities, field for walking dogs, 5 min walk to public park
	C CB		$10 per stay			laundry facilities, ½ acre fenced yard, 2 blocks to Carrie Blake Park (site of numerous dog shows)
B&B	C FB		$10 per stay	rm		½ mi to beach, ¼ mi to river & walking trail, vacation rental homes also available, call for rates

abbreviations used in this section   **217**

Sequim — Shelton

Juan De Fuca Cottages 182 Marine Dr Sequim, WA 9838	360-683-4433 www.dungeness.com/juandefuca	6 units $110–$190
Rancho Lamro B & B 1734 Woodcock Rd Sequim, WA 98382	360-683-8133	2 units $70–$75
Red Ranch Inn 830 W Washington St Sequim, WA 98382	360-683-4195 800-777-4195 www.redranch.com	55 units $44–$100
Sundowner Motel 364 W Washington St Sequim, WA 98382	360-683-5532 800-325-6966	33 units $35–$95
Canal Side Resort & Motel 21660 N US Highway 101 Shelton, WA 98584	360-877-9422	3 units $45–$75
City Center Best Rates Motel 128 E Alder St Shelton, WA 98584	360-426-3397 888-771-2378	13 units $33–$60
Lake Nahwatzel Resort 12900 W Shelton Matlock Rd Shelton, WA 98584	360-426-8323	2 units $55–$65
Rest Full Farm B & B W 2230 Shelton Valley Rd Shelton, WA 98584	360-426-8774	2 units $50–$60
Shelton Inn 628 W Railroad Ave Shelton, WA 98584	360-426-4468	30 units $43–$63
Super 8 Motel 2943 N View Cir, PO Box 267 Shelton, WA 98584	360-426-1654 800-800-8000 www.super8.com	38 units $45–$55

A: Where to Stay in Washington with Your Dog

food/bev	free	kitchen	pet fee	pool	spa	other features
	C	K			rm	dog allowed by advance reservation only, fully equipped kitchens, on 8 quiet acres, private beach access
B&B	C CB					located on 2¼ acres for walking dogs, close to beaches & trails
R&L	C CB	K	$6 per stay			open field for walking dogs, laundry facilities
	C	R M	$5 per day			dogs under 30 lbs only, area for walking dogs, close to public park & swim center
	C	R M				RV sites, 460 ft water frontage, area for walking dogs, oyster & clam beds, next to public boat launch
	C	M	$5 per day			grassy area for walking dogs, 5 min walk to public park & waterfront
R&L	C		$5 per day			cabins, RV & tent sites, 2 blocks to lakeside trail
B&B	C FB					well-behaved dogs by advance reservation only, must be on leash at all times, walking trails
	C	R	$5 per day	out htd		area for walking dogs, 5 min walk to public park
	C	R	$10-$20/stay			area for walking dogs, 1 mi to walking trail

abbreviations used in this section

Shoreline – Soap Lake

Shoreline Motel 16526 Aurora Ave N Shoreline, WA 98133	206-542-7777	18 units $45–$65
Lake Mayfield Motel 2911 US Highway 12 Silver Creek, WA 98585	360-985-2484	9 units $35–$55
Silver Lake Motel & Resort 3201 Spirit Lake Hwy Silver Lake, WA 98645	360-274-6141	11 units $14–$90
Cimarron Motel 9734 Silverdale Way NW Silverdale, WA 98383	360-692-7777 800-273-5076	63 units $51–$62
Sky River Inn 333 River Dr E, PO Box 280 Skykomish, WA 98288	360-677-2261 800-367-8194	18 units $60–$95
Country Man Bed & Breakfast 119 Cedar Ave Snohomish, WA 98290	360-568-9622 800-700-9622	3 units $75–$85
Inn at Snohomish 323 2nd St Snohomish, WA 98290	360-568-2208 800-548-9993	21 units $60–$90
Salish Lodge and Spa 6501 Railroad Ave SE, PO Box 1109 Snoqualmie, WA 98065	425-888-2556 800-272-5474 www.salishlodge.com	87 units $189–$349
Best Western Summit Inn 603 SR 906, PO Box 163 Snoqualmie Pass, WA 98068	425-434-6300 800-557-7829	82 units $69–$249
Lake Motel 322 Daisy St S (Hwy 17), PO Box 427 Soap Lake, WA 98851	509-246-1903	28 units $25–$35

A: Where to Stay in Washington with Your Dog

food/bev	free	kitchen	pet fee	pool	spa	other features
	C	K R M				laundry facilities, adjacent to open area for walking dogs
						area for walking dogs on 6 acres, ½ mi to lakeside parks & walking trails
	C	K				dogs allowed in cabins, RV & tent sites, lakeside area for walking dogs, boat rentals
	C CB	K	$10 per stay			laundry facilities, area for walking dogs, 2 blocks to waterfront walking trail
	C	K R M	$3 per day			riverfront location, adjacent to national wilderness regions, area for walking dogs
B&B	C CB FB					Victorian house, private baths, adjacent to public park, 3 blocks to riverfront park & trails
	C	R	ref dep		rm	small dogs allowed at manager's discretion by advance reservation only, next to public park
R&L	C		$50 per stay		sp rm	jacuzzi in all rooms, full service spa, steam, fireplaces, adjacent to public park & walking trails, open field
R&L	C	K	$10 per stay	out htd	sa tb	laundry facilities, area for walking dogs, ¼ mi to walking trails
		K				area for walking dogs, 1 block to public park, 5 blocks to lake

abbreviations used in this section   221

Soap Lake — Spokane

Notaras Lodge 13 Canna St N, PO Box 987 Soap Lake, WA 98851	509-246-0462	14 units $51–$150
Royal View Motel NE 4th Ave & SR 17, PO Box 968 Soap Lake, WA 98851	509-246-1831	19 units $39–$70
Tolo Vista Lodge 22 N Daisy, PO Box 386 Soap Lake, WA 98851	509-246-1512 877-399-1845 tolovist@televar.com	9 units $45–$95
Tumwata Lodge 340 Main St W, PO Box 927 Soap Lake, WA 98851	509-246-1416	12 units $45–$60
H & H Motel 101 E Water St, PO Box 613 South Bend, WA 98586	360-875-5523	16 units $34–$49
Russell House B & B 902 E Water St, PO Box F South Bend, WA 98586	360-875-6487 888-484-6907	4 units $60–$100
Seaquest Motel & Apartments 801 W 1st St, PO Box 309 South Bend, WA 98586	360-875-5349	16 units $35–$65
Bel-Air Motel 1303 E Sprague Ave Spokane, WA 99202	509-535-1677	17 units $35–$45
Bell Motel 9030 W Sunset Hwy Spokane, WA 99224	509-624-0852 800-223-1388	14 units $28–$55
Best Inn & Suites 6309 E Broadway Ave Spokane, WA 99212	509-535-7185 800-237-8466	73 units $49–$89

See pp. 90–91 for a key to the

A: Where to Stay in Washington with Your Dog

food/bev	free	kitchen	pet fee	pool	spa	other features
R&L	C	K	$10 per stay		rm	$50 deposit ($40 is refundable), mineral baths, massage therapist, nightclub, close to walking trails
	C	K				fully equipped kitchens, open field for walking dogs, 2 blocks to lake
	C	K				mineral water bath in each room, RV sites, kennels avail, gift shop, fly fishing shop, lakeside walking trails
		K		out htd		full kitchens, laundry facilities, RV sites, lakeside area for walking dogs
R&L		K				RV sites, close to "Rails to Trails" walking trail
B&B	C FB					1 RV site, laundry facilities, area for walking dogs, 2 blocks to public park
	C	K	$5 per day			bridal suite, walking trail through historic neighborhood, laundry, 20 min drive to ocean beaches
	C	R M	$6 per day			open area for walking dogs, RV sites, laundry facilities
	C	K R M	$5 per day			small dogs only, laundry facilities, fully equipped kitchens, RV sites, open fields for walking dogs
	C CB	K		out htd	sp	area for walking dogs, RV sites, laundry facilities, 3 mi to public park

abbreviations used in this section

Spokane

Best Inn & Suites 6309 E Broadway Ave Spokane, WA 99212	509-535-2442 800-237-8466	73 units $44–$99
Best Western Peppertree Airport Inn 3711 S Geiger Blvd Spokane, WA 99224 www.bestwesternwashington.com	509-624-4655 800-799-3933	100 units $59–$125
Best Western Pheasant Hill 12415 E Mission Ave Spokane, WA 99216 www.bestwesternwashington.com	509-926-7432	105 units $69–$179
Best Western Thunderbird Inn 120 W 3rd Ave Spokane, WA 99201 www.bestwesternwashington.com	509-747-2011 800-578-2473	89 units $65–$88
Best Western Trade Winds North 3033 N Division St Spokane, WA 99207 www.bestwesternwashington.com	509-326-5500 800-621-8593	63 units $59–$90
Budget Saver Motel-Spokane 1234 E Sprague Ave Spokane, WA 99202	509-534-0669	16 units $29–$43
Cavanaugh's Fourth Avenue 110 E 4th Ave Spokane, WA 99202	509-838-6101 800-325-4000	153 units $60–$89
Cavanaugh's Inn at the Park 303 W North River Dr Spokane, WA 99201	509-326-8000 800-325-4000	402 units $89–$199
Cavanaugh's Resident Court 1203 W 5th Ave Spokane, WA 99204	509-624-4142	35 units $39–$68
Cavanaugh's Ridpath Hotel 515 W Sprague Ave Spokane, WA 99201	509-838-2711 800-325-4000	342 units $70–$115

A: Where to Stay in Washington with Your Dog

food/bev	free	kitchen	pet fee	pool	spa	other features
	C CB	K		out htd	tb	exercise room, laundry facilities, area for walking dogs, close to public parks
	C CB	R M	$10 per day	in htd	sp	dogs under 10 lbs only, exercise room, laundry facilities, walking area
	C CB	R M		in htd	tb	laundry facilities, fitness center, 3 mi to Centennial Trail along river, 5 min to public park
R	C CB	R M	$10 per day	out htd	sp	exercise room, open area across street for walking dogs, 7 blocks to Centennial Trail along river
	C CB	R M	$20 ref dep	in htd	sa tb	laundry facilities, 2 blocks to public park
	C CB	K				1 or 2 dogs only, walking area behind motel, easy driving distance to riverfront park
R & L	C			out htd		laundry facilities, 8 blocks to riverfront park
R & L	C CB			in out htd	sp	across from riverfront park
	C	K	$50 ref dep	out	sp	laundry, quiet neighborhood for walking dogs, short drive to public park
R & L	C	R M	$200 ref dep	out htd		exercise room, laundry facilities, 4 blocks to riverfront park

abbreviations used in this section   225

Have Dog Will Travel—Washington Edition

Spokane

Cavanaugh's River Inn 700 N Division St Spokane, WA 99202	509-326-5577 800-325-4000	245 units $59–$240
Cedar Village Motel 5415 W Sunset Hwy Spokane, WA 99224	509-838-8558 800-700-8558	28 units $28–$55
Clinic Center Motel 702 S Mcclellan St Spokane, WA 99204	509-747-6081	31 units $34–$42
Cobblestone Bakery B & B Inn 620 S Washington St Spokane, WA 99204	509-624-9735	2 units $69–$119
Comfort Inn-North 7111 N Division St Spokane, WA 99208	509-467-7111 800-228-5150	96 units $39–$150
Comfort Inn-Valley 905 N Sullivan Rd Spokane, WA 99037	509-925-3838 800-228-5150	76 units $39–$150
Country Inn 3808 N Sullivan Spokane, WA 99216	509-893-0955	59 units $69–$129
Days Inn-Spokane Airport 4212 W Sunset Blvd Spokane, WA 99224	509-747-2021 800-329-7466 www.daysinn.com	132 units $52–$80
Doubletree Hotel-Spokane City Ctr 322 N Spokane Falls Ct Spokane, WA 99201	509-455-9600 800-222-tree	379 units $99–$119
Doubletree Hotel-Spokane Valley 1100 N Sullivan Rd Spokane, WA 99037	509-924-9000 800-222-tree	236 units $59–$118

See pp. 90-91 for a key to the

A: Where to Stay in Washington with Your Dog

food/bev	free	kitchen	pet fee	pool	spa	other features
R & L	C CB	K		out htd	tb	refrigerator & microwave avail on request, laundry facilities, close to Centennial Trail along river
	C	K	$5 per day			large yard for walking dogs, BBQ, picnic tables, gazebo, laundry facilities, RV sites
	C CB		$5 per day			large walking area, 2 blocks to public park
B B R	C CB FB					well-behaved dogs allowed at manager's discretion only, area for walking dogs, ½ mi to public park
	C CB		$5 per day	out htd	sp sa	courtyard & dog walking area on premises, laundry facilities, quiet neighborhood for longer walks
	C CB		$5 per day	out htd	sp sa	laundry facilities, dog walking area
	C CB	K		in htd	tb	laundry facilities, exercise room, area for walking dogs, short drive to public park
R & L	C CB	R M		out htd		laundry facilities, courtyard & open area for walking dogs, 4 mi to riverfront park
R & L	C	R M	$25 per day	in htd	sa	exercise room, laundry facilities, next to riverfront park
R & L	C	R M		out htd	sp	area for walking dogs, 1½ blocks to Centennial Trail along river

abbreviations used in this section

Have Dog Will Travel—Washington Edition

Spokane

Eastgate Motel 10625 E Trent Ave Spokane, WA 99206	509-922-4556	9 units $35–$75
Hampton Inn-Spokane 2010 S Assembly Rd Spokane, WA 99224	509-747-1100 800-426-7866	129 units $74–$91
Holiday Inn Express-Spokane Vly 9220 E Mission Ave Spokane, WA 99206	509-927-7100 800-465-4329	103 units $69–$149
Howard Johnson Inn-Downtown 211 S Division St Spokane, WA 99202	509-838-6630 800-446-4656	79 units $50–$80
Maple Tree Motel 4824 E Sprague Ave Spokane, WA 99212	509-535-5810	25 units $29–$45
Motel 6-Spokane 1919 N Hutchinson Rd Spokane, WA 99212	509-926-5399 800-466-8356 www.daysinn.com	92 units $40–$54
Motel 6-Spokane 1508 S Rustle Rd Spokane, WA 99224	509-459-6120 800-466-8356	120 units $45–$53
Oslo's Bed & Breakfast 1821 E 39th Ave Spokane, WA 99203	509-838-3175 888-838-3175	2 units $65–$85
Park Lane Motel Suites & RV Pk 4412 E Sprague Ave Spokane, WA 99212	509-535-1626 800-533-1626 www.parklanemotel.com	28 units $45–$105
Quality Inn Valley Suites-Spokane 8923 E Mission Ave Spokane, WA 99212	509-928-5218 800-777-7355	128 units $79–$300

See pp. 90-91 for a key to the

A: Where to Stay in Washington with Your Dog

food/bev	free	kitchen	pet fee	pool	spa	other features
	C	R M				area for walking dogs
R	C CB	K R	$50 ref dep	in htd	tb	smoking & nonsmoking pet rooms, fitness center, laundry, area for walking dogs, 5 min drive to park
	C CB	R M		in htd	tb	prefer dogs to be kept in travel kennel while in room, short drive to public park, laundry facilities
	C CB	R M	$5 per day		sp	area for walking dogs, 6 blocks to riverfront park
		K	$25 per stay			area for walking dogs
	C	R M				area for walking dogs, 1 mi to public park
	C	R M		out htd		1 dog per room under 30 lbs only, laundry facilities, area for walking dogs, 3 mi to riverfront park
B & B	C FB					dogs allowed at owner's discretion only, air-cond, ground floor rooms w/private bath, ½ block to park
	C CB	K			sa	laundry facilities, 18 RV sites, fenced grassy play area, ¾ mi to fairgrounds used for dog shows
	C CB	R M	$50 ref dep	in htd	sa tb	exercise room, laundry facilities, RV sites, dog walking area, close to Centennial Trail along river

abbreviations used in this section   **229**

Have Dog Will Travel—Washington Edition

Spokane

Ramada Inn-Spokane Airport 9000 Airport Rd, PO Box 19230 Spokane, WA 99219	509-838-5211 800-272-6232	165 units $65–$90
Ramada Limited Suites 9601 N Newport Hwy Spokane, WA 99218	509-468-4201 800-888-6630	76 units $55–$85
Ramada Ltd 123 S Post St Spokane, WA 99201	509-838-8504 800-272-6232	46 units $45–$70
Ranch Motel 1609 S Lewis St Spokane, WA 99224	509-456-8919	10 units $29–$35
Red Top Motel & Apartments 7217 E Trent Ave Spokane, WA 99212	509-926-5728	35 units $40–$125
Royal Scot Motel 20 W Houston Ave Spokane, WA 99208	509-467-6672 888-467-scot	39 units $40–$70
Select Inn Tiki Lodge 1420 W 2nd Ave Spokane, WA 99204	509-838-2026 800-246-6835	54 units $38–$52
Shangri-La Motel 2922 W Government Way Spokane, WA 99224	509-747-2066 800-234-4941	20 units $39–$76
Shilo Inn-Spokane 923 E 3rd Ave Spokane, WA 99202	509-535-9000 800-222-2244 www.shiloinns.com	105 units $69–$99
Skyline Motel 1724 S Geiger Blvd Spokane, WA 99224	509-747-8686	26 units $25–$35

See pp. 90-91 for a key to the

A: Where to Stay in Washington with Your Dog

food/bev	free	kitchen	pet fee	pool	spa	other features
R&L	C	K		in out htd	tb	exercise room, area for walking dogs
	C CB	R M	$10 per day	in htd	sp	laundry facilities, area for walking dogs
	C CB	R M	$5 per day			guest passes to local fitness center, 4 blocks to riverfront park & Centennial Trail
		K				area for walking dogs, laundry facilities, ½ mi to arboretum & walking trails
	C	K	$20 ref dep	out htd	rm	area for walking dogs
	C	R M	$10 per stay	out htd		small dogs only, area for walking dogs, 4 blocks to public park
R	C	R M		out htd		area for walking dogs, 6 blocks to public park
	C CB	K		out htd		next to greenbelt area w/walking trails to river
R&L	C FB	R M	$7 per day	in htd	sp sa	laundry facilities, exercise room, steam room
		K	ref dep			laundry facilities, open field for walking dogs, 1 mi to public park

abbreviations used in this section   **231**

Spokane – Stevenson

Solar World Estates Motel Alternat. 20 NE Pineridge Ct Spokane, WA 99208	509-468-1207 800-650-6530	56 units $39–$90
Spokane Apple Tree Inn 9508 N Division St Spokane, WA 99218	509-466-3020 800-323-5796	71 units $50–$82
Spokane House 4301 W Sunset Blvd Spokane, WA 99224	509-838-1471 800-550-7635	86 units $55–$75
Spokane Travelodge 33 W Spokane Falls Blvd Spokane, WA 99201	509-623-9727 800-578-7878	80 units $50–$70
Starlite Motel 3809 S Geiger Blvd Spokane, WA 99224	509-747-7186 800-772-7186	83 units $29–$50
Super 8 Motel 2020 N Argonne Rd Spokane, WA 99212	509-928-4888 800-800-8000 www.super8.com	187 units $53–$84
Super 8 Motel 11102 W Westbow Blvd Spokane, WA 99224	509-838-8800 800-800-8000 www.super8.com	80 units $45–$75
TradeWinds Motel 907 W 3rd Ave Spokane, WA 99201	509-838-2091 800-586-5397	59 units $40–$80
Purple Sage Motel 409 W 1st St, PO Box 76 Sprague, WA 99032	509-257-2507 877-957-2507 purplesagemotel@email.com	7 units $34–$45
The Timbers 200 SW Cascade, PO Box 435 Stevenson, WA 98648	509-427-5656	7 units $85–$250

A: Where to Stay in Washington with Your Dog

food/bev	free	kitchen	pet fee	pool	spa	other features
		K	$100 per stay		rm	$200 deposit ($100 is refundable), laundry facilities, monthly rates also available, 2 mi to riverfront park
	C CB	K	$25 ref dep	out htd		laundry facilities, designated pet walking area, 2 blocks to public park
R & L	C			out htd	sp	exercise room, live music, area for walking dogs, next to public arboretum & walking trails
	C CB	K	$10 per stay		rm	exercise room, laundry facilities, area for walking dogs, 4 blocks to public park
		K				area for walking dogs
R	C CB	R M	$25 ref dep			guest pass to fitness club, laundry facilities, RV sites, area for walking dogs, ½ mi to public park
	C CB	R M	$5 per day	in htd	tb	laundry facilities, open area for walking dogs
	C CB	R M		out htd	sp sa	exercise room, laundry facilities, 8 blocks to riverfront park
	C				rm	area for walking dogs, 2 mi to Sprague Lake
R	C	K			tb rm	on the Columbia River, adjacent to waterfront county park

abbreviations used in this section   **233**

Sultan — Tacoma

Dutch Cup Motel 918 Main St, PO Box 369 Sultan, WA 98294	360-793-2215 800-844-0488	22 units $53–$64
Krebs Mansion B & B 35820 Sultan Startup Rd Sultan, WA 98294	360-793-0447	4 units
BB Border Inn 121 Cleveland Ave, PO Box 178 Sumas, WA 98295	360-988-5800	21 units $35–$58
Sumner Motor Inn 15506 Main St E Sumner, WA 98390	253-863-3250	39 units $45–$66
Sun Valley Inn 724 Yakima Valley Hwy Sunnyside, WA 98944	509-837-4721	40 units $25–$60
Sunnyside Travelodge 408 Yakima Valley Hwy Sunnyside, WA 98944	509-837-7878 800-578-7878	73 units $38–$100
Town House Motel 509 Yakima Valley Hwy Sunnyside, WA 98944	509-837-5500	21 units $30–$60
Best Western Executive Inn-Fife 5700 Pacific Hwy E Tacoma, WA 98424	253-922-0080 800-938-8500 www.bestwesternwashington.com	139 units $85–$145
Best Western Tacoma Inn 8726 S Hosmer St Tacoma, WA 98444	253-535-2880 800-305-2880 www.bestwesternwashington.com	149 units $64–$99
Blue Spruce Motel 12715 Pacific Ave S Tacoma, WA 98444	253-531-6111	27 units $35–$60

See pp. 90-91 for a key to the

A: Where to Stay in Washington with Your Dog

food/bev	free	kitchen	pet fee	pool	spa	other features
R&L	C	K R M	$6 per day			area for walking dogs, 9 blocks to riverfront parks, 5 mi to walking trail
B&B	C CB			tb		area for walking dogs, close to riverfront & walking trails
R&L		R				open area for walking dogs, 3 blocks to public park
	C	K R M	$10 per stay			open fields for walking dogs, short drive to parks & lakes
	C CB	K		out		continental breakfast served on weekends only, area for walking dogs
R&L	C CB	K		out htd	sp rm	laundry facilities, area for walking dogs
	C	K				well-behaved short-haired dogs only, 1 block to public park
R&L	C	R	$25 per stay	in htd	sp	small area for walking dogs, 3 mi to waterfront park
R&L	C CB	K	$20 per stay	out htd	sp	area for walking dogs, laundry facilities, ¾ mi to lakeside park
	C	K	$5 per day			area for walking dogs, 5 minute drive to public park

abbreviations used in this section

Tacoma

Budget Inn-South Tacoma 1915 S Tacoma Way Tacoma, WA 98409	253-588-6615	50 units $40–$85
Comfort Inn-Tacoma 5601 Pacific Hwy E Tacoma, WA 98424	253-926-2301 800-228-5150	70 units $49–$69
Corporate Suites, Inc. 219 E Division Ct Tacoma, WA 98404	253-473-4105 800-255-6058 www.corporatesuites.com	21 units $54–$65
Days Inn-Fife 3021 Pacific Hwy E Tacoma, WA 98424	253-922-3500 800-329-7466 www.daysinn.com	185 units $60–$80
Days Inn-Tacoma 6802 Tacoma Mall Blvd Tacoma, WA 98409	253-475-5900 800-221-2680 www.daysinn.com	123 units $67–$129
La Quinta Inn 1425 E 27th St Tacoma, WA 98421	253-383-0146 800-531-5900	160 units $64–$99
Motel 6-Tacoma 1811 S 76th St Tacoma, WA 98408	253-473-7100 800-466-8356	120 units $46–$60
Quality Inn of Lakewood/Tacoma 9920 S Tacoma Way Tacoma, WA 98499	253-588-5241 800-600-9751	103 units $66–$79
Ramada Inn-Tacoma Dome 2611 East E St Tacoma, WA 98421	253-572-7272 800-272-6232	160 units $72–$250
Sheraton Tacoma Hotel 1320 Broadway Tacoma, WA 98402	253-572-3200 800-845-9466	319 units $92–$155

See pp. 90-91 for a key to the

A: Where to Stay in Washington with Your Dog

food/bev	free	kitchen	pet fee	pool	spa	other features
	C	K	$25 per stay			adult dogs only, area for walking dogs, laundry facilities, 2 mi to waterfront & public parks
	C CB	K	$15 per stay			quiet neighborhood for walking dogs, laundry facilities, 5 mi to Fairgrounds, 4 mi to Tacoma Dome
	C	K	$100 ref dep	out htd		$50 of the deposit is refundable, laundry facilities, area for walking dogs, 5 min drive to public park
R	C CB		$5 per stay	out htd		area for walking dogs
R	C	R M	$10 ref dep	out htd		exercise room, large yard for walking dogs, 10 min walk to park
R & L	C CB	R M		out htd	tb	dogs under 20 lbs only, exercise room, laundry facilities, area for walking dogs, short drive to parks
R & L	C			out htd	sp	large area for walking dogs, laundry facilities, 1 block to public park
R & L	C CB	K	$5 per day		rm	exercise room, laundry facilities, area for walking dogs
R & L			$10 per stay			small area for walking dogs, 5 min drive to public park, 10 min to waterfront
R & L	C	R M	$50 ref dep			dogs under 35 lbs only, discount at YMCA across street, small walking area, 3 mi to large waterfront park

abbreviations used in this section

Tacoma — Toppenish

Sherwood Inn 8402 S Hosmer St Tacoma, WA 98444	253-535-2800	120 units $54–$77
Shilo Inn-Tacoma 7414 S Hosmer St Tacoma, WA 98408	253-475-4020 800-222-2244 www.shiloinns.com	132 units $79–$99
Summertide Resort & Marina 15781 NE Northshore Rd Tahuya, WA 98588	253-925-9277 or 360-275-9313	3 units $75–$145
Circle H Holiday Ranch 810 Watt Canyon Rd Thorp, WA 98946	509-964-2000	4 units $85
Tradewinds On-The-Bay Motel 4305 Pomeroy Ln, PO Box 502 Tokeland, WA 98590	360-267-7500	17 units $65–$75
Red Apple Inn Highway 97 & 1st St, PO Box 453 Tonasket, WA 98855	509-486-2119	21 units $35–$76
Spectacle Falls Resort 879 Loomis Oroville Rd Tonasket, WA 98855	509-223-4141	4 units $50
El Corral Motel 61731 US Highway 97 Toppenish, WA 98948	509-865-2365	17 units $36–$45
Oxbow Motor Inn 511 S Elm St Toppenish, WA 98948	509-865-5800 888-865-5855	44 units $35–$49
Toppenish Inn Motel 515 S Elm St Toppenish, WA 98948	509-865-7444 800-222-3161	42 units $59–$82

See pp. 90-91 for a key to the

A: Where to Stay in Washington with Your Dog

food/bev	free	kitchen	pet fee	pool	spa	other features
R&L	C FB	RM	$15 per stay	out htd		area for walking dogs, 3 blocks to public park
	C CB	K RM	$7 per day	in htd	sp sa	laundry facilities, exercise room, steam room, area for walking dogs
		K				fully equipped cottages, 25 RV sites, laundry facilities, beachfront for walking dogs, short drive to park
		RM				cabins sleep 4-6, facilities for guests to bring their own horses, trails for walking-biking horseback riding
	C	K	$5 per day	out htd		fully equipped kitchens in all rooms, large "party room" w/kitchen, RV sites, beach for walking dogs
	C	K				adult dogs only, area for walking dogs
		K				fully equipped lakeside mobile homes by advance reservations only, lots of room for walking dogs
	C	RM				large area for walking dogs, 3 blocks to public park
	C CB	K	$5 per day			across street to public park
	C CB	RM	$5 per day	in htd	sp	small dogs only, exercise room, laundry facilities, area for walking dogs, public park across street

abbreviations used in this section   **239**

Have Dog Will Travel—Washington Edition

Tukwila — Union Gap

Best Western Southcenter 15901 W Valley Hwy Tukwila, WA 98188	425-226-1812 800-544-9863 www.bestwesternwashington.com	146 units $79–$120
Homestead Village Guest Studios 15635 W Valley Hwy Tukwila, WA 98188	425-235-7160	93 units $74–$94
Best Western Tumwater Inn 5188 Capitol Blvd S Tumwater, WA 98501	360-956-1235 800-848-4992 www.bestwesternwashington.com	90 units $58–$81
Lee Street Suites 348 Lee St SW Tumwater, WA 98501	360-943-8391	8 units $28–$49
Motel 6-Tumwater 400 Lee St SW Tumwater, WA 98501	360-754-7320 800-466-8356	119 units $38–$52
Shalimar Suites 5895 Capitol Blvd Tumwater, WA 98501	360-943-8391	17 units $28–$49
Idle-A-While Motel 505 N Highway 20, PO Box 667 Twisp, WA 98856	509-997-3222	25 units $45–$68
Sportsman Motel 1010 E Methow Valley Hwy, PO Box 98 Twisp, WA 98856	509-997-2911	8 units $35–$50
De Koeyer Hot Tub Cabins 6730 E SR 106, PO Box 182 Union, WA 98592	360-898-3434	9 units $90–$175
Days Inn-Yakima 2408 Rudkin Rd Union Gap, WA 98903	509-248-9700 800-348-9701 www.daysinn.com	118 units $47–$66

See pp. 90-91 for a key to the

A: Where to Stay in Washington with Your Dog

food/bev	free	kitchen	pet fee	pool	spa	other features
R & L	C	RM	$25 ref dep	out htd	sp sa tb	dogs under 20 lbs only, exercise room, laundry facilities, next to walking trail
	C CB	K	$75 per stay			weekly rates, laundry facilities, across street from walking trail that leads to public park
	C CB	RM	$5 per stay		sa tb	exercise room, laundry facilities, dog walking service avail, natural area for walking dogs, near parks
		K	$2-$5/ day			fully furnished apartments, 4 night min stay, laundry facilities, wooded area for walking dogs
	C			out htd		picnic area, laundry facilities, 5 min drive to riverside park & walking trails
		K	$2-$5/ day			fully furnished apartments, laundry facilities, 4 night min stay, close to semi-wooded area for walking dogs
	C CB	K	$3 per day		sa tb	cottages w/fully equipped kitchens, motel units, picnic area, BBQ, 5 acres for walking dogs, near parks
		K	$3 per day			large open area for walking dogs, RV sites, ¾ mi to riverside park & walking trails
	C	K				cabins w/private hot tubs, access to public swimming pool, small area for walking dogs, near nature trail
	C CB	K	$10 per day	out htd	rm	$25 refundable damage deposit, laundry facilities, grassy area for walking dogs

abbreviations used in this section   241

Union Gap – Vancouver

La Casa Motel 2703 Main St Union Gap, WA 98903	509-457-6147	25 units $35–$45
Super 8 Motel-Yakima 2605 Rudkin Rd Union Gap, WA 98903	509-248-8880 800-800-8000 www.super8.com	95 units $39–$78
Hotel Usk 410 River Rd Usk, WA 99180	509-445-1526 888-423-8084	8 units $38–$64
Jump Off Joe Lake Resort 3290 E Jump Off Joe Rd Valley, WA 99181	509-937-2133	4 units $45–$60
Best Inn & Suites 221 NE Chkalov Dr Vancouver, WA 98684	360-256-7044 800-426-5110	116 units $52–$139
Best Western Ferryman's Inn 7901 NE 6th Ave Vancouver, WA 98665	360-574-2151 www.bestwesternwashington.com	132 units $54–$68
Guest House Motel 11504 NE 2nd St Vancouver, WA 98684	360-254-4511	47 units $40–$65
Homewood Suites 701 SE Columbia Shores Blvd Vancouver, WA 98661	360-750-1100 800-call-home	104 units $99–$169
Quality Inn-Vancouver 7001 NE Highway 99 Vancouver, WA 98665	360-696-0516 888-696-0516	72 units $54–$95
Red Lion Hotel at the Quay (formerly Doubletree at the Quay) 100 Columbia St, Vancouver, WA 98660	360-694-8341 800-222-tree	160 units $69–$120

See pp. 90-91 for a key to the

A: Where to Stay in Washington with Your Dog

food/bev	free	kitchen	pet fee	pool	spa	other features
	C	K		out htd		large yard for walking dogs, ½ block to greenway & pond for swimming
	C		$25 ref dep	in htd		laundry facilities, area for walking dogs, 2 blocks to greenway trail along river
	C					area for walking dogs, close to riverfront
		K	$5 per day			lakefront cabins w/fully equipped kitchens, convenience store, area for walking dogs
	C CB	K	$15 per day	in htd	sp	exercise room, area for walking dogs, ½ mi to public park
	C CB	K	$3 per day	out		laundry facilities, area for walking dogs, 1 mi to walking trail
	C	R M				small dogs only, area for walking dogs, 3 blocks to public park
	C CB	K	$10 per day	out htd	sp	$10/day pet fee plus one-time $25 cleaning fee, laundry facilities, fully equipped kitchens, riverside trail
	C CB	K	$5 per day	out htd	sp	laundry facilities, large grassy area for walking dogs, 4 blocks to public park
R & L	C	K	$15 per stay	out htd		adjacent to walking trail along river, 5 blocks to public park

abbreviations used in this section

Have Dog Will Travel—Washington Edition

Vancouver — Vashon Island

Residence Inn by Marriott 8005 NE Parkway Dr Vancouver, WA 98662	360-253-4800 800-331-3131	120 units $79–$139
Riverside Motel 4400 Columbia House Blvd Vancouver, WA 98661	360-693-3677	17 units $38–$45
Shilo Inn-Downtown Vancouver 401 E 13th St Vancouver, WA 98660	360-696-0411 800-222-2244 www.shiloinns.com	118 units $65–$99
Shilo Inn-Hazel Dell/Vancouver 13206 NE Highway 99 Vancouver, WA 98686	360-573-0511 800-222-2244 www.shiloinns.com	66 units $65–$85
Value Motel 708 NE 78th St Vancouver, WA 98665	360-574-2345	120 units $22–$40
Vancouver Lodge 601 Broadway St Vancouver, WA 98660	360-693-3668	45 units $45–$85
Vantage Motel 551 Main St Vantage, WA 98950	509-856-2230	20 units $54–$89
Angels of the Sea B & B 26431 99th Ave SW Vashon Island, WA 98070	206-463-6980 800-798-9249 www.angelsofthesea.com	3 units $75–$125
Betty MacDonald Farm B & B 12000 99th Ave SW Vashon Island, WA 98070	206-567-4227 888-eat-n-sleep www.bettymacdonald.com	2 units $110–$130
Emerald Isle Guest House 10520 SW 140th St Vashon Island, WA 98070	206-567-5133	1 unit $100

See pp. 90-91 for a key to the

A: Where to Stay in Washington with Your Dog

food/bev	free	kitchen	pet fee	pool	spa	other features
	C CB	K	$10 per day	out htd	sp	exercise room, laundry facilities, area for walking dogs, near corporate park w/walking paths
		K	$5 per day			1 or 2 nights only w/$10 refundable deposit, area for walking dogs, ½ mi to public park
	C CB	R M	$7 per day	out htd	sp sa	laundry facilities, steam room
	C CB	R M	$7 per day	in htd	sp sa	laundry facilities, steam room, area for walking dogs
			$5 per day	out	rm	pool open May 15-Sept 15, laundry facilities, area for walking dogs, short drive to public park
	C	R M	$8 per day		tb	small area behind motel for walking dogs, 2 blocks to public park
			$5 per day	in htd		laundry facilities, convenience store, area for walking dogs along Columbia River
B&B	C FB					private entrances, fenced yard, laundry, guest privileges at country club, short walk to beach & trails
B&B	C CB	K				loft & fully equipped cottage, dogs allowed in covered porch but not inside house, 6 acres, private beach
	C	K	$20 per stay			private cottage w/fully equipped kitchen sleeps 6, meadow for walking dogs, close to beaches

abbreviations used in this section

Have Dog Will Travel—Washington Edition

Vashon Island — Walla Walla

Old Tjomsland House B & B 17011 Vashon Hwy SW PO Box 913, Vashon Island, WA 98070	206-463-5275 888-255-2706	2 units $85–$150
Swallow's Nest Guest Cottages 6030 SW 248th St Vashon Island, WA 98070 www.vashonislandcottages.com	206-463-2646 800-269-6378	8 units $75–$95
Van Gelder's Retreat PO Box 1328 Vashon Island, WA 98070	206-463-3684	3 units $75–$85
A & H Motel 2599 E Isaacs Ave Walla Walla, WA 99362	509-529-0560	9 units $26–$35
Best Western Walla Walla Suites Inn 7 E Oak St Walla Walla, WA 99362 www.bestwesternwashington.com	509-525-4700 800-528-1234	78 units $59–$89
Capri Motel 2003 E Melrose St Walla Walla, WA 99362	509-525-1130 800-451-1139	37 units $34–$75
City Center Motel 627 W Main St Walla Walla, WA 99362	509-529-2660	17 units $36–$175
Colonial Motel 2279 E Isaacs Ave Walla Walla, WA 99362	509-529-1220	17 units $35–$60
Hawthorne Inn & Suites 520 N 2nd Ave Walla Walla, WA 99362	509-525-2522 800-527-1133	61 units $69–$159
Howard Johnson Express Inn 325 E Main St Walla Walla, WA 99362	509-529-4360	85 units $72–$140

See pp. 90-91 for a key to the

A: Where to Stay in Washington with Your Dog

food/bev	free	kitchen	pet fee	pool	spa	other features
B&B	C FB	K				2 bdrm suite w/separate entrance, 1 bdrm cottage, dog must be in travel kennel, meadow for walking
	C	K	$10 per day		tb	dogs allowed in 3 cottages, hot tub privileges avail $5 per person, close to public parks & beaches
	C	K		out htd	sp	breakfast avail at additional charge, kitchens & private entrances, large open field for walking dogs
		RM				small dogs only, area for walking dogs
	C CB	RM	$5 per day	in htd	sp	laundry facilities, grassy area for walking dogs, close to walking trail around golf course
	C	K	$5 per stay	out htd		small area for walking dogs, ½ mi to public park w/ponds
	C		ref dep	out htd		rooms & furnished apartments, garden area for walking dogs, 2 blocks to public park
	C	RM				large landscaped yard for walking dogs, 1 block to public park & walking trail
	C CB	K		in htd	tb	laundry facilities, area for walking dogs, 1 mi to public park
	C CB	K		out htd	sp rm	laundry facilities, area for walking dogs, 1 to 2 mi to public park & walking trails

abbreviations used in this section   247

Walla Walla — Wenatchee

Sicyon Gallery B & B 1283 Star St Walla Walla, WA 99362	509-525-2964	1 unit $55
Super 8 Motel-Walla Walla 2315 Eastgate St N Walla Walla, WA 99362	509-525-8800 800-800-8000 www.super8.com	100 units $50–$75
Vagabond Inn 305 N 2nd Ave Walla Walla, WA 99362	509-529-4410 888-529-4161	35 units $30–$75
Walla Walla Travelodge 421 E Main St Walla Walla, WA 99362	509-529-4940 800-578-7878	39 units $40–$70
Rama Inn 544 6th St Washougal, WA 98671	360-835-8591	26 units $52–$60
Tower House Bed & Breakfast 305 W Ash, PO Box 129 Waterville, WA 98858	509-745-8320	2 units $45
Avenue Motel 720 N Wenatchee Ave Wenatchee, WA 98801	509-663-7161 800-733-8981	39 units $50–$66
Comfort Inn-Columbia River 815 Wenatchee Ave Wenatchee, WA 98801	509-662-1700 800-228-5150	81 units $59–$89
Doubletree Hotel 1225 N Wenatchee Ave Wenatchee, WA 98801	509-663-0711 800-222-tree	149 units $69–$89
Economy Inn 700 N Wenatchee Ave Wenatchee, WA 98801	509-663-8133 800-587-6348	41 units $40–$100

A: Where to Stay in Washington with Your Dog

food/bev	free	kitchen	pet fee	pool	spa	other features
B&B	C FB					breakfast served indoors or outside in sculpture garden, walking trail, less than 1 mi to Pioneer Park
	C		$25 ref dep	in htd	sp	laundry facilities, small area for walking dogs, 1 mi to public park
	C CB	K	$10 per day	out htd	tb	
	C	R	$5 per day	out htd	sp	small dogs only, microwave avail at front desk, small area for walking dogs, ½ mi to public park
	C	R M	$2 per day			area for walking dogs, 1 mi to riverfront walking area, laundry facilities
B&B	C FB					advance reservations required, turn of the century home, large yard, close to public parks
	C	K		out htd	sp	park-like setting, area for walking dogs, 4 blocks to public park
	C CB	R M	$15 per stay	in htd	sp	exercise room, laundry facilities, ½ mi to public park & walking trail
R&L	C CB	R M		out htd	sp	next to walking path & public park
	C CB	K	$10 per day	out htd		laundry facilities, 4 blocks to public park

abbreviations used in this section

Wenatchee — Westport

Hawthorn Inn & Suites 1905 N Wenatchee Ave Wenatchee, WA 98801	509-664-6565 800-527-1133 www.bestwesternwashington.com	65 units $74–$140
Hill Crest Motel 2921 School St Wenatchee, WA 98801	509-663-5157	16 units $48–$70
Holiday Lodge 610 N Wenatchee Ave Wenatchee, WA 98801	509-663-8167 800-722-0852	59 units $38–$75
Lyles Motel 924 N Wenatchee Ave Wenatchee, WA 98801	509-663-5155 800-582-3788	23 units $36–$70
Orchard Inn 1401 N Miller St Wenatchee, WA 98801	509-662-3443 800-368-4571	103 units $49–$78
Starlite Motel 1640 N Wenatchee Ave Wenatchee, WA 98801	509-663-8115 800-668-1862	34 units $40–$60
Warm Springs Inn B & B 1611 Love Ln Wenatchee, WA 98801	509-662-8365 800-543-3645 www.warmspringsinn.com	5 units $85–$120
Welcome Inn at Wenatchee Ctr 232 N Wenatchee Ave Wenatchee, WA 98801	509-663-7121 800-561-8856	38 units $49–$65
Westcoast Wenatchee Ctr Hotel 201 N Wenatchee Ave Wenatchee, WA 98801	509-662-1234 800-426-0670	147 units $99–$200
Alaskan Motel 708 N 1st St, PO Box 314 Westport, WA 98595	360-268-9133	11 units $45–$125

A: Where to Stay in Washington with Your Dog

food/bev	free	kitchen	pet fee	pool	spa	other features
	C FB	K R M		in htd	sp sa rm	24-hr pool-spa-sauna, fitness center, hot breakfast buffet, laundry facilities, close to walking area
	C	K		out		area for walking dogs, ½ mi to public park
	C CB	R M		out htd	sa tb	laundry facilities, lawn area for walking dogs, 2 blocks to public park
	C	K	ref dep	out htd	tb	adult dogs only, dog run available, laundry facilities, 1 block to public park
	C	R M	$25 ref dep	out htd	tb	adjacent to walking trail along the river
	C	K R M		out htd	sp	snacks avail in lobby, laundry facilities, 2 blocks to public park
B&B	C FB				tb	ground floor room w/outside entrance on 10 acres along river for walking dog
	C	R M	$5 per day	out		easy walk to riverfront park
R&L	C	R	$50 ref dep	in out htd	sp	exercise room, 2 blocks to riverfront park
		K	$6-$10/day			rooms & 2 separate houses, area nearby for walking dogs, must NOT walk them on the motel lawn

abbreviations used in this section   **251**

Westport

Breakers Motel 971 N Montesano St, PO Box 1279 Westport, WA 98595	360-268-0848 800-898-4889	18 units $54–$72
Coho Charters Motel & Rv Park 2501 N Nyhus, PO Box 1087 Westport, WA 98595	360-268-0111 800-572-0177	28 units $49–$89
Cranberry Motel & RV Park 920 S Montesano St, PO Box 589 Westport, WA 98595	360-268-0807	14 units $35–$40
Frank L Motel & Aquatic Gardens 725 S Montesano St Westport, WA 98595	360-268-9200	13 units $40–$110
Harbor Resort 871 E Neddie Rose Dr, PO Box 312 Westport, WA 98595	360-268-0169 www.harborresort.com	14 units $49–$110
Ken's Kourt Motel 2339 Nyhus St N, PO Box 868 Westport, WA 98595	360-268-9633	17 units $25–$55
Mariners Cove Inn 303 W Ocean Ave Westport, WA 98595	360-268-0531	9 units $39–$49
Mc Bee's Silver Sands Motel 1001 S Montesano St Westport, WA 98595	360-268-9029	19 units $48–$66
Ocean Avenue Inn 275 W Ocean Ave, PO Box 571 Westport, WA 98595	360-268-9278 888-692-5262	12 units $49–$135
Pacific Motel & RV Park 330 S Forrest St Westport, WA 98595	360-268-9325	12 units $54–$64

See pp. 90-91 for a key to the

A: Where to Stay in Washington with Your Dog

food/bev	free	kitchen	pet fee	pool	spa	other features
		C	K	$6 per day			area for walking dogs, next to public park
		C		$10 per day			dogs under 10 lbs only, area for dogs, walking path thru dunes to beach
		C	K				small dogs only, RV sites, large area for walking dogs, ½ mi to public park
		C CB	K	$5 per day			designated pet area on premises, 1 mi to walking trail & ocean access
			K	$10 per day		rm	motel units & cottages, waterfront area w/paved beach trail for walking dogs
			K R M				close to open field and beach for walking dogs
		C	K R				gazebo, picnic area w/BBQ, area for walking dogs, 6 blocks to beach, close to 2 state parks
		C					dogs under 10 lbs only, area for walking dogs, 5 min drive to beach
		C	K	$10 per day			area for walking dogs, ½ mi to ocean
			K	$5 per day	out		small short-haired dogs allowed in 2 units only, close to walking trails

abbreviations used in this section   253

Westport — Winthrop

Sands Motel & Rv Park 1416 S Montesano St, PO Box 2044 Westport, WA 98595	360-268-0091	12 units $35–$55
Seagull's Nest Motel 830 N Montesano St, PO Box 2516 Westport, WA 98595	360-268-9711 888-613-9078	16 units $39–$69
Shipwreck Motel 2653 N Nyhus St, PO Box 494 Westport, WA 98595	360-268-9151 888-225-2313	35 units $45–$70
Surf Spray Motel & Rv Park 949 S Montesano St, PO Box 1677 Westport, WA 98595	360-268-9149 888-600-9149	10 units $42–$85
Llama Ranch Bed & Breakfast 1980 Highway 141 White Salmon, WA 98672	509-395-2786	7 units $69–$99
Eight Bar B Motel 718 E Main, Wilbur, WA 99185	509-647-2400	15 units $30–$70
Settle Inn Motel 303 NE Main, Wilbur, WA 99185	509-647-2100	11 units $35–$45
Best Western Cascade Inn 960 W Highway 20, PO Box 813 Winthrop, WA 98862	509-996-3100 800-468-6754 www.bestwesternwashington.com	63 units $50–$150
Duck Brand Hotel & Restaurant 248 Riverside Ave, PO Box 238 Winthrop, WA 98862	509-996-2192 800-996-2192	6 units $56–$66
River Run Inn 27 Rader Rd Winthrop, WA 98862	509-996-2173 800-757-2709 www.methow.com/~riverrun/	18 units $65–$90

A: Where to Stay in Washington with Your Dog

food/bev	free	kitchen	pet fee	pool	spa	other features
	C	K				area for walking dogs, RV sites, 6 blocks to state park
	C	K R	$6 per day			across street from public park, 1 mi to paved beach trail
	C	K	$5 per day			across street from beach
		K	$10 per day			fully equipped kitchens, laundry facilities, lawn, BBQ & picnic area, crab cooker, short drive to beach
B&B	C FB					100 acres, ponds & creeks, walking trails, mountain views, resident llamas
	C	K R M	$5 per stay	out htd		½ mi to public park
	C	K				area for walking dogs, 3 blocks to public park
	C CB	R M	$10 per day	out htd	tb	riverfront picnic & BBQ area, laundry facilities, adjacent to walking trails
R						private decks, large area for walking dogs, across street from river, ½ mi to public park
	C	K		in htd	tb	cabins w/patios & private decks, on 11 riverfront acres for walking dogs

abbreviations used in this section 255

Have Dog Will Travel—Washington Edition

Winthrop — Yakima

Virginian Resort 808 N Cascade Highway 20, PO Box 237 Winthrop, WA 98862	509-996-2535 800-854-2834 www.methow.com/~virgnian	37 units
Westar Lodge & Retreat 386 W Chewuch Rd, PO Box 87 Winthrop, WA 98862	509-996-2697 800-854-2834	2 units $150–$500
Winthrop Inn 960 Highway 20, PO Box 265 Winthrop, WA 98862	509-996-2217 800-444-1972	30 units $45–$100
Wolfridge Resort 412B Wolf Creek Rd Winthrop, WA 98862	509-996-2828 800-237-2388 www.wolfridgeresort.com	17 units $69–$192
Lakeside Motel 785 Lake Shore Dr, PO Box 737 Woodland, WA 98674	360-225-8240	13 units $36–$60
Lewis River Inn 1100 Lewis River Rd Woodland, WA 98674	360-225-6257 800-543-4344	49 units $46–$69
Scandia Motel 1123 Hoffman St Woodland, WA 98674	360-225-8006	13 units $32–$40
Woodlander Inn 1500 Atlantic Ave Woodland, WA 98674	360-225-6548 800-444-9667	61 units $40–$60
Bali Hai Motel 710 N 1st St Yakima, WA 98901	509-452-7178	28 units $25–$38
Best Western Oxford Inn 1603 Terrace Heights Dr Yakima, WA 98901	509-457-4444	96 units $55–$80

See pp. 90-91 for a key to the

A: Where to Stay in Washington with Your Dog

food/bev	free	kitchen	pet fee	pool	spa	other features
R	C	K	$5 per day	out htd	tb	motel rooms and cabins, walking trails, ¾ mi to city park, close to state park
		K R M	$5 per day			riverside lodge sleeps up to 30, cottage sleeps 7, laundry facilities, fields & trails for walking dogs
	C CB	R M	$7 per day	out htd	tb	located on the Methow River, near walking-biking-cross country skiing trails
	C	K	$10 per day	out htd	sp	log townhouses, walking-hiking-biking trails, close to river
		R	$5-$7/day			dogs MUST be kept off furniture & beds, 2½ acres for walking dogs, across street from park & lake
	C	R M	$6 per day			area for walking dogs, 6 blocks to public park
	C	K R M	$6 per day			small area for walking dogs, 5 min walk to public park
	C CB	R M	$5 per day	in htd	sp	area for walking dogs, RV sites, short drive to public park
	C	R M	$3 per day	out		4 mi to Yakima Greenway trail
	C CB	K		out htd	sp	adjacent to Yakima Greenway trail along the river, laundry facilities

abbreviations used in this section   257

Have Dog Will Travel—Washington Edition

Yakima

Best Western Oxford Suites 1701 Terrace Heights Dr Yakima, WA 98901	509-457-9000 800-404-7848	107 units $69–$149
Best Western Peppertree Yakima Inn 1614 N 1st St Yakima, WA 98901	509-453-8898 800-238-7234 www.bestwesternwashington.com	73 units $59–$89
Birchfield Manor 2018 Birchfield Rd Yakima, WA 98901	509-452-1960 800-375-3420	11 units $95–$195
Cavanaughs At Yakima Ctr 607 E Yakima Ave Yakima, WA 98901	509-248-5900 800-325-4000	153 units $65–$200
Cavanaughs Gateway Hotel 9 N 9th St Yakima, WA 98901	509-452-6511 800-325-4000	171 units $59–$200
Comfort Suites 3702 Fruitvale Blvd Yakima, WA 98902	509-249-1900 800-228-5150	59 units $69–$169
Doubletree Hotel-Yakima Valley 1507 N 1st St Yakima, WA 98901	509-248-7850 800-222-8733	208 units $55–$135
Holiday Inn Express-Yakima 1001 East A St Yakima, WA 98901	509-249-1000 800-465-4329	87 units $63–$83
Motel 6-Yakima 1104 N 1st St Yakima, WA 98901	509-454-0080 800-466-8356	95 units $35–$40
Mystery Manor B & B 3109 S Wiley Rd Yakima, WA 98903	509-966-9971	4 units $45–$65

See pp. 90-91 for a key to the

A: Where to Stay in Washington with Your Dog

food/bev	free	kitchen	pet fee	pool	spa	other features
	C FB	R M	$15 per stay	in htd	tb	dogs under 20 lbs only, adjacent to Yakima Greenway trail along the river, laundry facilities
	C CB	R M	$8 per day	in htd	sp	dogs under 8 lbs only, 24-hour pool & spa, laundry facilities, open lot for walking dogs, short drive to park
B&B	C FB		ref dep		rm	dogs allowed in 2 rooms w/private fenced patios, lots of natural area for walking dogs
R&L	C	R M	$10 per stay	out htd		10-15 min walk to Yakima Greenway trail along river
R&L	C	K R M	$10 per day	out htd	sp	laundry facilities, 5 min walk to Yakima Greenway trail along river
	C CB	R M		in htd	sp	24 hour exercise room, laundry facilities, 2 blocks to Yakima Greenway trail
R&L	C	R M		out htd	sp	complimentary cookies & dog treats, gift shop, fitness center, 5 min walk to Yakima Greenway trail
	C CB	R M	$6 per day	in out htd	sp tb	exercise room, laundry facilities
	C			out htd		laundry facilities, area for walking dogs, 2 mi to Yakima Greenway trail
B&B	C FB			in htd		"Dinner & Murder Mystery Show" 1st Saturday of ea month, massage therapist, walking area for dogs

abbreviations used in this section   259

Have Dog Will Travel—Washington Edition

Yakima — Zillah

Nendels Inn-Yakima 1405 N 1st St Yakima, WA 98901	509-453-8981 800-547-0106	53 units $39–$66
Quality Inn-Yakima 12 Valley Mall Blvd Yakima, WA 98903	509-248-6924 800-510-5670	86 units $59–$79
Red Apple Motel 416 N 1st St Yakima, WA 98901	509-248-7150	60 units $30–$90
Red Carpet Motor Inn 1608 Fruitvale Blvd Yakima, WA 98902	509-457-1131 800-457-5090	29 units $39–$68
Sun Country Inn 1700 N 1st St Yakima, WA 98901	509-248-5650 800-559-3675	70 units $52–$66
Tourist Motor Inn 1223 N 1st St Yakima, WA 98901	509-452-6551	70 units $29–$60
Western Motel 1202 Fruitvale Blvd Yakima, WA 98902	509-452-1007	14 units $27–$35
Prairie Hotel 701 Prairie Park Ln NE, PO Box 5210 Yelm, WA 98597	360-458-8300	23 units $50–$110
Comfort Inn Zillah 911 Vintage Valley Pkwy Zillah, WA 98953	509-829-3399 800-501-5433	40 units $59–$79

See pp. 90-91 for a key to the

A: Where to Stay in Washington with Your Dog

food/bev	free	kitchen	pet fee	pool	spa	other features
	C CB	R M		in htd	tb	24 hour pool & hot tubs, small dogs only, small area for walking dogs, short drive to Yakima Greenway
R & L	C CB	R M	$10 per day	out htd		laundry facilities, area on premises for walking dogs, 2 mi to Yakima Greenway walking trail
	C CB	R M	$5 per day	out htd		laundry facilities, small area for walking dogs, short drive to public park
	C	K	$5 per stay	out htd	sa	laundry facilities, small open area for walking dogs, short walk to riverside trail & public park
	C CB	K	$5 per day	out htd	sa	laundry facilities, small area for walking dogs, 1 block to Yakima Greenway trail
	C CB	K	$5 per day	out htd		laundry facilities, 6 blocks to Yakima Greenway trail
		K	$5 per day			4 mi to Yakima Greenway & public park
	C	K	$ per stay			call for pet fee, 7 acres natural area for walking dogs, 4 blocks to walking trail
	C CB	R M	$5 per stay	in htd	tb rm	cookies in evening, laundry facilities, area for walking dogs, walking trails within ½ mi

abbreviations used in this section

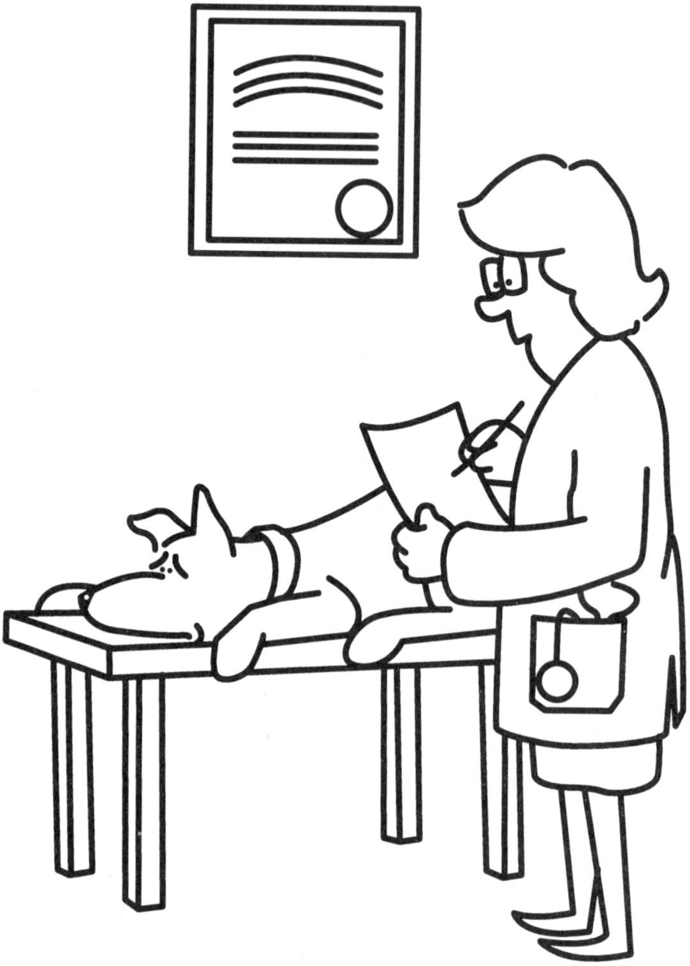

B: Emergency Clinics

Time is a critical factor when your pet needs emergency medical care. Your best bet for quickly finding a veterinary clinic is the local phone book. Even though the nearest clinic may not be open at the moment, many do offer 24 hour emergency service. When you call after normal business hours, their answering service takes down your name, the nature of the emergency, and the phone number you're calling from. That information is immediately relayed to the doctor who is "on call" at the time. He or she then calls you back with either instructions for handling the situation yourself or directions for meeting the doctor at the clinic.

Always call ahead, even during the clinic's normal business hours. That gives their staff a chance to prepare so that any lifesaving procedures that the doctor may deem necessary will be ready the minute your pet arrives. They can also give directions so that you don't waste time or get lost along the way.

Some of these emergency clinics are open around the clock. Other "after-hour" clinics are open only on weeknights, weekends and holidays, often sharing their facilities with unrelated daytime clinics (which are identified in parentheses below).

Washington's 24 hour and after-hour clinics:

Auburn   253–939–6272
After Hours Animal Emergency Clinic
718 Auburn Way N
        Mon–Fri 6 PM–8 AM
        Sat Noon–Mon 8 AM
        Holidays 24 hours
(Day use: Auburn Veterinary Hospital,
    253–833–4510)

Bellevue   425–641–8414
After Hours Animal Emergency Clinic
2975 156th St SE
        Mon–Fri 6 PM–8 AM
        Sat Noon–Mon 8 AM
        Holidays 24 hours
(Day use: Arrowwood Animal Hospital,
    425–746–6557)

Everett   425–258–4466
Animal Emergency Clinic of Everett
3625 Rucker Ave
        Mon–Fri 6 PM–8 AM
        Sat 1 PM–Mon 8 AM
        Holidays 24 hours
(Day use: Diamond Veterinary Hospital,
    425–252–1106)

B: Emergency Clinics

Issaquah 425–392–8888
Alpine Animal Hospital
888 NW Sammamish Rd
      24 hours/day, 365 days/year

Kennewick 509–783–7391
Mid–Columbia Pet Emergency Service
8620 W Gage Blvd
      Mon–Thur 5:30 PM–8 AM
      Fri 5:30 PM–Mon 8 AM
      Holidays 24 hrs
(Day use: Meadow Hills Veterinary Center,
      509–783–0399)

Lynnwood 425–745–6745
Animal Emergency Service
19511 24th Ave W
      Mon–Thur 6 PM–8 AM
      Fri 6 PM–Mon 8 AM
      Holidays 24 hours
(Day use: Alderwood Companion Animal Hospital,
      425–775–7655)

Olympia 360–709–0108
Olympia Pet Emergency Clinic
1602 Harrison Ave NW
      Mon–Fri 6 PM–7:30 AM
      Sat Noon–Mon 7:30 AM
      Note: Please call ahead!
(Day use: West Olympia Pet Hospital,
      360–352–4414)

Have Dog Will Travel—Washington Edition

Poulsbo 206–842–6684
Animal Emergency & Trauma Center
Poulsbo Village Shopping Center
>Mon–Fri 5 PM–8:30 AM
>Sat Noon–Mon 8:30 AM
>Holidays 24 hours

Additional local phone lines: 895–8050, 697–7771

Poulsbo 360–692–6162
Animal Hospital of Central Kitsap
10310 Central Valley Rd NE
>24 hours/day, 365 days/year

Close to Silverdale & Bremerton, call for directions

Seattle 206–634–9000
Emerald City Emergency Clinic
4102 Stone Way North
>Mon–Fri 6 PM–8 AM
>Sat Noon–Mon 8 AM
>Holidays 24 hours

(Day use: Animal Surgical Clinic of Seattle,
    206–545–4322)

Snohomish 360–563–5300
Small Animal Emergency Clinic of PSCVM
11308 92nd SE
>Mon–Fri 6 PM–8 AM
>Sat Noon–Mon 8 AM
>Holidays 24 hours

(Day use: Pilchuck Veterinary Hospital,
    360–568–3113)

B: Emergency Clinics

Spokane   509–326–6670
Pet Emergency Clinic
21 East Mission Ave
>Mon–Fri 5 PM–8 AM
>Fri 5 PM–Mon 8 AM
>Holidays 24 hours
(Day use: Veterinary Referral Service,
509–324–0055)

Tacoma   253–474–0791
Pierce County Animal Emergency Clinic
5608 S Durango
>Mon–Thur 6 PM–7:30 AM
>Fri 6 PM–Mon 7:30 AM
>Holidays 24 hours

Tacoma   253–983–1000
Puget Sound Pet Pavilion
2505 S 80th St
>24 hours/day, 365 days/year

Vancouver   360–694–3007
Emergency Veterinary Service, Inc.
6818 E 4th Plain Blvd Ste C
>Mon–Thur 5:30 PM–8 AM
>Fri 5:30 PM–Mon 8 AM
>Holidays 24 hours

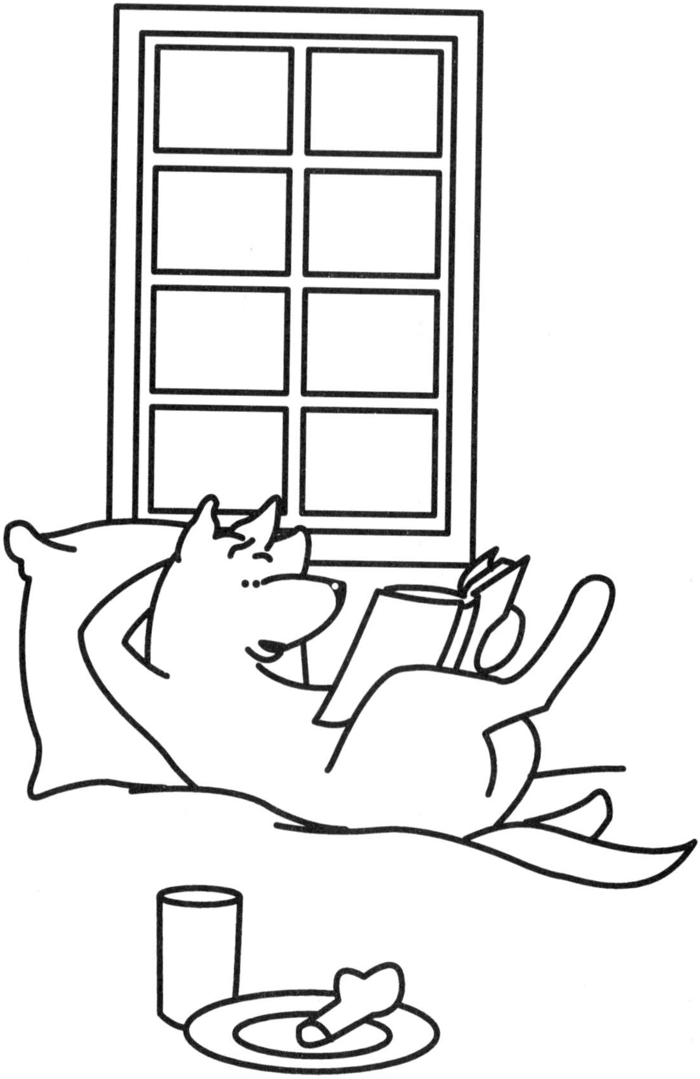

C: Some Useful Books

During the writing of this book, I discovered a number of other useful volumes about dogs. Their topics range from dog training to first aid procedures to why your best pal thinks like a dog instead of a human. To learn more, check these books out—you'll find a wealth of information just waiting for you at the library or bookstore.

Here are some personal favorites:

ASPCA Complete Dog Care Manual by Bruce Fogle, D.V.M. This oversized book is full of photographs that beautifully illustrate dog behavior, body language, training methods, and first aid techniques.

Dogs & Kids, Parenting Tips by Bardi McLennan. Lots of helpful information for integrating a dog—and especially a puppy—into your family. Includes some great insights into solving or preventing common behavior problems.

Have Dog Will Travel—Washington Edition

Dogs and the Law by Anmarie Barrie, Esq. This slim volume will give you a real education on your rights and responsibilities as a dog owner.

Dr. Jim's Animal Clinic for Dogs by Jim Humphries, D.V.M. Written in the form of questions and answers from the author's talk radio show. Humorous style makes this book easy to read as well as informative.

Dr. Pitcairn's Complete Guide to Natural Health for Dogs & Cats by Richard H. Pitcairn, D.V.M., Ph.D. and Susan Hubble Pitcairn. This is one volume that is used *a lot* in our household. Full of information about how important a nutritious diet is for your pet's lifelong health, it even includes recipes for preparing nutritionally balanced dog food, whether you are dealing with pet allergies or just want to explore alternatives to commercial dog chow. Also includes an extensive reference section on common health problems as well as medical emergencies.

I Just Got a Puppy. What Do I Do? by Mordecai Siegal and Matthew Margolis. Zeroes right in on what the new owner of a puppy needs to do, know, provide, and train to bring up your new "baby."

The Canine Good Citizen by Jack and Wendy Volhard. The authors' training methods are based on understanding how your dog views the world: what factors motivate him to either good or bad behavior, and how you can steer him toward the behavior you want.

C: Some Useful Books

The Dog Care Book by Sheldon L. Gerstenfeld, V.M.D. This medical reference book includes a wonderfully clear set of diagnostic charts that help you determine whether your dog's emergency situation is minor, serious, or life-threatening—and what to do about it.

The Home Pet Vet Guide—Dogs by Martin I. Green. Another great guide to emergency first aid procedures, organized alphabetically by topic. Clear line drawings and concise instructions tell you exactly what you need to know when dealing with a medical crisis.

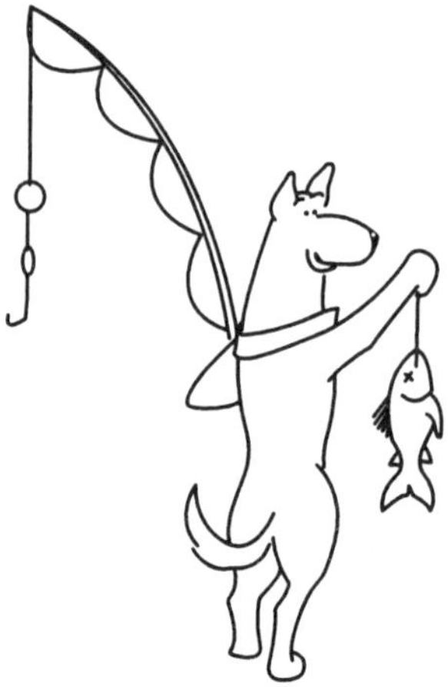

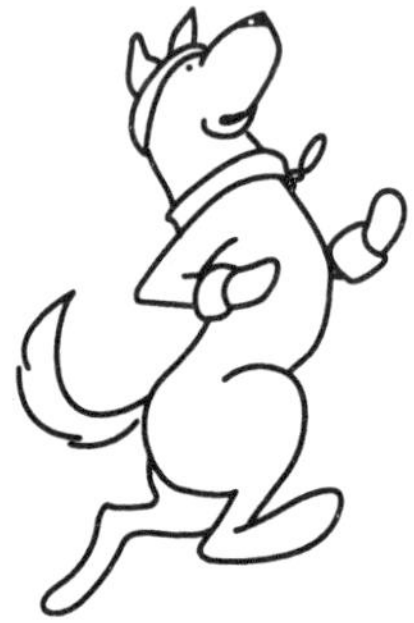

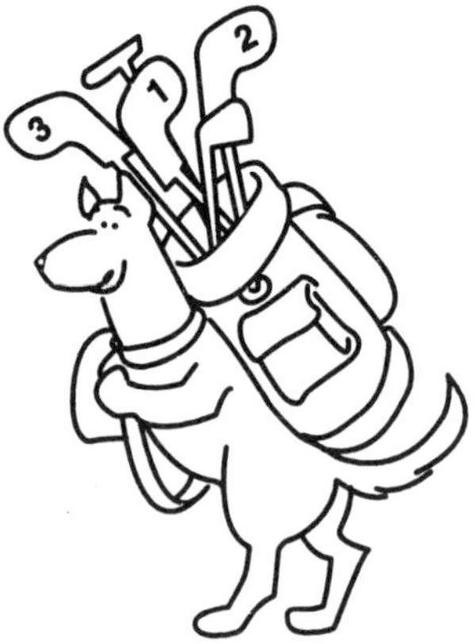
3
1
2

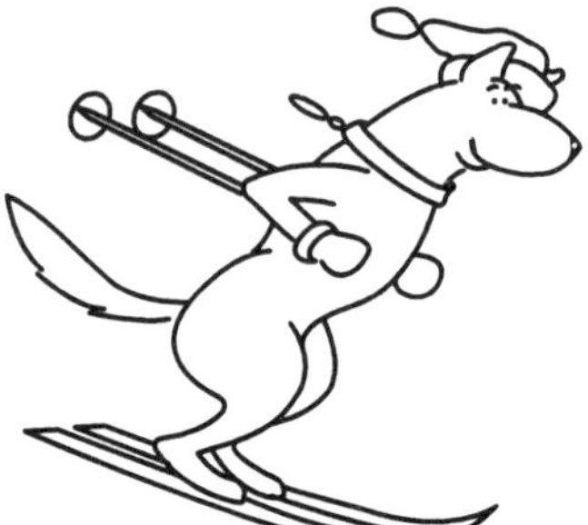

D: Listings Index

The following list contains the same entries shown in the main directory on pp. 89–261, but this time they are sorted alphabetically by business name—in case you know the name of a particular establishment but aren't sure in exactly which city it is located.

Numbers
49er Motel & RV Park, Chewelah 112
7 West Motel, Castle Rock 110

A
A & H Motel, Walla Walla 246
A Cab in the Woods, Rockport 204
A-View Mobile Home Park, Clallam Bay 114
Acorn Motor Inn, Oak Harbor 176
Airport Motel, Pasco 188
Airport Plaza Hotel, Seattle 206
Ala Cozy Motel, Coulee City 120

Aladdin Motor Inn, Port Townsend 194
Alaskan Motel, Westport 250
Alexis Hotel, Seattle 206
Alice Bay Bed & Breakfast, Bow 108
Aloha Motel, Bellingham 104
Alpen Inn, Leavenworth 154
Alpine Chalets, Leavenworth 154
Alpine Rivers Inn, Leavenworth 154
Amanda Park Motel & Rv Park, Amanda Park 96
Anaco Inn, Anacortes 96
Anacortes Inn, Anacortes 98
Anchorage Cottages, Long Beach 158
Andre Court, Clallam Bay 114
Angel Cottage B & B, Langley 152
Angels of the Sea B & B, Vashon Island 244
Annapurna Inn & Spa, Port Townsend 194
Anthony's Home Court Motel, Long Beach 158
Arlington Motor Inn, Arlington 100
Art's Place B & B, La Conner 150
Aster Inn, Cle Elum 114
Astor Motel, Clarkston 114
Aurora Seafair Inn, Seattle 206
Avenue Motel, Wenatchee 248

B

Bagby's Town Motel, Forks 134
Bailey Motor Inn, Olympia 182
Bainbridge House, Bainbridge Island 100
Bali Hai Motel, Yakima 256
Bali Hi Motel, Richland 202
Barchris Motel, Goldendale 140

D: Listings Index

Barn Motor Inn, Prosser 196
Barnacle Motel, Moclips 166
Barney's Cafe & Motel, Kettle Falls 150
Bartwood Lodge, Eastsound 124
Bay Motel & Marina, Sekiu 214
Bayside Motor Inn, Blaine 106
BB Border Inn, Sumas 234
Beach Cabin, Langley 152
Beach Front Vacation Rentals, Ocean Shores 178
Beach It Rentals, Long Beach 158
Beachfront Mobile Homes, Chelan 112
Beachwood Resort, Copalis Beach 120
Beaver Lodge Resort, Colville 116
Bedfinders, Leavenworth 154
Bel-Air Motel, Spokane 222
Belfair Motel, Belfair 102
Bell Motel, Spokane 222
Benny's Colville Inn, Colville 118
Best Inn & Suites, Ritzville 204
Best Inn & Suites, Spokane 222, 224
Best Inn & Suites, Vancouver 242
Best Western Aladdin Motor Inn, Kelso 144
Best Western Aladdin Motor Inn, Olympia 182
Best Western Baron Inn, Monroe 166
Best Western Cascade Inn, Winthrop 254
Best Western College Way Inn, Mount Vernon 172
Best Western Cottontree Inn, Mount Vernon 172
Best Western Executel, Federal Way 130
Best Western Executive Inn-Fife, Tacoma 234
Best Western Ferryman's Inn, Vancouver 242
Best Western Hallmark Inn, Moses Lake 168

Best Western Harbor Plaza, Oak Harbor 176
Best Western Heritage Inn, Kent 148
Best Western Kennewick Inn, Kennewick 146
Best Western Kirkland Inn, Kirkland 150
Best Western Lakeside Lodge, Chelan 112
Best Western Lakeway Inn, Bellingham 104
Best Western Lakewood Motor Inn, Lakewood 152
Best Western Lincoln Inn, Othello 186
Best Western Lynnwood/N Seattle, Lynnwood 164
Best Western Oxford Inn, Yakima 256
Best Western Oxford Suites, Yakima 258
Best Western Park Center Hotel, Enumclaw 128
Best Western Park Plaza, Puyallup 198
Best Western Peppertree Airport Inn, Spokane 224
Best Western Peppertree Yakima Inn, Yakima 258
Best Western Pheasant Hill, Spokane 224
Best Western Prosser Inn, Prosser 196
Best Western Sequim Bay Lodge, Sequim 216
Best Western Shores Motel, Grayland 142
Best Western Southcenter, Tukwila 240
Best Western Summit Inn, Snoqualmie Pass 220
Best Western Tacoma Inn, Tacoma 234
Best Western Thunderbird Inn, Spokane 224
Best Western Tower Inn, Richland 202
Best Western Trade Winds North, Spokane 224
Best Western Tulalip Inn, Marysville 164
Best Western Tumwater Inn, Tumwater 240
Best Western Walla Walla Suites Inn, Walla Walla 246
Best Western Wesley Inn, Gig Harbor 138
Betty MacDonald Farm B & B, Vashon Island 244
Bev's Beach Bungalow, Seaview 214

D: Listings Index

Birch Bay Vacation Rental Cottages, Blaine 106
Birchfield Manor, Yakima 258
Bishop Victorian Guest Suites, Port Townsend 194
Black Beach Resort, Republic 200
Blair House Bed & Breakfast, Friday Harbor 136
Blue Lake Resort, Coulee City 120
Blue Mountain Motel, Dayton 122
Blue Pacific Motel & RV Park, Ocean City 176
Blue Spruce Motel, Tacoma 234
Blue Top Motel & RV Park, Coulee City 120
Blue Willow Bed & Breakfast, Seattle 206
Boggan's Oasis, Anatone 98
Boulevard Motel, Long Beach 158
Box Canyon Resort & Motel, Ione 144
Breakers Motel, Long Beach 160
Breakers Motel, Westport 252
Brewster Motel, Brewster 108
Bridge Motel, Seattle 208
Brigadoon Bed & Breakfast, Sequim 216
Brightwater House B & B, Forks 134
B's Getaway B & B, Clinton 116
Budget Inn, Kelso 144
Budget Inn, Longview 162
Budget Inn-South, Tacoma 236
Budget Saver Motel, Spokane 224

C

C B's Motel, Easton 124
C-View Resort, Sekiu 216
Cabana Motel, Othello 186
Camaray Motel, Oroville 184

Canal Side Resort & Motel, Shelton 218
Cape Motel & RV Park, Neah Bay 174
Capri Motel, Walla Walla 246
Carson Mineral Hot Springs Resort, Carson 110
Carstens Bed & Breakfast, Pullman 196
Cascade Inn, Bellingham 104
Cascade Mountain Inn, Cle Elum 114
Cavanaugh's at Capital 8, Olympia 182
Cavanaugh's At Columbia Ctr, Kennewick 146
Cavanaughs At Yakima Ctr, Yakima 258
Cavanaugh's Fourth Avenue, Spokane 224
Cavanaughs Gateway Hotel, Yakima 258
Cavanaugh's Inn at the Park, Spokane 224
Cavanaugh's On Fifth Avenue, Seattle 208
Cavanaugh's Resident Court, Spokane 224
Cavanaugh's Ridpath Hotel, Spokane 224
Cavanaugh's River Inn, Spokane 226
Cedar House Inn B & B, Point Roberts 190
Cedar Village Motel, Spokane 226
Cedars Inn, East Wenatchee 124
Center Lodge Motel, Grand Coulee 140
Centralia Travelodge, Centralia 110
Chalet Motel, Cle Elum 116
Chalet Village, Ocean Shores 178
Chautauqua Lodge Resort, Long Beach 160
Chieftain Motel, Bremerton 108
Childs' House, Olalla 182
Chinook Motel, Port Angeles 190
Chopaka Lodge, Loomis 162
Cimarron Motel, Silverdale 220
Circle H Holiday Ranch, Tacoma 238

D: Listings Index

Circle Motel, Metaline Falls 166
City Center Best Rates Motel, Shelton 218
City Center Motel, Bingen 106
City Center Motel, Marysville 164
City Center Motel, Walla Walla 246
Clark's Cabins & Resort, Rockport 204
Cle Elum Travelodge Inn, Cle Elum 116
Clinic Center Motel, Spokane 226
Coachman Inn Motel, Bellingham 104
Coastal Cottages of Ocean Park, Ocean Park 178
Cobblestone Bakery B & B Inn, Spokane 226
Coho Charters Motel & Rv Park, Westport 252
Colonial Motel, Lakewood 152
Colonial Motel, Walla Walla 246
Columbia Motor Inn, Kennewick 146
Columbia-Pacific Motel, Ilwaco 142
Colwell Motor Inn, Ritzville 204
Comfort Inn, Auburn 100
Comfort Inn, Colville 118
Comfort Inn, Ellensburg 126
Comfort Inn, Federal Way 130
Comfort Inn, Kennewick 146
Comfort Inn, Kent 148
Comfort Inn, Mount Vernon 172
Comfort Inn, Tacoma 236
Comfort Inn, Zillah 260
Comfort Inn-Columbia River, Wenatchee 248
Comfort Inn-North, Spokane 226
Comfort Inn-Valley, Spokane 226
Comfort Suites, Yakima 258
Conconully Motel, Conconully 118

Corporate Suites, Tacoma 236
Coulee House Motel, Coulee Dam 120
Country Bed & Breakfast, Pullman 196
Country Inn, Spokane 226
Country Man Bed & Breakfast, Snohomish 220
Cranberry Motel & RV Park, Westport 252
Crowne Plaza Hotel, Seattle 208

D
Davenport Motel, Davenport 122
Days Inn, Bellingham 104
Days Inn, Centralia 110
Days Inn, Mount Vernon 172
Days Inn, Tacoma 236
Days Inn-Fife, Tacoma 236
Days Inn-South Seattle, Kent 148
Days Inn-Spokane Airport, Spokane 226
Days Inn-Yakima, Union Gap 240
Dayton Motel, Dayton 122
De Koeyer Hot Tub Cabins, Union 240
Deer Harbor Inn, Deer Harbor 124
Deer Meadows Motel, Davenport 122
Der Ritterhof Motor Inn, Leavenworth 156
Dew Drop Inn, Forks 134
Dibble House B & B, Seattle 208
Discovery Inn Condominium, Ocean Shores 180
Discovery Inn, Friday Harbor 136
Doe Bay Village Resort, Olga 182
Doubletree Hotel Bellevue Ctr, Bellevue 102
Doubletree Hotel, Kelso 146
Doubletree Hotel, Pasco 188

D: Listings Index

Doubletree Hotel, Wenatchee 248
Doubletree Hotel-Seattle Airport, Seattle 208
Doubletree Hotel-Spokane City Ctr, Spokane 226
Doubletree Hotel-Spokane Valley, Spokane 226
Doubletree Hotel-Yakima Valley, Yakima 258
Downtown Motel, Colville 118
Drake's Landing, Langley 152
Driftwood Inn Resort Motel, Birch Bay 106
Duck Brand Hotel & Restaurant, Winthrop 254
Dunes Motel, Bremerton 108
Dungeness Bay Motel, Sequim 216
Dutch Cup Motel, Sultan 234

E
Eagle's Nest Alder Lake Motel, Eatonville 126
East Wenatchee Motor Inn, East Wenatchee 124
Eastgate Motel, Spokane 228
Econo Lodge, Fife 132
Econo Lodge, Sequim 216
Economy Inn, Wenatchee 248
Edgewater Inn, Long Beach 160
Edmonds Harbor Inn, Edmonds 126
Eight Bar B Motel, Wilbur 254
El Corral Motel, Toppenish 238
Elwha Resort, Port Angeles 190
Emerald Isle Guest House, Vashon Island 244
Empire Motel, Ritzville 204
Enchanted B & B, Freeland 136
Entiat Valley Motel, Entiat 128
Everett Inn, Everett 128
Everett/Broadway Travelodge, Everett 128

Evergreen Motel, Morton 168
Evergreen Motor Inn, Leavenworth 156
Executive Inn Express, Ferndale 132

F
Fairgrounds Inn, Monroe 168
Ferryman's Inn, Centralia 110
Forks Motel, Forks 134
Fort Clarke Motel, Lakewood 152
Four Seasons Olympic Hotel, Seattle 208
Frank L Motel & Aquatic Gardens, Westport 252
Fraternity Snoqualmie Park, Issaquah 144
Frontier Inn Motel, Republic 202

G
Gallery Suite B & B, Langley 154
Game Ridge Motel, Rimrock 204
Garden of Angels Guest House, Freeland 136
Gibson's North Fork Lodge, Conconully 118
Gig Harbor Motor Inn, Gig Harbor 138
Glacier Creek Lodge, Glacier 140
Golden Kent Motel, Kent 148
Golden Key Motel, Clarkston 114
Golden Spur Motor Inn, Newport 174
Grand Mound Motel, Centralia 110
Grandview Inn Motel & RV Park, Kettle Falls 150
Grandview Motel, Grandview 140
Grandview Orchard Inn B & B, Cashmere 110
Grayland Bed & Breakfast, Grayland 142
Grays Harbor Hostel, Elma 128
Greathouse Motel, Sequim 216

D: Listings Index

Green Gables Motel, Kennewick 146
Grey Gull Motel, Ocean Shores 180
Groveland Cottage B & B, Sequim 216
Guemes Island Resort, Anacortes 98
Guest House Motel, Vancouver 242
Guesthouse Inn, Port Orchard 194

H

H & H Motel, South Bend 222
Hampton Inn, Spokane 228
Hanford Castle B & B, Oakesdale 176
Harbinger Inn B & B, Olympia 184
Harbor House Bed & Breakfast, Blaine 106
Harbor Lights, Ilwaco 144
Harbor Resort, Westport 252
Harborside Inn, Port Townsend 194
Harbour Inn Motel, Freeland 136
Harrison House Suites, Friday Harbor 138
Hartman's Log Cabin Resort, Inchelium 144
Hawthorn Inn & Suites, Pullman 196
Hawthorn Inn & Suites, Wenatchee 250
Hawthorne Inn & Suites, Seattle 208
Hawthorne Inn & Suites, Walla Walla 246
Heidi's Inn, Ilwaco 144
Herb's Motel & Charters, Sekiu 216
Heritage Suites, Moses Lake 168
Heron Beach Inn On Ludlow Bay, Port Ludlow 194
Hi-Tide Ocean Beach Resort, Moclips 166
Highland House, Clarkston 114
Hill Crest Motel, Wenatchee 250
Hillside Motel, Mount Vernon 172

Hilton-Seattle Airport, Seattle 208
Historic Lake Crescent Lodge, Port Angeles 190
Historic Sou'wester Lodge, Seaview 214
Hoh Humm Ranch, Forks 134
Holiday Inn Express, Bellingham 104
Holiday Inn Express, Kennewick 146
Holiday Inn Express, Longview 162
Holiday Inn Express, Moses Lake 168
Holiday Inn Express, Pullman 196
Holiday Inn Express, Yakima 258
Holiday Inn Express-Spokane Vly, Spokane 228
Holiday Inn-SeaTac, Seattle 208
Holiday Lodge, Wenatchee 250
Holiday Motel, Anacortes 98
Holly Motel, Olympia 184
Home By The Sea Cottages, Clinton 116
Homestead Guest Studios, Bellevue 102
Homestead Guest Studios, Mountlake Terrace 174
Homestead Village Guest Studios, Bellevue 102
Homestead Village Guest Studios, Tukwila 240
Hometel Inn, Fife 132
Homewood Suites Hotel, Seattle 208
Homewood Suites, Vancouver 242
Homewood Suites-Tukwila, Seattle 210
Hotel Monaco, Seattle 210
Hotel Packwood, Packwood 186
Hotel Usk, Usk 242
Howard Johnson, Auburn 100
Howard Johnson, Chehalis 112
Howard Johnson Express Inn, Walla Walla 246
Howard Johnson Inn, Kent 148

D: Listings Index

Howard Johnson Inn-Downtown, Spokane 228
Howard Johnson, SeaTac 206
Hudgens Haven, Edmonds 126
Hudson Hotel, Longview 162
Hudson Manor Motel, Longview 162
Hueter Haus, Camano Island 110
Hummingbird Inn, Roslyn 206

I

Idle-A-While Motel, Twisp 240
Illahee Manor, Bremerton 108
IMA El Rancho Motel, Moses Lake 168
Imperial Inn, Moses Lake 170
Indian Valley Motel & RV Park, Port Angeles 190
Inn at Burg's Landing B & B, Anderson Island 98
Inn At Friday Harbor, Friday Harbor 138
Inn At Gig Harbor, Gig Harbor 138
Inn at Moses Lake, Moses Lake 170
Inn At Port Gardner, Everett 130
Inn at Snohomish, Snohomish 220
Inn Vienna Woods B & B, Leavenworth 156
Interstate Inn, Moses Lake 170
Inverness Inn, Langley 154
Ione Motel & Trailer Park, Ione 144
Iron Springs Ocean Beach Resort, Copalis Beach 120
Island Country Inn, Bainbridge Island 100
Island Tyme Bed & Breakfast, Langley 154
Islands Inn, Anacortes 98

J

Jack's RV Park & Motel, Conconully 118

Jameson Lake Resort North End, Mansfield 164
Jerry's Landing Resort, Elk 126
Juan De Fuca Cottages, Sequim 218
Jump Off Joe Lake Resort, Valley 242

K
K & E Motor Inn, Edmonds 126
K-Diamond-K Guest Ranch, Republic 202
Kalaloch Lodge, Forks 134
Kelly's Resort, Chelan 112
Ken's Kourt Motel, Westport 252
Kettle Falls Inn, Kettle Falls 150
King City Truck Stop, Pasco 188
King's Arms Motel, Seattle 210
King's Motel, Enumclaw 128
Kings Motor Inn, Fife 132
Kinney Suites, Leavenworth 156
Klondike Motel, Republic 202
Kozy Kabins & RV Park, Conconully 118
Krebs Mansion B & B, Sultan 234

L
La Casa Motel, Union Gap 242
La Conner Country Inn, La Conner 150
La Push Ocean Park Resort, La Push 152
La Quinta Inn, Kirkland 150
La Quinta Inn, Seattle 210
La Quinta Inn, Tacoma 236
La Residence Suite Hotel, Bellevue 102
Lake Campbell Lodging, Anacortes 98
Lake Mayfield Motel, Silver Creek 220

D: Listings Index

Lake Motel, Soap Lake 220
Lake Nahwatzel Resort, Shelton 218
Lake Pateros Motor Inn, Pateros 190
Lake Quinault Lodge, Quinault 198
Lake Wenatchee Hide-A-Ways, Leavenworth 156
Lakeshore Resort Motel, Moses Lake 170
Lakeside Motel, Loon Lake 164
Lakeside Motel, Woodland 256
Lantern Park Motel, Airway Heights 96
Lariat Motel, Ephrata 128
Last Resort, Roslyn 206
Leavenworth Village Inn, Leavenworth 156
Lee Street Suites, Tumwater 240
Leirvangen Bed & Breakfast, Leavenworth 156
Lewis River Inn, Woodland 256
Lighthouse Motel, Long Beach 160
Linda's Low Tide Motel, Copalis Beach 120
Llama Ranch Bed & Breakfast, White Salmon 254
Lochaerie Resort, Amanda Park 96
Log Cabin Resort, Port Angeles 192
Love's Victorian B & B, Deer Park 124
Lyles Motel, Wenatchee 250

M

M & M Motel, Connell 118
Mac's Motel, Bellingham 104
Madigan Motel, Lakewood 152
Main Stay B & B, Coulee City 120
Manitou Lodge B & B, Forks 134
Manor Inn & Inside Out, La Conner 150
Manor Lodge Motel, Pullman 198

Maple Grove Motel, Quilcene 198
Maple Tree Motel, Spokane 228
Maples Motel, Moses Lake 170
Mariners Cove Inn, Westport 252
Marriott Seattle Sea Tac, Seattle 210
Marshall Lake Resort, Newport 176
Maunu Mountcastle Motel, Raymond 200
Mazama Country Inn, Mazama 166
Mc Bee's Silver Sands Motel, Westport 252
Medici Motel & Campground, Randle 200
Microtell Inn & Suites, Auburn 100
Midway Inn, Bremerton 108
Mike's Beach Resort, Lilliwaup 158
Mill Creek Inn, Forks 134
Miller Tree Inn, Forks 134
Mini-Rate Motel, SeaTac 206
Moby Dick Hotel, Nahcotta 174
Moclips Motel, Moclips 166
Monarch Manor Rentals–B&B, Bainbridge Island 102
Monte Square Motel, Montesano 168
Moses Lake Travelodge, Moses Lake 170
Mossyrock Inn, Mossyrock 172
Motel 6, Bellingham 104
Motel 6, Centralia 112
Motel 6, Clarkston 114
Motel 6, Kelso 146
Motel 6, Kirkland 150
Motel 6, Moses Lake 170
Motel 6, Pasco 188
Motel 6, Richland 202
Motel 6, Spokane 228

D: Listings Index

Motel 6, Tacoma 236
Motel 6, Tumwater 240
Motel 6, Yakima 258
Motel 6-Everett North, Everett 130
Motel 6-Everett South, Everett 130
Motel 6-SeaTac Airport, Seattle 210
Motel 6-SeaTac South, Seattle 210
Motel 6-Seattle South, Seattle 210
Motel 6-Tacoma/Fife, Fife 132
Motel International, Blaine 106
Motel Nicholas, Omak 184
Motel Puyallup, Puyallup 198
Mount Adams Motel & RV Park, Randle 200
Mount Valley Vista B & B, Peshastin 190
Mountain View Cedar Lodge, Eatonville 126
Mountain View Inn, Granite Falls 142
Mountain View Lodge, Packwood 186
Mt Baker Chalet, Glacier 140
Mt Si Motel, North Bend 176
Mt View Inn, Buckley 110
Mystery Manor B & B, Yakima 258

N

Natapoc Lodging, Leavenworth 156
Natchez Hotel, Naches 174
Nautilus Hotel, Ocean Shores 180
Nendels Inn, Auburn 100
Nendels Inn, Kennewick 146
Nendels Inn, Pullman 198
Nendels Inn, Yakima 260
New Horizon Motel, Federal Way 130

Newport City Inn, Newport 176
Nites Inn Motel, Ellensburg 128
No Cabbages' Bed & Breakfast, Gig Harbor 138
Nordic Inn Motel, Aberdeen 96
Nordlig Motel, Chewelah 114
North Beach Inn, Eastsound 124
North Beach Motel, Ocean City 176
North Shore Cottages, Eastsound 126
Northern Inn, Republic 202
Northwest Motor Inn, Puyallup 198
Notaras Lodge, Soap Lake 222

O
Oasis Budget Inn, Moses Lake 170
Obertal Motor Inn, Leavenworth 156
Ocean Avenue Inn, Westport 252
Ocean Crest Bed & Breakfast, Port Angeles 192
Ocean Crest Resort, Moclips 166
Ocean Lodge, Long Beach 160
Ocean Park Resort, Ocean Park 178
Ocean Shores Motel, Ocean Shores 180
Ocean Spray Motel, Grayland 142
Ocean View Resort Homes, Ocean Shores 180
Odessa Motel, Odessa 182
Okanogan Cedars Inn, Okanogan 182
Old Alcohol Plant Lodge & Marina, Port Hadlock 192
Old Brook Inn B & B, Anacortes 98
Old Tjomsland House B & B, Vashon Island 246
Olde Glencove Hotel B & B, Gig Harbor 140
Olson's Vacation Cabins, Forks 136
Olympic Inn Motel, Aberdeen 96

D: Listings Index

Olympic Suites, Forks 136
Omak Inn, Omak 184
Omak Rodeway Inn & Suites, Omak 184
Orchard Inn, Wenatchee 250
Oslo's Bed & Breakfast, Spokane 228
Our Place At The Beach, Long Beach 160
Ovenell's Heritage Inn B & B, Concrete 118
Oxbow Motor Inn, Toppenish 238
Oyster Bay Inn, Bremerton 108

P

Pacific Motel & RV Park, Westport 252
Pacific Sands, Ocean City 176
Pacific View Motel, Long Beach 160
Palace Hotel, Port Townsend 194
Pargardens Bed & Breakfast, Seattle 210
Park Lane Motel Suites & RV Pk, Spokane 228
Park Motel, Centralia 112
Parkhurst Motel, Elma 128
Paulson's Play House, Ocean Park 178
Pend O'reille Apts/Historic Miners Hotel, Metaline Falls 166
Pensione Nichols, Seattle 210
Peppertree West Motor Inn, Centralia 112
Peters Inn, Packwood 186
Phippen's Bed & Breakfast, Leavenworth 156
Pine Cottage B & B, Langley 154
Pine Point Resort, Republic 202
Pioneer Motel, Pomeroy 190
Plum Tree Motel & Apt Rentals, Montesano 168
Point Hudson Resort, Port Townsend 194

Polynesian Resort, Ocean Shores 180
Pond Motel, Port Angeles 192
Ponderosa Motel, Goldendale 140
Ponderosa Motor Lodge, Okanogan 182
Portside Inn, Port Angeles 192
Poulsbo Inn, Port Townsend 196
Prairie Hotel, Yelm 260
Primrose Path Cottage, Langley 154
Prosser Motel, Prosser 196
Puget View Guesthouse B & B, Olympia 184
Purple House Bed & Breakfast, Dayton 122
Purple Sage Motel, Sprague 232

Q
Quality Inn of Lakewood/Tacoma, Tacoma 236
Quality Inn Paradise Creek, Pullman 198
Quality Inn Valley Suites, Spokane 228
Quality Inn, Vancouver 242
Quality Inn, Yakima 260
Quality Inn-Baron Suites, Bellingham 104
Quilcene Hotel, Quilcene 198

R
Rabbit On The Green B & B, Langley 154
Rainbow Beach Resort, Inchelium 144
Rama Inn, Washougal 248
Ramada Inn, Des Moines 124
Ramada Inn, Seattle 212
Ramada Inn-Clover Island, Kennewick 148
Ramada Inn-Spokane Airport, Spokane 230
Ramada Inn-Tacoma Dome, Tacoma 236

D: Listings Index

Ramada Limited Suites, Spokane 230
Ramada Ltd, Spokane 230
Ranch Motel, Spokane 230
Rancho Lamro B & B, Sequim 218
Red Apple Inn, Oroville 186
Red Apple Inn, Tonasket 238
Red Apple Motel, Yakima 260
Red Carpet Motor Inn, Yakima 260
Red Lion Hotel at the Quay, Vancouver 242
Red Lion Hotel, Port Angeles 192
Red Lion Hotel, Richland 202
Red Lion Inn, Aberdeen 96
Red Ranch Inn, Sequim 218
Red Top Motel & Apartments, Spokane 230
Remax San Juan Island Vacation Rentals, Friday Harbor 138
Residence Inn by Marriott, Bellevue 102
Residence Inn by Marriott, Bothell 108
Residence Inn by Marriott, Lynnwood 164
Residence Inn by Marriott, Seattle 212
Residence Inn by Marriott, Vancouver 244
Residence Inn by Marriott-South, Seattle 212
Rest Full Farm B & B, Shelton 218
Reynold's Resort, Nespelem 174
Richland Hampton Inn, Richland 202
River Run Inn, Winthrop 254
River's Edge Lodge, Leavenworth 158
Riverside Motel, Vancouver 244
Roadrunner Truckers Motel, Federal Way 130
Rockcreek Manor B & B, Rockford 204
Rodeway Inn & Suites, Leavenworth 158

Rodeway Inn, Bellingham 104
Rodeway Inn, Lynnwood 164
Rodeway Inn-SeaTac, Seattle 212
Rose Cottage, Seaview 214
Rose Motel, Lynnwood 164
Rosebrook Inn, Cheney 112
Roslyn Inns, Roslyn 206
Royal Arms Apartments & Motel, Seattle 212
Royal Coachman Motor Inn, Fife 132
Royal Motel, Omak 184
Royal Motor Inn, Everett 130
Royal Scot Motel, Spokane 230
Royal View Motel, Soap Lake 222
Russell House B & B, South Bend 222

S
Sage 'n' Sand Motel, Moses Lake 170
Sage 'n Sun Motel, Pasco 188
Saimons Hide-A-Ways, Leavenworth 158
Salish Lodge and Spa, Snoqualmie 220
San Juan Motel, Anacortes 98
Sand Dollar Inn, Pacific Beach 186
Sandpiper Beach Resort, Pacific Beach 186
Sands Motel & Rv Park, Westport 254
Sands Motel, Long Beach 160
Sands Resort, Ocean Shores 180
Sands Royal Pacific Motel, Ocean Shores 180
Sandstone Motel, Hoquiam 142
Scandia Motel, Woodland 256
Scottish Lodge Motel, Ferndale 132
Sea Nest in Long Beach, Ocean Park 178

D: Listings Index

Seagull's Nest Motel, Westport 254
Seaquest Motel & Apartments, South Bend 222
Seasons Motel, Morton 168
Seattle North Travelodge, Edmonds 126
Seaview CoHo Motel, Seaview 214
Seaview Motel & RV Park, Seaview 214
Select Inn Tiki Lodge, Spokane 230
Serenity Pines Waterfront Cottages, Freeland 136
Settle Inn Motel, Wilbur 254
Shafer-Baillie Mansion, Seattle 212
Shakti Cove Cottages, Ocean Park 178
Shalimar Suites, Tumwater 240
Shaman Motel, Long Beach 160
Shangri-La Downtown Motel, Bellingham 106
Shangri-La Motel, Spokane 230
Shaniko Suites Motel, Kennewick 148
Shelton Inn, Shelton 218
Sheraton Tacoma Hotel, Tacoma 236
Sherwood Inn, Tacoma 238
Shilo Conference Hotel, Richland 204
Shilo Inn, Moses Lake 170
Shilo Inn, Spokane 230
Shilo Inn, Tacoma 238
Shilo Inn-Downtown, Vancouver 244
Shilo Inn-Hazel Dell/Vancouver, Vancouver 244
Ship Harbor Inn, Anacortes 98
Shipwreck Motel, Westport 254
Shore Line Motel, Pacific Beach 186
Shoreline Motel, Shoreline 220
Shoreline Resort, La Push 152
Sicyon Gallery B & B, Walla Walla 248

Silver King Motel, Ocean Shores 180
Silver Lake Motel & Resort, Silver Lake 220
Silver Moon Resort, Belfair 102
Skagit Motel, Sedro Woolley 214
Sky River Inn, Skykomish 220
Skyline Motel, Spokane 230
Slater Heritage House B & B, Ferndale 132
Sleepy Hollow Motel, Naselle 174
Smiley's Colonial Motel, Kingston 150
Smokey Point Motor Inn, Arlington 100
Snug Harbor Marina Resort, Friday Harbor 138
Solar World Estates Motel Alternative,
    Airway Heights 96
Solar World Estates Motel Alternative, Spokane 232
South Fork Moorage House Boat, Conway 120
Spectacle Falls Resort, Tonasket 238
Spokane Apple Tree Inn, Spokane 232
Spokane House, Spokane 232
Spokane Travelodge, Spokane 232
Sportsman Motel, Twisp 240
Sportsmen Motel, Port Angeles 192
Spring Inn, Leavenworth 158
Stagecoach Inn, Darrington 122
Stagecoach Inn, Fife 134
Stampede Motel, Omak 184
Starlite Motel, Pasco 188
Starlite Motel, Spokane 232
Starlite Motel, Wenatchee 250
Stewart Lodge, Cle Elum 116
Still Waters Bed & Breakfast, Olalla 182
Stiltner Motel, Morton 168

D: Listings Index

Stormking Spa at Mt Rainier, Ashford 100
Summerfield Suites, Seattle 212
Summertide Resort & Marina, Tacoma 238
Sumner Motor Inn, Sumner 234
Sun Country Inn, Yakima 260
Sun Valley Inn, Sunnyside 234
Sundowner Motel, Quincy 198
Sundowner Motel, Sequim 218
Sunland Motor Inn, Moses Lake 172
Sunny Bay Cottage, Gig Harbor 140
Sunnyside Travelodge, Sunnyside 234
Sunrise Motel & Resort, Hoodsport 142
Sunrise Resort-Lake Sawyer, Black Diamond 106
Sunset Beach Cottage, Clinton 116
Sunset Motel, Clarkston 114
Sunset View Resort, Ocean Park 178
Super 8 Motel, Bremerton 108
Super 8 Motel, Ellensburg 128
Super 8 Motel, Federal Way 132
Super 8 Motel, Ferndale 132
Super 8 Motel, Kelso 146
Super 8 Motel, Kennewick 148
Super 8 Motel, Lacey 152
Super 8 Motel, Moses Lake 172
Super 8 Motel, Port Angeles 192
Super 8 Motel, Shelton 218
Super 8 Motel, Spokane 232
Super 8 Motel, Walla Walla 248
Super 8 Motel-SeaTac, Seattle 212
Super 8 Motel-Yakima, Union Gap 242
Surf Motel & Cottages, Grayland 142

Surf Spray Motel & Rv Park, Westport 254
Sutton Bay Resort, Newman Lake 174
Swallow's Nest Guest Cottages, Vashon Island 246
Swan Hotel, Port Townsend 194
Sweetwater Cottage, Clinton 116

T
Tall Timber Motel, Randle 200
Tapadera Inn, Kennewick 148
Tatoosh Meadows Resort & Rentals, Packwood 186
The Guest House, Deming 124
The Logs Resort, Deming 124
The Timbers, Stevenson 232
Three Rivers Inn, Sedro Woolley 214
Three Rivers Resort, Forks 136
Thunderbird Motel, Aberdeen 96
Thunderbird Motel, Long Beach 160
Thunderbird Motel, Pasco 188
Thurston House Bed & Breakfast, Maple Falls 164
Timber Lodge Motel, Cle Elum 116
Timberline Inn, Hoquiam 142
Timberline Motel, Peshastin 190
Timberline Village Motel, Packwood 188
Tolo Vista Lodge, Soap Lake 222
Toppenish Inn Motel, Toppenish 238
Totem Trail Motel & Conf Ctr, Rockport 204
Tourist Motor Inn, Yakima 260
Tower House Bed & Breakfast, Waterville 248
Town Chalet Motor Hotel, Longview 162
Town House Motel, Longview 162
Town House Motel, Sunnyside 234

D: Listings Index

TradeWinds Motel, Spokane 232
Tradewinds On-The-Bay Motel, Tokeland 238
Traditional Inns, Quincy 200
Trail West Motel, Grand Coulee 140
Trave-Lure Motel, Aberdeen 96
Travel House Inn, Bellingham 106
Travel Inn Motel, Pasco 188
Travelodge by the Space Needle, Seattle 212
Travelodge, Everett 130
Travelodge, Renton 200
Tri-Cities Sleep Inn, Pasco 188
Tryon by the Beach, Long Beach 162
Tucker House Bed & Breakfast, Friday Harbor 138
Tumbleweed Motel, Connell 118
Tumwata Lodge, Soap Lake 222
Tyee Motel & Restaurant, Coupeville 122
Tyee Motel, Neah Bay 174
Tyrolean Ritz Hotel, Leavenworth 158

U

U & I Rivers Edge Motel, Okanogan 182
Uptown Inn, Port Angeles 192

V

Vagabond Inn, Seattle 212
Vagabond Inn, Walla Walla 248
Val U Inn, Auburn 100
Val-U Inn, Bellingham 106
Val-U Inn, Kent 148
Valley View Motel, Port Townsend 196
Value Motel, Vancouver 244

Van Gelder's Retreat, Vashon Island 246
Van Riper's Resort & Charter, Sekiu 216
Vancouver Lodge, Vancouver 244
Vantage Motel, Vantage 244
Victorian Bed & Breakfast, Coupeville 122
Victorian Rose, Oak Harbor 176
Victorian Suite at the Club, Port Townsend 196
Victoria's Cottage, Coulee Dam 120
Village Motor Inn, Marysville 166
Vineyard Inn, Pasco 190
Virginian Resort, Winthrop 256
Vista Motel, Port Orchard 194

W

Walla Walla Travelodge, Walla Walla 248
Warm Springs Inn B & B, Wenatchee 250
Washington Hotel, Metaline Falls 166
Waterfront Bed & Breakfast, Bainbridge Island 102
Weinhard Hotel, Dayton 122
Welcome Inn at Wenatchee Ctr, Wenatchee 250
Welcome Motor Inn, Everett 130
West Bay Park On Deer Lake, Loon Lake 164
West Beach Resort, Eastsound 126
West Wind Motel, Renton 200
West Winds Motel, Mount Vernon 172
West Winds Resort Motel, Ocean City 178
Westar Lodge & Retreat, Winthrop 256
Westcoast Bellevue Hotel, Bellevue 102
Westcoast SeaTac Hotel, Seattle 214
Westcoast Wenatchee Ctr Hotel, Wenatchee 250
Westerly Motel, Ocean Shores 180

D: Listings Index

Western Motel, Yakima 260
Westgate Motel & Trailer Court, Ocean Park 178
Westin Hotel, Seattle 214
Westside Motor Inn, Ritzville 204
Westview Motel, Blaine 108
Westward Hoh Resort, Forks 136
Westwynd Motel, Gig Harbor 140
Whale's Tale, Long Beach 162
Whiskey Creek Beach, Port Angeles 192
Whispering Firs B & B, Mount Vernon 172
White Spot Motel, Salkum 206
White Swan Guest House, Mount Vernon 174
White Willow Motel & Camp, Fruitland 138
Wild Lily Cabins B & B, Index 144
Willis Motel, Raymond 200
Willow Springs Motel, Cheney 112
Wind Blew Inn Motel, Cle Elum 116
Wind River Motel, Carson 110
Windsong Bed & Breakfast, Orcas Island 184
Winters' Summer Inn B & B, Sekiu 216
Winthrop Inn, Winthrop 256
Wolfgang's Riverview Inn, Curlew 122
Wolfridge Resort, Winthrop 256
Woodland Motel, Randle 200
Woodlander Inn, Woodland 256

Y

Y Motel, Hoquiam 142
Yett Beach House, Long Beach 162

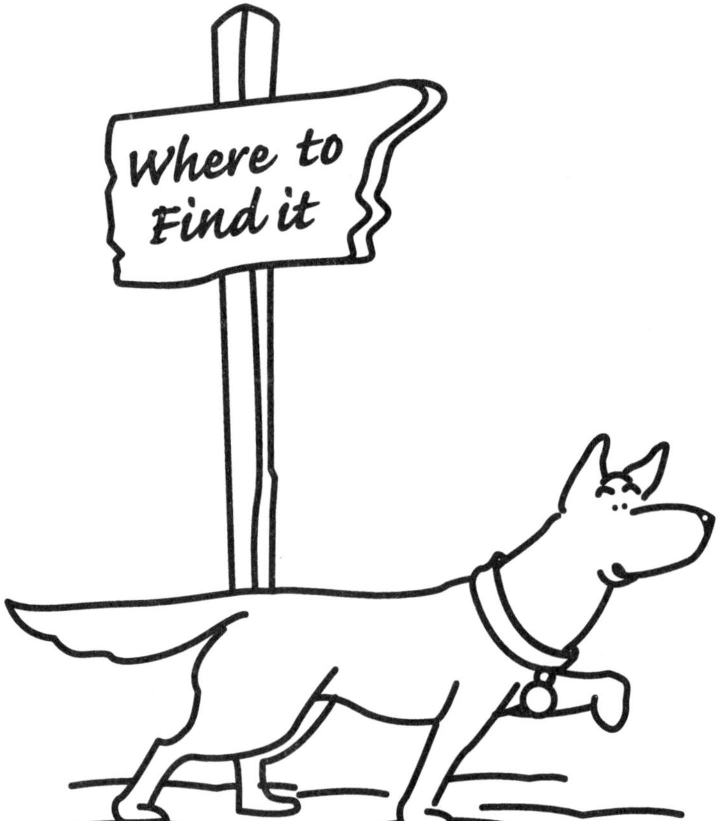
Where to
Find it

E: Topics Index

A
activated charcoal 52, 64
adhesive tape 52, 60, 68
advance reservations 39, 42, 89
after hour veterinary clinics 264
aggression 32
airline crate 16
alcohol 70
alone in room 34, 43
alphabetical listings,
    business name 273
    city name 89
antibacterial ointment 51, 68
antifreeze 65
applying a splint 60
applying a tourniquet 60

artificial respiration 57
ASPCA , tranquilizers 51

B
bandages, elastic 52
barking 34, 43
basic commands
    how to train 29
    recommended 25
beach tips 47
bedding 20, 42
bedsheet 20, 43
boarding kennel 15, 28
breathing, abnormal
    choking 55
    heatstroke 73
    how to restart 57
    internal bleeding 61
    poisoning 62

303

shock 66
while muzzled 59
broken bones 59
brush & comb 21
burns 67

C

candy, for car sickness 51, 71
car rides
    tips 39
    training 35
car sickness
    avoiding 36, 44, 47
    cleanup supplies 22
    treating 71
cardiac massage 57
cats, traveling with 7
charcoal 52, 64
checking into room 42
checklist
    first aid kit 51
    life-threatening emergency 53
    packing list 23
    preventing a lost dog 77
    trip preparations 5
    when to bring your dog—or not 6

where to put lost dog posters 84
chew toys 23, 43
chocolate 51, 71
choking 55
cleaning up
    after relief stops 41
    at the beach 47
    before going indoors 45
    brush & comb 21
    dog towels 20
    supplies to pack 22
collar
    for training 10
    permanent 9
color, mouth & gums
    heatstroke 73
    internal bleeding 61
    normal 50
    shock 66
Come command 30
commands
    how to train 29
    recommended 25
contact poison 62
controlling aggression 32
cotton-tipped swabs 52
crate, travel 16, 20, 35
cup, paper or plastic 52

E: Topics Index

cuts & scrapes 68

D

diarrhea
    heatstroke 73
    treating 72
disposable scoopers 22
Dispoz-A-Scoop 22
distilled water 19
distractions while
    training 29
dog license 11
dog towels 20, 45, 47, 75
dog-friendly
    accommodations 89
Down command 31
drinking water 19
drowning 56

E

ears, foreign objects in
    69
elastic bandages 52, 68
electrical burns 67
emergency, lifesaving
    procedures 53
emergency veterinary
    clinics 263
external bleeding 60
eye drops 52, 69

eyes, foreign objects in
    69

F

first aid kit 15, 51
first aid procedures 49
fishhooks 55, 70
flashlight 23
flea treatments 16
food
    mealtimes 43
    packing 18
foreign objects 69
frostbite 75

G

garage sales 19, 20
gasoline 70
gauze pad 52, 60, 67, 68
good behavior 25
grooming aids 21, 47

H

hazards
    burns 67
    choking 55
    heat buildup 41, 72
    hypothermia 74
    poisoning 62
    underfoot 46, 72
health certificate 14, 51

heart, how to restart 57
heat buildup in car 41, 73
heatstroke 73
Heel command 31
honey, for car sickness 51, 71
houseboat, listing 120
how to:
    apply a splint 60
    apply a tourniquet 60
    give artificial respiration 57
    give cardiac massage 57
    handle a life-threatening emergency 53
    move an injured dog 65
    restrain an injured dog 59
    treat for shock 66
hydrogen peroxide 52, 64, 68, 71
hypothermia 74

I
ice cream 71, 74
ice pack 52, 67, 73
ID tags

dog license 11
microchip 13
permanent 11
temporary travel 12
immunization records 14
internal bleeding, symptoms 61

K
Kaopectate 52, 72
kennel
    boarding 28
    portable travel 16

L
leash
    at motel 44
    in car 40
    packing 10
    rest stops 41
    training 31
    when in public 45
leaving dog alone in room 34
legal liability 43
license 11
listings, sorted by:
    business name 273
    city name 89

E: Topics Index

listings,
   houseboat 120
   nudist park 144
lost dog
   checklist for
      preventing 77
   packing master
      poster 51
   preparing poster in
      advance 78
   putting up posters 83
   radio/TV
      announcements
      83
   reward 12
   searching for 82
Lyme disease 71

M

master poster,
   completing when
   needed 83
master poster, lost dog
   78
medical records 14, 51
medications 16, 51
microchip ID 13, 83
milk 64
mouth, color
   heatstroke 73
   internal bleeding 61

   normal 50
   shock 66
moving an injured dog
   65
muzzle 52, 59

N

nail polish remover 70
Neosporin 51, 68
nervous in car 35, 40
nervous stomach 36
No command 30
normal body
   temperature 53
nudist park, listing 144

O

obedience
   before & after 26
   classes 28
   definition 25
   reviewing commands
      37
ointment, antibacterial
   51
olive oil 52, 64
open car window 40

P

packing
   bedding 20

307

cleanup supplies 22
collar & leash 9
first aid kit 15
flashlight 23
food 18
grooming aids 21
towels 20
travel papers 14
water 19
packing checklist 23
Panalog 51, 68
pet-safe antifreeze 65
petroleum jelly 52, 53, 70
phone
   destination 12, 83, 84
   home or answering machine 78, 85
photo of your pet 78, 84
pickup truck 41
placemat 18, 43
plastic bags 22
pliers 52, 70
poison 62
pooper scoopers 22, 41, 42, 44
porcupine quills 70
posters, lost dog
   distributing 83
   in travel papers 51
   making copies 84

preparing in advance 78
prescription medications 16, 51
preventing lost dog, checklist 77

R

rabies tag 12
records, medical 14
removing foreign objects 69
reservations 39, 42, 89
rest stops 37, 41
restraining an injured dog 59
restraints 17
reviewing commands 37, 41
reward for lost dog 12
riding in car 35, 39
Rocky Mountain spotted fever 71
room
   checking in 42
   leaving dog alone 34, 43
   reservations 39, 42, 89

E: Topics Index

S
safety
    hazards underfoot 46
    heat buildup 41, 72
    leash 40
    muzzle 52, 59
    open car window 40
    pickup truck 41
    restraints 17
scanning, microchip ID 13
scissors 52
screens, car window 18, 40
searching for lost dog 82
seat belts 17
shampoo 21
sheet, protective 20, 43
shock
    burns 67
    internal bleeding 61
    symptoms of 66
    treating 66
Sit command 30
splint, applying 60
splinters 69
spoon, dosage 52
squirt bottle 34
Stay command 31
stomach upsets
    at beach 47
    drinking water 19
    nervous in car 36
    treating 71
stretcher 52, 59, 61, 65
Susie's Country Inn 28
swallowed poison 63
symptoms of:
    broken bones 59
    choking 55
    heatstroke 73
    internal bleeding 61
    poisoning 62
    serious illness 72
    shock 66

T
tags
    permanent ID 11
    rabies 12
    travel 12
tape, adhesive 52
temperature
    how to take 53
    inside parked car 73
    normal 53
thermometer 52, 53, 73, 75
ticks 70
tote bag
    checklist 23
    garage sales 20

tourniquet 60
towels, cleanup 20, 45, 47, 74, 75
training
  aggression 32
  barking 34
  basic 29
  car travel 35
tranquilizers 51
travel crate
  choosing 16
  sleeping 20
  time-out 35
travel ID tags 12
travel papers 14, 51, 82
traveling with your cat 7
treating
  broken bones 59
  burns 67
  choking 55
  cuts & scrapes 68
  diarrhea 72
  drowning 56
  external bleeding 60
  frostbite 75
  heatstroke 73
  hypothermia 74
  internal bleeding 61
  poison, contact 62
  poison, swallowed 63
  removing foreign objects 69
  shock 66
  upset stomach 71
tweezers 52, 70

U

upset stomach 71

V

vaccination records 14
veterinary emergency clinics 263
vomiting
  antifreeze 65
  car sickness 71
  collecting poison sample 63
  heatstroke 73
  internal bleeding 61
  poisoning 62
  salt water 47
  stopped breathing 57
  while muzzled 59
vomiting, induced 64

W

walking
  hazards underfoot 46
  on motel grounds 44

E: Topics Index

warning
   antifreeze 65
   chocolate 71
   electrical cord 67
   open car window 40
   parked car 41, 73
   pickup truck 41
   toilet water 19
water
   diarrhea 72
   distilled 19
   in room 19, 43
   on day trips 45
   packing 19
   rest stops 41
   upset stomach 71
well-behaved traveler 3
what to do in a life-threatening emergency 53
where to stay, listings 89
window, open 40
window screens 18, 40

Z

zip-top plastic bags
   cleanup 22
   packing 52
   poison sample 63

Ginger & Spike Publications

P O Box 937
Wilsonville, OR 97070-0937
barbwhit@teleport.com

voice 503/625-3001
fax 503/625-3076
toll-free 888-255-8030

Yes! — I want to order Have Dog Will Travel

Name _____

Address _____

City/state/zip _____

Daytime phone number _____

$14.95 for one copy (postage paid)
Buy 2 and save— 2 copies for just $25

____ copies **Have Dog Will Travel—Oregon Edition**

____ copies **Have Dog Will Travel—Washington Edition**

Shipping: $ _____ **Free!**

Total amount of order $ _____

Mail order form with check or money order to:

    Ginger & Spike Publications
    PO Box 937
    Wilsonville, OR 97070-0937

Credit card orders: call toll-free 888/255-8030
    or fax order form to 503/625-3076

Credit card no. _____

Circle one: Visa / MC / AMEX   exp date _____

Signature _____